Lab Manual for
Guide to Computer Forensics and Investigations,
Fifth Edition

Andrew Blitz

CENGAGE
Learning·

Australia • Brazil • Mexico • Singapore • United Kingdom • United States

CENGAGE
Learning®

Lab Manual for Guide to Computer Forensics and Investigations, Fifth Edition

Andrew Blitz

SVP, GM Skills & Global Product Management: Dawn Gerrain

Product Director: Kathleen McMahon

Product Team Manager: Kristin McNary

Senior Director, Development: Marah Bellegarde

Product Development Manager: Leigh Hefferon

Senior Content Developer: Michelle Ruelos Cannistraci

Development Editor: Lisa M. Lord

Senior Product Assistant: Abigail Pufpaff

Marketing Director: Michele McTighe

Senior Marketing Manager: Eric LaScola

Senior Production Director: Wendy Troeger

Production Director: Patty Stephan

Senior Content Project Manager: Brooke Greenhouse

Managing Art Director: Jack Pendleton

Manufacturing Planner: Ron Montgomery

Quality Assurance Tester: Serge Palladino

Cover image(s): © Mega Pixel/ Shutterstock

For product information and technology assistance, contact us at **Cengage Learning Customer & Sales Support, 1-800-354-9706**

For permission to use material from this text or product, submit all requests online at **cengage.com/permissions.** Further permissions questions can be e-ºmailed to **permissionrequest@cengage.com**

Library of Congress Control Number: 2014958600

ISBN: 978-1-2850-7581-5
Package ISBN: 978-1-2850-7908-0

Cengage Learning
20 Channel Center Street
Boston, MA 02210
USA

Cengage Learning is a leading provider of customized learning solutions with employees residing in nearly 40 different countries and sales in more than 125 countries around the world. Find your local representative at **www.cengage.com.**

Cengage Learning products are represented in Canada by Nelson Education, Ltd.

To learn more about Cengage Learning, visit **www.cengage.com** Purchase any of our products at your local college store or at our preferred online store **www.cengagebrain.com**

Notice to the Reader

Printed in the United States of America
Print Number: 01 Print Year: 2015

CONTENTS

INTRODUCTION

The hands-on labs in this manual are designed to give you additional skills to reinforce the concepts covered in *Guide to Computer Forensics and Investigations, Fifth Edition*. Practicing these skills is necessary to become a digital forensics investigator. This book assumes a beginning to intermediate level of experience in operating systems and networking, and you should have experience in computer hardware equivalent to the coverage in the CompTIA A+ certification curriculum. If you don't have this background, reviewing a supplemental book, such as *A+ Guide to IT Tech Support, Ninth Edition*, by Jean Andrews, can help you understand the concepts and techniques in the labs.

FEATURES

The labs feature step-by-step procedures with screenshots to illustrate the steps. They're designed to be finished within typical class periods and have been tested in classes taught during the past six years. Each lab ends with challenging review questions that require you to analyze the evidence files. This lab manual works best in a classroom setting with an instructor or a facilitator to help guide students.

To help you understand digital forensics, this lab manual includes many features designed to enhance your learning experience:

- *Lab objectives*—Each lab has an introduction with background information, if needed, and a list of learning objectives.

- *Materials required*—Every lab includes information on hardware, software, and other materials you need to do the lab.

- *Completion times*—Every lab has an estimated completion time so that you can plan your activities more accurately.

- *Step-by-step instructions*—Logical step-by-step instructions guide you through the hands-on activities in each lab.

- *Review questions*—Questions help reinforce concepts covered in the lab.

- *Software and student data files*—This book includes a DVD containing student data files and free software for use with the labs.

HARDWARE REQUIREMENTS

- An Intel Core i3, i5, or i7 64-bit processor
- 8 to 12 GB RAM suggested
- 1 TB free hard drive space
- Screen resolution: 1920 × 1080 or better
- A DVD-ROM dual-layer drive

SOFTWARE REQUIREMENTS

To do the labs, you need the following software: AccessData FTK Imager and Registry Viewer (downloaded from *http://accessdata.com*), Autopsy 3.1.2 for Windows (downloaded from *www.sleuthkit.org*), DB Browser for SQLite (downloaded from *http://sqlitebrowser.org*), Digital Evidence and Forensics Toolkit (DEFT; downloaded from *www.deftlinux.net*), and VirtualBox (downloaded from *www.virtualbox.org*). In addition, you use forensic images downloaded from *http://digitalcorpora.org*. The following software is included on the DVD: Mini-WinFE, OSForensics, ProDiscover Basic, and WinHex. However, you need the Windows 8 or 8.1 Professional installation DVD (an activation or product identification not required) to create the WinFE tool. The labs in this book are designed to work in Windows 8 or 8.1 (64-bit). The Home editions of Windows OSs aren't supported and might not produce accurate or similar results. To use virtualization software, such as VirtualBox, computers should have an Intel 3 GHz or faster Core i7 or Xeon 64-bit processor that supports virtualization and at least 8 GB RAM and 500 GB free hard drive space. However, the completion times listed for each lab might increase by 25%, depending on the computer's performance.

All labs have been tested with Windows 8 and 8.1 Professional (64-bit). (*Note*: ProDiscover Basic is no longer offered free, and there's no technical support for the 8.2.0.2 version included on the DVD.) Software versions are subject to change without notice, and any changes could render some lab steps incorrect. Instructors might want to recommend using the software on the accompanying DVD to make sure steps correspond to what's in the lab manual.

The following companies have granted permission to include their products with this lab manual: AccessData Group, Inc. (*http://accessdata.com*, FTK Imager and Registry Viewer), ARC Group of New York (*www.arcgroupny.com/products/prodiscover-basic*, ProDiscover Basic), PassMark Software (*www.osforensics.com*, OSForensics), and X-Ways AG (*www.x-ways.net*, WinHex).

CLASSROOM SETUP GUIDELINES

This lab manual assumes Windows has been installed and doesn't require computers to be networked unless shared resources (such as printers), ExamView exams, or Internet access are needed. Lab managers can install all the software included on the DVD on a Windows computer and use imaging software, such as Symantec Ghost, to push the images out to networked computers. Several labs use very large forensic images, ranging from 3 to 4 GB, and processing them might take 4 hours or more, depending on computer performance. Starting these labs before the end of the class day and allowing them to run overnight is the recommended method.

ABOUT THE AUTHOR

Andrew Blitz teaches computer science at Florida Southwestern State College and Broward College in Florida. He has more than 35 years of experience in electronics, computer hardware, data communications, computer forensics, and information security. Andrew has designed and taught online and on-site classes in computer/cyber forensics, networking, information security, ethical hacking, cryptography, and A+ hardware and software. He has been teaching for more than 15 years and holds a B.S. and M.S. in computer science and is currently a doctoral candidate in information systems at Nova Southeastern University.

ACKNOWLEDGMENTS

Thank you to the professionals at Cengage Learning for their expertise and commitment to quality. In particular, thank you to Kristin McNary, Product Team Manager; Michelle Ruelos Cannistraci, Senior Content Developer; Lisa Lord, Development Editor; and Serge Palladino, Manuscript Quality Assurance. I would also like to thank the reviewers: Steve Bale, Truckee Meadows Community College; Gary Kessler, Embry-Riddle Aeronautical University; and Tenette Prevatte, Fayetteville Technical Community College. Thanks to my friends Amelia Phillips and Bill Nelson for help and guidance in creating this book. Finally, I want to thank my beloved wife, Laurie, for all her support during this project and dedicate this book to the memory of her parents, Miriam and Murray Siederman, who always believed in me.

CHAPTER ONE

UNDERSTANDING THE DIGITAL FORENSICS PROFESSION AND INVESTIGATIONS

Labs included in this chapter:

- Lab 1.1 Installing OSForensics in Windows
- Lab 1.2 Installing FTK Imager
- Lab 1.3 Installing ProDiscover Basic
- Lab 1.4 Installing AccessData Registry Viewer

Lab 1.1 Installing OSForensics in Windows

Objectives

Investigating digital evidence takes time because of the large storage capacity of modern hard disk drives. In addition, operating systems (OSs) and applications are typically large collections of files and executable programs that work together to form a user interface. OSForensics combines an extensive array of digital forensics tools into a single stand-alone software suite. It enables investigators to analyze storage devices and search for files, folders, e-mails, documents, pictures, and any remaining evidence that might have been deleted and document their findings.

Forensics investigators need to search large volumes of data stored on different types of storage media, such as CDs and DVDs, flash drives, and hard disk drives, for potential digital evidence. In many criminal cases, the suspect might have attempted to delete a file or modify it in some way to prevent other users from seeing it. OSForensics can recover deleted or corrupted files and display the contents, even if they're encrypted with a password. Additional features, such as keyword searching, enable investigators to search for specific words related to the crime or search for number patterns that might reveal telephone or credit card numbers.

OSForensics also creates hash values for every file so that investigators can search for known file types, changed or altered files, malware, and legitimate application and OS files. File hashes are mathematically derived hexadecimal values that uniquely identify both known and unknown files. Hashing is an important feature because it preserves the chain of custody by making sure files haven't been altered or changed and recovered evidence doesn't change over time. OSForensics also supports creating hash sets that allow investigators to import known OS and application hash values into OSForensics to distinguish them from potential file evidence. In this lab, you install OSForensics in Windows to begin investigating digital evidence.

After completing this lab, you will be able to:

- Install OSForensics on a Windows 8 or 8.1 Professional computer
- Explain the OSForensics features that help forensic investigators recover digital evidence

Materials Required

This lab requires the following:

- The `osf.exe` installation file on the DVD
- The `OSFHashSet.zip` file (for your Windows version) on the DVD
- Windows 8 or 8.1 Professional

Estimated completion time: **10–15 minutes**

Activity

In this lab, you install OSForensics:

1. Open File Explorer, and copy the **osf.exe** file on the DVD to the **Documents** folder on your computer. Right-click this file and click **Run as administrator** to begin the installation. In the User Account Control dialog box, click **Yes** to continue.

2. Click **Next** in the Setup - OSForensics dialog box to continue.

3. In the License Agreement window, click the **I accept the agreement** option button, and then click **Next**.

4. In the Select Destination Location window, shown in Figure 1-1, click **Next** to continue. In the Select Start Menu Folder window, click **Next**.

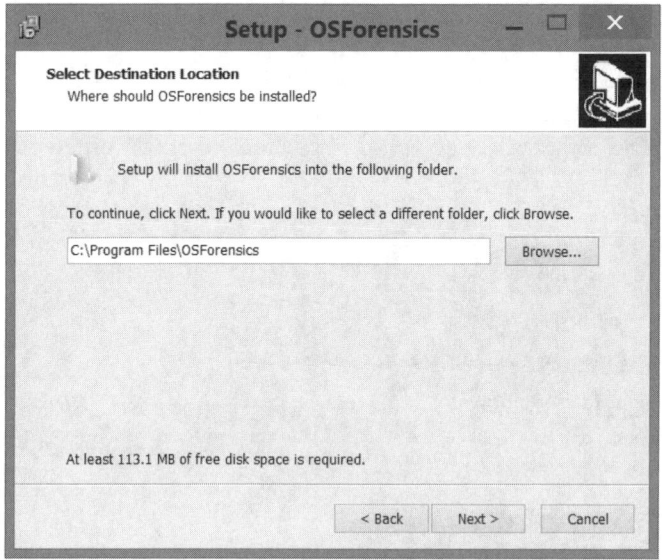

Figure 1-1   The Select Destination Location window

Source: PassMark Software, www.osforensics.com

5. In the Select Additional Tasks window, leave the **Create a desktop icon** check box selected, as shown in Figure 1-2, and click **Next** to continue. Click **Install** in the Ready to Install window to finish the installation.

6. In the Information window, click **Next**. Leave the **Launch OSForensics** check box selected, and click **Finish** to install the program. When the program starts automatically, click the **Continue Using Free Version** button. (You might need to do this each time you run OSForensics.) Exit OSForensics.

7. In File Explorer, browse to the DVD and find the correct OSFHashSet.zip file for your version of Windows. Right-click this file and click **Extract All**.

8. In the Select a Destination and Extract Files window that opens, type **C:\ProgramData\ PassMark\OSForensics\hashSets** in the "Files will be extracted to this folder" text box, and leave the **Show extracted files when complete** check box selected (see Figure 1-3).

9. Click **Extract**. After Windows extracts the files, you can view them in the C:\ProgramData\PassMark\OSForensics\hashSets folder (see Figure 1-4). Installing hash sets allows you to identify known files, such as OS and program files, during an investigation. Close any open windows, and leave your computer running for the next lab.

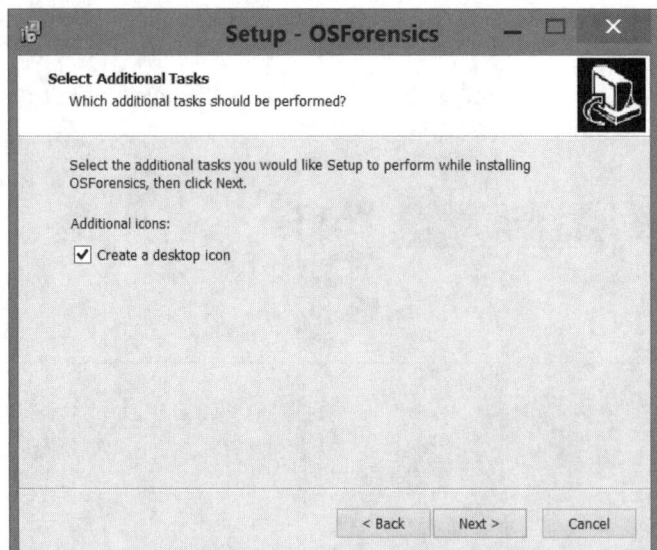

Figure 1-2   The Select Additional Tasks window

Source: PassMark Software, www.osforensics.com

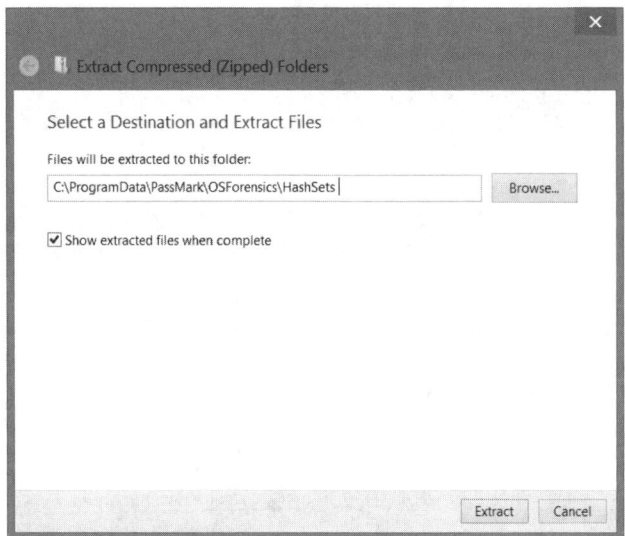

Figure 1-3   Extracting compressed files

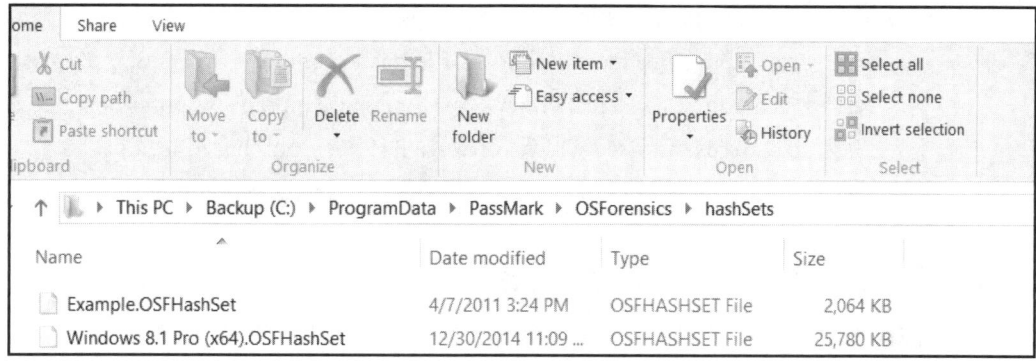

Figure 1-4   Extracted files in the hashSets folder

Review Questions

1. Why is OSForensics an important forensics tool?

   a. It can be used to troubleshoot a computer.

   b. It can be used to test a computer's operability.

   c. It can be used to help digital forensics investigators locate potential evidence.

   d. It can be used to recover human DNA.

2. OSForensics can search for which of the following types of files? (Choose all that apply.)

   a. E-mail

   b. Graphics

   c. Deleted files

   d. Registry files

3. What's a file hash?

   a. A hexadecimal value obtained mathematically from a file

   b. The name of a software program's vendor or manufacturer

   c. The size of the computer's hard disk

   d. The file size of potential evidence

4. Which of the following statements is true?

   a. File hash information can be found in File Explorer.

   b. File hashes can verify that the chain of custody has been maintained.

   c. File hashes can indicate that software has been purchased legally.

   d. File hashing values aren't important to a digital investigator.

5. OSForensics uses hash sets for what purpose?

    a. Hash sets are used to identify known file hashes used by OSs and applications.

    b. Hash sets are used to identify the OS version in use on the computer being investigated.

    c. Hash sets are used to see which software has been purchased legally.

    d. Hash sets are used to copy evidence from the investigated computer to a USB drive.

Lab 1.2 Installing FTK Imager

Objectives

Forensics investigators are required to protect the integrity of digital evidence from the time it's seized until the end of the trial. This protection, known as "maintaining the chain of custody," ensures that the original data hasn't been changed during the investigation. Forensics investigators duplicate digital evidence by using a bit-stream process called "imaging," which preserves the original evidence along with other system files and duplicates the entire storage device with files intact to another lab storage device. Imaging allows examining the duplicated storage device without the risk of damaging potential digital evidence. This bit-stream process makes an exact byte-for-byte copy of the original storage device, which preserves the physical and logical file locations and any unpartitioned space. This process is important because remnants of deleted files still exist on a storage device until they're overwritten during computer operations. The file remnants can be searched and repaired to recover deleted files and make them readable. Imaging also generates file hashes that can be used to identify potential evidence and validate its integrity throughout the investigative process.

FTK Imager can also be used to preview digital files to determine whether evidentiary data exists before starting an extensive investigation. If potential forensic data is located, FTK Imager can then forensically duplicate the storage device to process the data safely. FTK Imager supports the following file systems: Microsoft FAT12, FAT16, FAT32, and NTFS; Linux/UNIX Ext2, Ext3, and Ext4; and Mac HFS and HFS+. It can produce hard disk formats supported by FTK, EnCase, OSForensics, Expert Witness, Linux dd, Symantec Ghost, SMART, and VMware. Although FTK Imager can copy encrypted files, it can't actually decrypt them. In this lab, you install FTK Imager in Windows.

After completing this lab, you will be able to:

* Install FTK Imager in Windows
* Explain the purpose of using an imager tool to copy digital evidence

Materials Required

This lab requires the following:

* Windows 8 or 8.1 Professional

Estimated completion time: **10 minutes**

Activity

In this lab, you install FTK Imager:

1. Start a Web browser, go to **http://accessdata.com/product-download**, and download FTK Imager 3.3.0. Follow instructions to register the product. Right-click the installation file and click **Run as administrator** to begin the installation.

2. Click **Run** in the Open File Security Warning message box, if necessary, and click **Yes** in the UAC message box.

3. In the welcome window of the AccessData FTK Imager - InstallShield Wizard, click **Next**. In the License Agreement window, click the **I accept the terms in the license agreement** option button, and then click **Next** to continue. In the Destination Folder window, click **Next**.

4. Click **Install** to install the software.

5. When the installation has finished, click to clear the **Launch AccessData FTK Imager** check box, and click **Finish** to complete the installation. Close any open windows, and leave your computer running for the next lab.

Review Questions

1. FTK Imager can be used to search all the following except what?

   a. Deleted files

   b. Documents

   c. Graphics

   d. Encrypted files

2. FTK Imager is used primarily to produce which of the following?

   a. Hard disk images that can be analyzed by forensics software

   b. Forensic evidence

   c. Computer manufacturer information

   d. DNA evidence

3. Why do forensics investigators work with bit-stream images?

   a. Image files are smaller than the actual hard disk files.

   b. Only image files contain forensic evidence.

   c. An image file can be examined without damaging the original evidence.

   d. The original storage device can't be analyzed without the original computer.

4. FTK Imager can detect and view encrypted files. True or False?

5. Bit-stream imaging is the process of _____.

   a. creating hash values from files on a storage device

   b. extracting readable information from encrypted files

   c. duplicating data on storage devices for forensic analysis

   d. determining the forensic nature of digital evidence

Lab 1.3 Installing ProDiscover Basic

Objectives

Forensics investigators often use more than one forensics tool to analyze stored files and search for potential evidence. ProDiscover Basic is a popular forensics tool with many features, such as the capability to produce file hashes, and includes several search tools designed for security. It's used by law enforcement agencies, system administrators, consultants, and forensic accountants to search digital evidence and gather the data needed for civil or criminal litigation. In addition, ProDiscover includes incident response and intrusion detection features for generating reports on intruders attempting to take control of network resources. It also supports searching entire storage disks for existing and deleted files, graphics, Internet history, and Windows Registry keys. It supports searching the FAT12, FAT16, FAT32, NTFS, Sun Solaris UFS, and Ext2 and Ext3 file systems; basic and dynamic disks; and RAID disk drives.

ProDiscover can also extract Exchangeable Image File (Exif) format information, including the camera model, shutter speed, and lens as well as the date and time a photo was taken. This information can be useful in determining which camera took a picture. In addition, it can export Windows disk images to a VMware virtual machine file. Virtualization is the process of running a guest OS inside a host OS, which enables forensics investigators to view an image as a computer running within another computer. In this lab, you install ProDiscover in Windows.

After completing this lab, you will be able to:

- Install ProDiscover Basic in Windows
- Explain the features of ProDiscover Basic

Materials Required

This lab requires the following:

- Windows 8 or 8.1 Professional
- The ProDiscover Basic installation file on the DVD

 Two versions of ProDiscover are included on the DVD. Use `ProDiscoverRelease8202Basicx86.zip` for 32-bit Windows systems and `ProDiscoverRelease8202Basicx64.zip` for 64-bit Windows systems.

> Estimated completion time: **15–20 minutes**

Activity

In this lab, you install ProDiscover Basic:

1. Open File Explorer, and copy the **ProDiscoverRelease8202Basicx86.zip** or **ProDiscoverRelease8202Basicx64.zip** file on the DVD to the Documents folder on your computer. Right-click this file and click **Extract All** to extract the contents.

2. When the Select a Destination and Extract Files window opens, click **Browse**. Navigate to and click the **Documents** folder, click **OK**, and then click **Extract** to extract the installation files.

3. In File Explorer, right-click `ProDiscoverRelease8202Basicx86.exe` or `ProDiscoverRelease8202Basicx64.exe` and click **Run as administrator** to begin installing ProDiscover Basic. In the UAC message box, click **Yes**.

4. The Install Wizard starts. This process might take a few minutes. Click **Next** in the Welcome to the InstallShield Wizard for ProDiscover Basic 8.2.0.2 window to continue.

5. In the License Agreement window, click the **I accept the terms in the license agreement** option button, and then click **Next**. In the Readme Information window, click **Next** to continue.

6. In the Customer Information window, type your full name in the User Name text box, and then click **Next**.

7. In the Destination Folder dialog box, accept the default location, and then click **Next** to continue.

8. In the InstallShield Wizard Completed window, click **Finish**. Close any open windows, and leave your computer running for the next lab.

Review Questions

1. ProDiscover can be used to search all the following file systems except _____.

   a. FAT16

   b. HFS+

   c. NTFS

   d. FAT32

2. The Exif format contains information on which of the following? (Choose all that apply.)

   a. Date and time a photo was taken

   b. The shutter speed

   c. When the camera was purchased

   d. The camera model

3. ProDiscover can search digital devices for which of the following? (Choose all that apply.)

   a. Macintosh files

   b. RAID data

   c. Linux files

   d. UNIX files

4. ProDiscover isn't capable of producing file hash values. True or False?

5. Which of the following statements is correct?

   a. ProDiscover can decrypt encrypted Microsoft Word documents.

   b. ProDiscover can decrypt encrypted Microsoft Excel spreadsheets.

   c. ProDiscover can decrypt encrypted e-mail files.

   d. ProDiscover can't decrypt any encrypted files.

Lab 1.4 Installing AccessData Registry Viewer

Objectives

The Windows Registry is the central repository that stores options and settings for hardware, OS software, and user-specific information, such as account usernames and hashed passwords. It's responsible for booting into the Windows environment based on user preferences and contains valuable forensic information. AccessData Registry Viewer enables forensics investigators to view the Registry's contents and search for data such as recently opened files, removable storage devices, user account names, deleted files in the Recycle Bin, and other potential evidence. Although the Registry includes file information, such as timestamps, it doesn't actually store files—only their physical locations. Because of Windows protection systems, you can't view Registry information in the Windows Registry Editor without tools such as Registry Viewer.

The Registry contains five critical system folders (hives) with detailed information on the system state of a Windows computer at any point, including devices that might have been attached and later removed or deleted. Therefore, a forensics analysis of the Registry can yield information that has been deliberately destroyed to hide the details of a crime. The Registry also contains a history of Web sites visited, Internet queries including timestamps, and a list of all programs installed on the computer. In this lab, you install AccessData Registry Viewer in Windows.

After completing this lab, you will be able to:

- Install Registry Viewer in Windows
- Explain the purpose of Registry Viewer

Materials Required

This lab requires the following:

- Windows 8 or 8.1 Professional

> Estimated completion time: **10 minutes**

Activity

In this lab, you install Registry Viewer:

1. Start a Web browser, go to **http://accessdata.com/product-download**, and download Registry Viewer 1.8.0.5. Follow instructions to register the product. Right-click the installation file and click **Run as administrator** to start the installation. Click **Yes** in the UAC message box.

2. Click **Next** in the AccessData Registry Viewer - InstallShield Wizard welcome window.

3. In the License Agreement window, click the **I accept the terms in the license agreement** option button, and then click **Next**.

4. In the Destination Folder window, accept the default destination folder **C:\Program Files\ AccessData,** and then click **Next.**

5. Click **Install,** and then click **Finish.** Registry Viewer is now installed, and your desktop should include icons for OSForensics, FTK Imager, ProDiscover Basic, and AccessData Registry Viewer. Close any open windows, and shut down your computer.

Review Questions

1. The Windows Registry is responsible for which of the following?

    a. Registering Windows software with Microsoft

    b. Creating the NTFS file system

    c. Booting into the Windows environment

    d. Deleting files and folders

2. The Registry contains valuable forensics information, such as which of the following? (Choose all that apply.)

    a. Account usernames and hashed passwords

    b. Where software was purchased

    c. When files were created or deleted

    d. Duplicate copies of Microsoft Word documents

3. Registry Viewer can recover forensics information, such as _____, that can't be viewed in Windows Registry Editor.

    a. when software was purchased

    b. what software is considered illegal

    c. the version of the HFS+ file system

    d. a history of Web sites visited

4. Which of the following statements is true?

    a. The Registry contains information on the Windows environment.

    b. The Registry contains a list of Linux files.

    c. The Registry doesn't contain useful forensics information.

    d. The Registry doesn't contain hard disk information that has been deleted.

5. The Registry is composed of _____ hives containing system data.

    a. three

    b. seven

    c. five

    d. four

THE INVESTIGATOR'S OFFICE AND LABORATORY

Labs included in this chapter:

- Lab 2.1 Securely Wiping a USB Drive
- Lab 2.2 Using ProDiscover Basic to Image a USB Drive
- Lab 2.3 Converting a ProDiscover Basic Image to a .dd Image
- Lab 2.4 Imaging Evidence with FTK Imager
- Lab 2.5 Viewing Images in FTK Imager

Lab 2.1 Securely Wiping a USB Drive

Objectives

Sometimes data must be deleted from a storage device securely to prevent recovering sensitive or secret files. Simply deleting files isn't enough to remove file data because when a file is deleted from a storage device, only the pointer to the file location is removed. The Master File Table (MFT), which stores the physical location of files in the file system, is updated to reflect the free space. The MFT is a separate structure in the NTFS file system; it's not the Recycle Bin. File information might remain on a computer even if it has been deleted from the Recycle Bin. Therefore, deleted data might still exist on a computer until all remnants have been overwritten by new data.

Deleted files often aren't overwritten immediately, and forensics software can be used to recover file remnants and reconstruct an original file by a process known as "data carving." Unless remnants are overwritten with other data, there's no guarantee that the deleted files can't be retrieved and viewed. Therefore, secure destruction of digital data often requires writing a series of 0 or 1 bits to the storage device to overwrite any file remnants.

The National Institute of Standards and Technology (NIST) 800-88 standard requires seven wiping passes over existing data before the data can be considered unrecoverable on storage devices. ProDiscover includes a disk wipe tool designed to erase storage media completely; it conforms to NIST standards and prevents any forensic recovery. Before digital evidence can be copied to a storage device for forensic analysis, all previous data stored on the device must be erased completely. In this lab, you securely wipe data from a USB drive to prepare it for forensic imaging.

After completing this lab, you will be able to:

- Wipe a storage device securely
- Explain the purpose of wiping a storage device

Materials Required

This lab requires the following:

- Windows 8 or 8.1 Professional
- Data files in the C2Proj1 folder on the DVD
- A USB drive with data on it that can be erased
- ProDiscover Basic

> Estimated completion time: **60–120 minutes,** depending on the size of your USB drive

Activity

In this lab, you wipe the contents of a USB drive by using ProDiscover Basic:

1. Log on to your computer, and insert a USB drive containing files you don't need.

2. Right-click the **ProDiscover Basic** desktop icon and click **Run as administrator** to start ProDiscover Basic. Click **Yes** in the User Account Control (UAC) message box.

3. In the Launch Dialog dialog box, click the **Don't show this dialog in the future** check box, and then click **Cancel** to close the Open dialog box. Click **Tools, Secure Wipe** from the ProDiscover menu.

4. In the Secure Wipe Disk dialog box, click the **Disk to Wipe** list arrow, and click the drive letter corresponding to the USB drive. Verify that you have selected the correct drive letter to prevent accidentally erasing any other attached storage device. In the Number of Passes list box, type 7, and then click **Start** to begin the process.

5. Click **OK** in the ProDiscover message box to bypass the warning that all data will be securely wiped. The Securely Deleting file message is displayed in the lower-left corner to indicate that disk files are being wiped.

6. When the disk has been wiped seven times, you see the message "The selected disk has been securely wiped." Click **OK**, and exit ProDiscover Basic.

7. Open File Explorer, and then right-click the USB drive and click **Format**.

8. In the Format dialog box, click **NTFS** in the File system list box, and type **EVIDENCE** in the Volume label text box. Click **Start** to format the USB drive. Click **OK** in the Format Removable Disk message box.

9. When the format is finished, click **OK** in the Formatting Removable Disk message box, and close the Format dialog box. Copy the 11 files from the **C2Proj1** folder on the DVD accompanying this book. This folder is your original source of digital evidence. Label the storage device, and don't write any more files to it.

10. Close any open windows, and leave your computer running for the next lab.

Review Questions

1. Which statement about deleted files is true?

   a. Deleted files can be rebuilt from remnants that haven't been overwritten.

   b. After a file has been deleted from the Recycle Bin, it can't be recovered.

   c. After a file pointer has been deleted in the MFT, it can't be recovered.

   d. The MFT isn't updated until all file remnants have been overwritten with new data.

2. When a file is deleted from a storage device, only the pointer to the file location is removed. True or False?

3. According to NIST standards, how many wipes should be done to erase data completely?

   a. Three

   b. One

   c. Two

   d. Seven

4. Which of the following statements about the MFT is true?

   a. The MFT is overwritten each time a file is deleted.

   b. The MFT is updated to indicate free space when files are deleted.

   c. The MFT and the Recycle Bin are the same file structure.

   d. The MFT isn't used in the NTFS file system.

5. Secure destruction of digital data requires doing which of the following?

   a. Overwriting the MFT

   b. Writing 0s and 1s to the storage device to overwrite file remnants

   c. Writing information in the MFT to file remnant locations

   d. Deleting files from the Recycle Bin

Lab 2.2 Using ProDiscover Basic to Image a USB Drive

Objectives

When computers and devices are seized during a forensics investigation, the process of extracting information includes using disk imaging to make a bit-stream copy of the original storage media. Disk imaging builds forensically sound bit-for-bit copies of the evidence data, including the MFT with all physical file locations containing data or remnants and unallocated free space on the hard disk. After the original medium is duplicated, investigators can safely analyze the file structure and recover potential forensics evidence without the danger of destroying it during the process. Additionally, disk imaging maintains the chain of custody by protecting the evidence from any changes that might render it unusable in court.

ProDiscover Basic supports importing several types of image file formats, including .dd, .eve, .cmp, .pdg, and .pds. In this lab, you simulate seizing digital evidence on the USB drive you prepared in Lab 2.1 and build a ProDiscover Basic .eve image to search for existing or deleted files. This process is the same procedure you follow during an actual investigation, except you use a write-blocker in actual investigations to prevent any changes to the original evidence during the acquisition. A write-blocker is a hardware or software component inserted between the original storage device and the computer creating the image to prevent what's on the original storage device from being overwritten, which violates the chain of custody.

After completing this lab, you will be able to:

- Explain the purpose of disk imaging
- Make a bit-stream image of a USB drive or a similar storage device

Materials Required

This lab requires the following:

- Windows 8 or 8.1 Professional
- ProDiscover Basic
- The USB drive prepared in Lab 2.1

Estimated completion time: **10–20 minutes**

Activity

In this lab, you image the USB drive you prepared in Lab 2.1:

1. Insert the USB drive containing evidence into your computer.

2. In File Explorer, create a folder called **Work** in your C drive, and then create a subfolder named **Labs** in the Work folder. The Work\Labs folder is used throughout this book for lab files. In C:\Work\Labs, create three subfolders called **Cases**, **Data**, and **Evidence**.

3. Double-click the **ProDiscover Basic** desktop icon. Click **Action**, **Capture Image** from the menu.

4. In the Capture Image dialog box, click the **Source Drive** list arrow, and then click the drive letter for the USB drive.

5. Click the **double arrow** button next to the Destination text box, click **Choose Local Path**, and navigate to and click the **C:\Work\Labs\Evidence** folder. In the Save As dialog box, type **C2Proj2** in the File name text box (see Figure 2-1), and click **Save**.

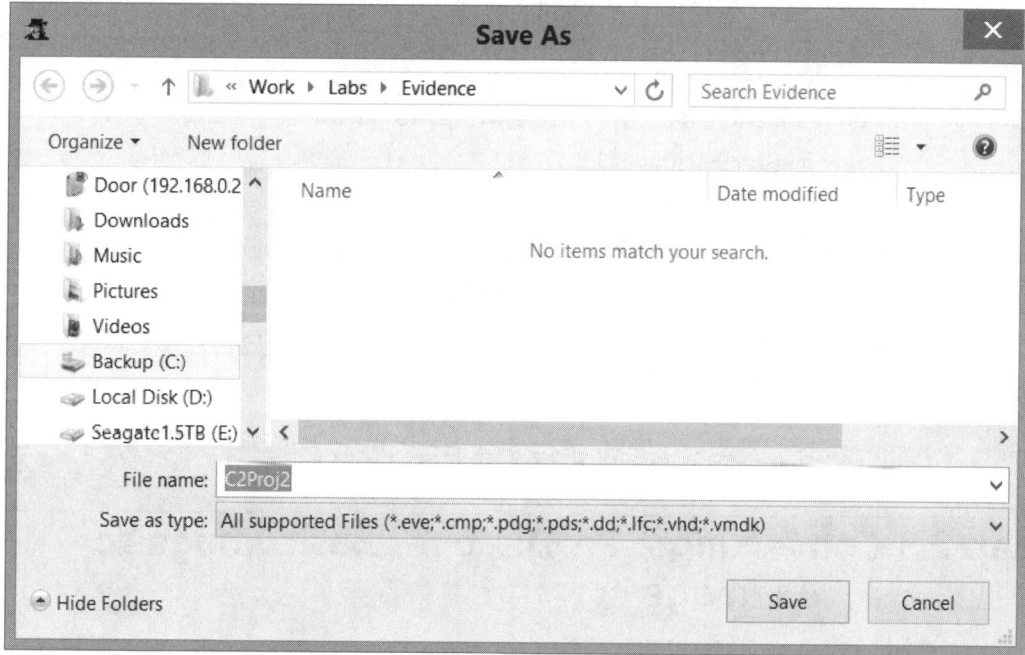

Figure 2-1   Selecting a destination for case files

6. In the Capture Image dialog box, type your full name in the Technician Name text box, and type **C2Proj2** in the Image Number text box. Click **OK** to continue.

7. When the imaging is finished, click **OK**. Navigate to and click the **C:\Work\Labs\Evidence** folder in File Explorer, and confirm that the C2Proj2.eve image has been created.

8. Close File Explorer, and leave ProDiscover Basic running for the next lab.

Review Questions

1. ProDiscover Basic supports all the following image formats except _____.

   a. `.dd`

   b. `.eve`

   c. `.pdg`

   d. `.vhd`

2. Disk images don't include the MFT. True or False?

3. Which statement about a ProDiscover Basic image is true?

   a. It doesn't copy the MFT because it isn't needed during analysis.

   b. It copies the MFT and any unallocated free space from the original storage device.

   c. It can't be used during forensic analysis.

   d. It contains only data; it doesn't include unallocated free space.

4. What's the purpose of a write-blocker?

   a. Preventing any data on the original storage device from being overwritten, which would violate the chain of custody

   b. Preventing any data from being written to the forensic image

   c. Creating file hash values

   d. Duplicating the MFT

5. What's the purpose of disk imaging? (Choose all that apply.)

   a. Allowing investigators to calculate hash values

   b. Giving investigators a way to analyze data without destroying potential evidence on the original medium

   c. Maintaining the chain of custody

   d. Creating extra copies to share with other investigators

Lab 2.3 Converting a ProDiscover Basic Image to a `.dd` Image

Objectives

Forensics investigators often use more than one suite of software tools to search for digital evidence because using multiple tools can yield more evidence than using just one tool and is useful for validating results. In addition, they should be able to use different imaging tools in case they need faster duplications in some settings or need tools optimized for specific file systems, such as NTFS or HFS. However, forensics tools typically produce files that aren't compatible with other software tools. For example, ProDiscover Basic produces images in its proprietary `.eve` format that other software might not be able to read. However, ProDiscover Basic can convert `.eve` images to other formats, such as the `.dd` format supported by most forensics software. The `.dd` format produces a bit-by-bit copy of a storage device's contents and can be read by Windows, Linux, UNIX, and Mac OS X.

ProDiscover Basic also supports converting .eve images to ISO, .dd to ISO, and .dd to VMware virtual hard disks. ISO images are files stored in an uncompressed format; they're used to burn a DVD or CD and make it installable or bootable. A VMware virtual hard disk can be viewed as a virtual machine that appears as an OS running in another OS, which enables forensics investigators to run a disk image as though it were connected to the original computer. In this lab, you convert a ProDiscover Basic image to a .dd format that's imported into FTK Imager in Lab 2.4.

After completing this lab, you will be able to:

- Describe ProDiscover Basic's conversion tools
- Convert an .eve image to a .dd image in ProDiscover Basic

Materials Required

This lab requires the following:

- Windows 8 or 8.1 Professional
- ProDiscover Basic
- The C2Proj2.eve file created in Lab 2.2

Estimated completion time: **5–10 minutes**

Activity

In this lab, you convert the C2Proj2.eve image to a .dd format:

1. Double-click the **ProDiscover Basic** desktop icon, if necessary. Click **Tools** on the menu, point to **Image Conversion Tools**, and then click **Convert ProDiscover Image to "DD"**, as shown in Figure 2-2.

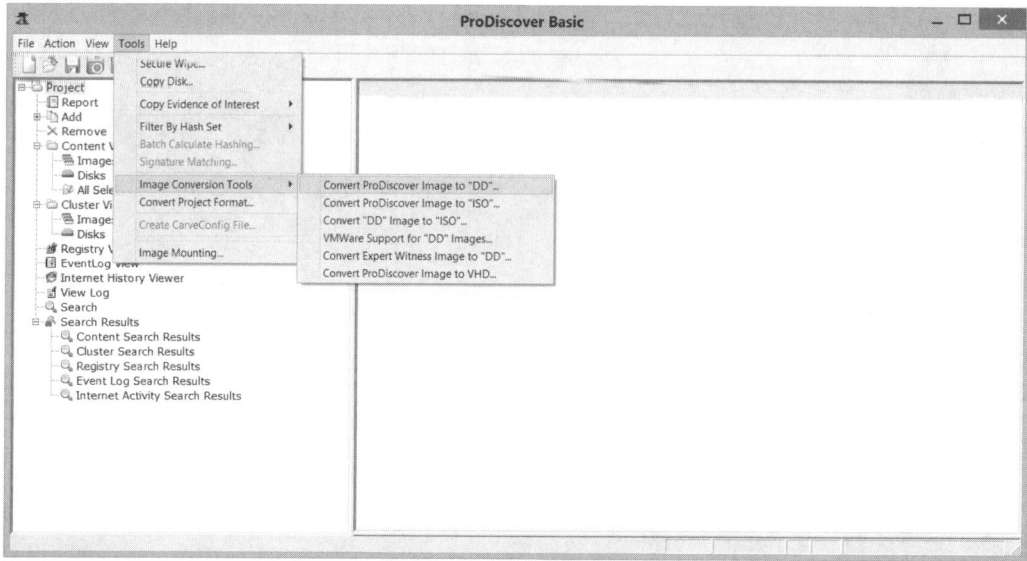

Figure 2-2   Converting a ProDiscover image to the .dd format

2. In the Convert ProDiscover Image to 'DD' Image dialog box, click the **Browse** button, navigate to and click the **C:\Work\Labs\Evidence** folder, and click the **C2Proj2.eve** file to enter the path and filename in the Source ProDiscover Image text box (see Figure 2-3).

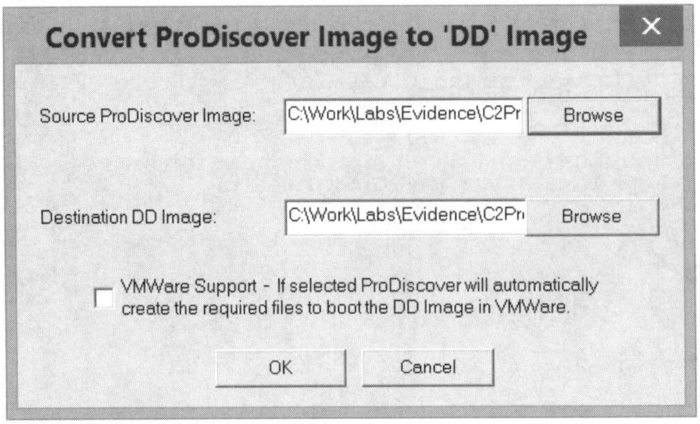

Figure 2-3   Finishing the format conversion
©2015 The ARC Group of New York

3. Click **OK**. The blue bar in the lower-right corner indicates that the file conversion is in progress.

4. When the conversion is finished, navigate to and click the **C:\Work\Labs\Evidence** folder in File Explorer, and confirm that the C2Proj2.dd image has been created. The image's file size should be approximately the size of the storage device, not the data.

5. Close File Explorer, and exit ProDiscover Basic. Leave your computer running for the next lab.

Review Questions

1. Which image format can be read by Windows, Linux, UNIX, and Mac OS X?

   a. .dd

   b. .eve

   c. .pdg

   d. .mft

2. An ISO image is stored as which of the following?

   a. Compressed format

   b. Proprietary format

   c. Uncompressed format

   d. Hashed format

3. ProDiscover Basic can perform which of the following image conversions?

    a. ISO to .dd

    b. VMware to .dd

    c. .eve to ISO

    d. .eve to .E01

4. ProDiscover images are the same size as the total size of all evidence files on the original source. True or False?

5. Forensics investigators should be familiar with more than one forensics analysis tool so that they can maintain the chain of custody. True or False?

Lab 2.4 Imaging Evidence with FTK Imager

Objectives

AccessData FTK Imager creates bit-stream images in raw (.dd), Smart (.s01), and .E01 formats and enables investigators to extract Registry files from a Windows computer and import them into Registry-viewing tools, such as AccessData Registry Viewer, for recovering passwords or encrypted files.

Unlike ProDiscover, FTK Imager isn't optimized to search through large volumes of data to find evidence. Instead, it has verification features, such as MD5 and SHA-1 hashing calculations that provide redundant verification to show that files haven't been altered during imaging. FTK Imager does have some basic search features and can be used to look for deleted files or identify encrypted files. It's available in a "lite" version that can be placed on removable media to make it portable; it also makes it possible for investigators to extract files without booting the suspect's computer. In this lab, you identify files that have been deleted on a USB drive.

After completing this lab, you will be able to:

* List the image formats FTK Imager supports
* Use FTK Imager to image a USB drive

Materials Required

This lab requires the following:

* Windows 8 or 8.1 Professional
* FTK Imager
* The USB drive prepared in Lab 2.1

Estimated completion time: **30–40 minutes**

Activity

In this lab, you delete two files on the EVIDENCE drive you created in Lab 2.1, and then image the USB drive with FTK Imager to produce an .E01 image:

1. Open File Explorer, and browse to the USB drive. Delete the **Qtr 1 Emp.xls** and **Online.docx** files on the USB drive, and then close File Explorer.

2. Double-click the **FTK Imager** desktop icon. Click **Yes** in the UAC message box, if necessary. Click **File, Create Disk Image** from the menu.

3. In the Select Source dialog box, click the **Logical Drive** option button, and then click **Next**.

4. In the Select Drive dialog box, click the **EVIDENCE [NTFS]** source drive in the drop-down list box, and then click **Finish** to continue.

5. In the Create Image dialog box, click **Add**. In the Select Image Type dialog box, click the **E01** option button, and then click **Next** to continue.

6. In the Evidence Item Information dialog box, type **C2Proj4** in the Case Number and Evidence Number text boxes. Enter your full name in the Examiner text box, and type **USB image with deleted files** in the Notes text box, as shown in Figure 2-4. Click **Next** to continue.

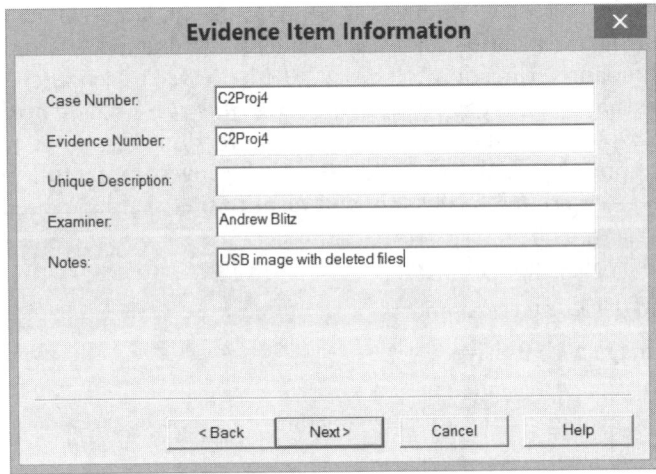

Figure 2-4   Entering evidence item information
©2015 AccessData Group, Inc. All Rights Reserved.

7. In the Select Image Destination dialog box, click the **Browse** button, navigate to and click the **C:\Work\Labs\Evidence** folder, click **OK**, and type **C2Proj4** in the Image Filename text box (see Figure 2-5). Click **Finish**.

8. In the Create Image dialog box, click **Start**. When the imaging process is finished, the results are displayed along with the computed MD5 and SHA-1 hashes (see Figure 2-6), which verify the forensic image's integrity. Click **Close** in the Drive/Image Verify Results and Creating Directory Listing dialog boxes. The C2Proj4.E01 file is used in Lab 2.5. Leave FTK Imager running for the next lab.

Select Image Destination
Image Destination Folder
C:\Work\Labs\Evidence
Browse
Image Filename (Excluding Extension)
C2Proj4
Image Fragment Size (MB)
For Raw, E01, and AFF formats: 0 = do not fragment
1500
Compression (0=None, 1=Fastest, ..., 9=Smallest)
6
Use AD Encryption
< Back
Finish
Cancel
Help

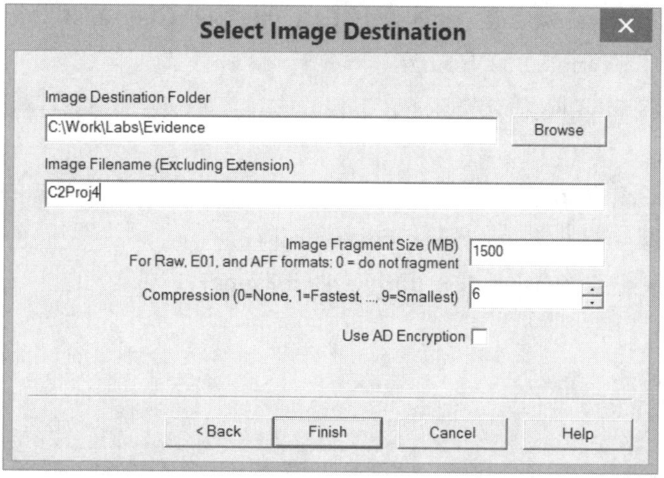

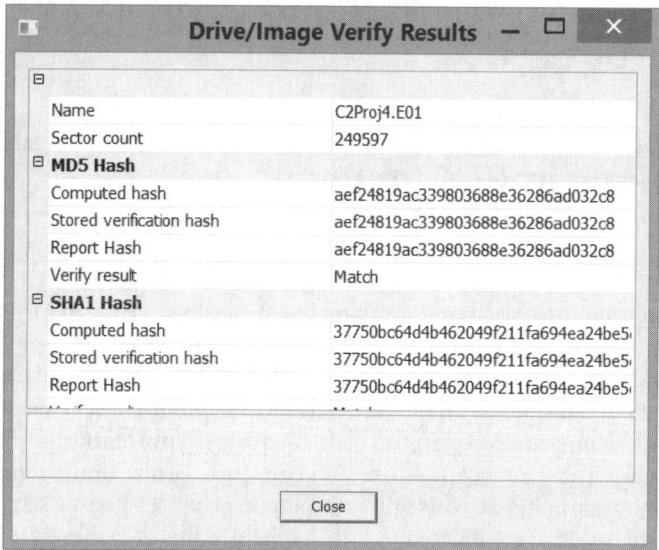

Figure 2-5 Selecting the image destination

Drive/Image Verify Results
Name C2Proj4.E01
Sector count 249597
MD5 Hash
Computed hash aef24819ac339803688e36286ad032c8
Stored verification hash aef24819ac339803688e36286ad032c8
Report Hash aef24819ac339803688e36286ad032c8
Verify result Match
SHA1 Hash
Computed hash 37750bc64d4b462049f211fa694ea24be5
Stored verification hash 37750bc64d4b462049f211fa694ea24be5
Report Hash 37750bc64d4b462049f211fa694ea24be5
Close

Figure 2-6 Verifying the results

Review Questions

1. FTK Imager can produce all the following image formats except __________.
   a. `.E01`
   b. `.dd`
   c. `.s01`
   d. `.eve`

2. Which of the following features isn't available in FTK Imager? (Choose all that apply.)

   a. Creating images in raw and `.E01` formats

   b. Being optimized to search large volumes of data

   c. Creating `.eve` image files

   d. Extracting Windows Registry files

3. FTK Imager Lite is designed to be portable. True or False?

4. FTK Imager calculates which hash values during file imaging?

   a. MD5

   b. SHA-5

   c. DD5

   d. `.eve`

5. Why does FTK Imager calculate two hash values?

   a. So that they can be read by older versions of Microsoft Office

   b. To provide redundant verification that files haven't been altered during imaging

   c. For use in other forensics tools

   d. None of the above

Lab 2.5 Viewing Images in FTK Imager

Objectives

FTK Imager has features that are useful for forensic analysis of disk images, such as calculating hash values and viewing file formats based on their file structures. You can also use FTK Imager to search for existing and deleted files on disk images and view data in its readable state as well as hexadecimal bytes written to the disk. In addition, FTK Imager displays information on physical and logical data blocks, including bad blocks and unallocated blocks that can be helpful in recovering deliberately corrupted disk partitions. This feature is also useful in narrowing the search scope for evidence because you can quickly determine whether any data has been deleted from a disk image. In this lab, you examine the `C2Proj4.E01` image to locate and export the two files that were deleted in Lab 2.4 before the USB drive was imaged.

After completing this lab, you will be able to:

- View images in FTK Imager for preliminary analysis
- Locate deleted files and export them for further analysis

Materials Required

This lab requires the following:

- Windows 8 or 8.1 Professional
- Microsoft Office 2007, 2010, or 2013 (or open-source software capable of reading Office files)

- FTK Imager
- The C2Proj4.E01 image from Lab 2.4

Estimated completion time: **10–15 minutes**

Activity

In this lab, you add the USB image created in Lab 2.4 and look for two deleted files:

1. Double-click the **FTK Imager** desktop icon, if necessary, and click **File, Add Evidence Item** from the menu.

2. In the Select Source dialog box, click the **Image File** option button, and then click **Next**.

3. In the Select File dialog box, click **Browse**, navigate to and click the **C:\Work\Labs\ Evidence** folder, click the **C2Proj4.E01** file, and then click **Open**. Click **Finish**.

4. In the Evidence Tree pane, expand the **C2Proj4.E01, EVIDENCE [NTFS]**, and [**root**] folders, and then click the [**root**] folder to view the files on the imaged drive. Notice that the deleted Qtr 1 Emp.xls and Online.docx files show a red X in the File List pane (see Figure 2-7). FTK Imager was able to recover these deleted files from the USB drive, even though they weren't visible in File Explorer.

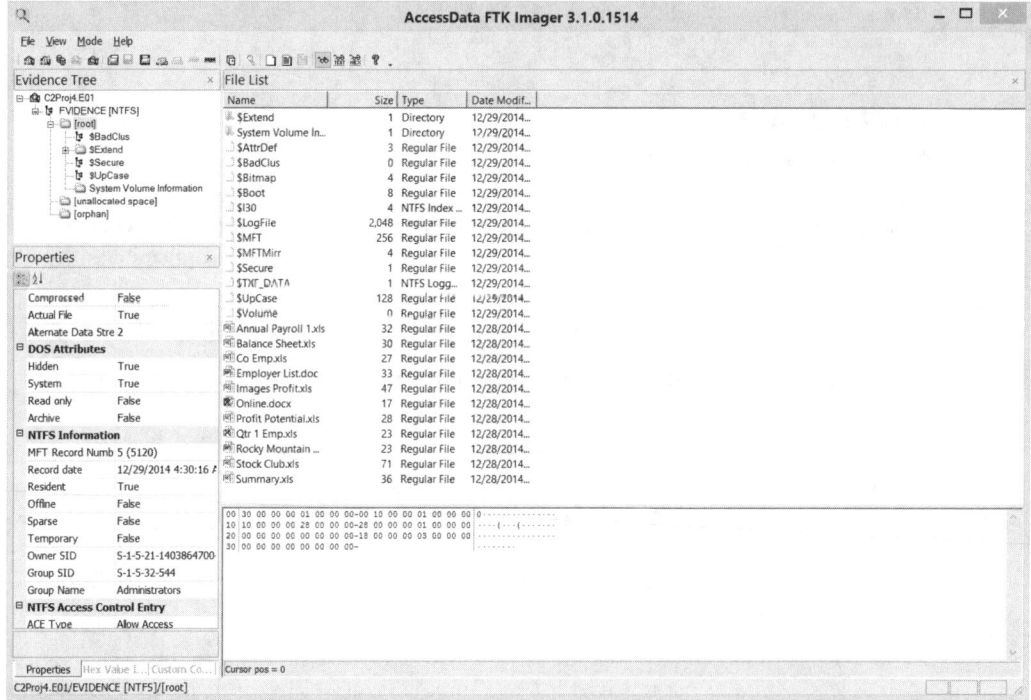

Figure 2-7   Viewing files on an imaged drive

5. In the File List pane, Ctrl+click the **Qtr 1 Emp.xls** and **Online.docx** deleted files. Right-click the **Online.docx** file and click **Export Files**, as shown in Figure 2-8.

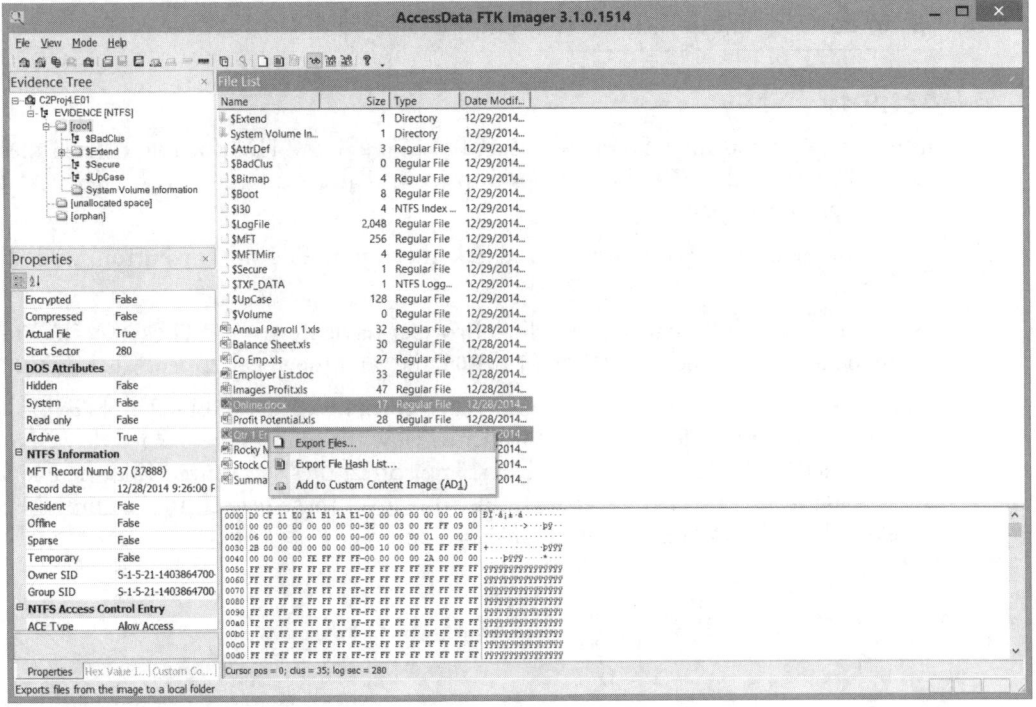

Figure 2-8   Exporting files

©2015 AccessData Group, Inc. All Rights Reserved.

6. In the Browse For Folder dialog box, navigate to and click the **C:\Work\Labs\Evidence** folder, click **OK** to export the files, and then click **OK** in the Export Results dialog box.

7. In the File List pane, Ctrl+click the **Qtr 1 Emp.xls** and **Online.docx** deleted files. Right-click the **Online.docx** file and click **Export File Hash List**.

8. In the Save As dialog box, type **C2Proj4 deleted file hashes** in the File name text box, and then click **Save**.

9. Answer the following review questions, and when you're finished, exit FTK Imager. In File Explorer, navigate to and click the **C:\Work\Labs\Evidence** folder. Find and double-click the exported **C2Proj4 deleted file hashes.csv** file to open it in Excel. Review the Excel spreadsheet listing the two deleted files and their MD5 and SHA-1 hashes. Expand the columns, if needed, to view the full hash values, as shown in Figure 2-9, and then exit Excel.

10. In File Explorer, locate the C2Proj2.dd and C2Proj2.eve images. Notice that the image size is about the same for each image type. Now find the C2Proj4.E01 image, and notice that it's much smaller. FTK Imager creates a compressed image yet preserves all the evidence.

11. Close any open windows.

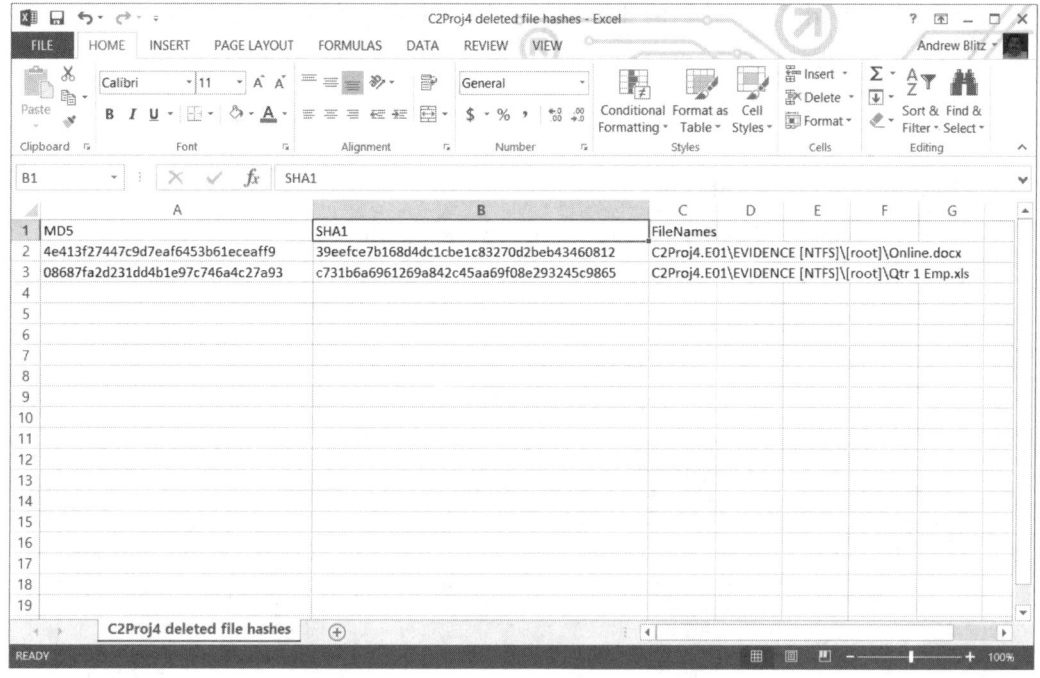

Figure 2-9   Viewing deleted file hashes

Review Questions

1. How many Excel files were recovered in the C2Proj4.E01 image?

   a. 3

   b. 7

   c. 11

   d. 4

2. How many deleted files were recovered in the C2Proj4.E01 image?

   a. 2

   b. 7

   c. 11

   d. 4

3. What's the filename of the deleted Excel file in the C2Proj4.E01 image?

   a. Annual Payroll 1.xls

   b. Profit Potential.xls

   c. Qtr 1 Emp.xls

   d. Online.xls

4. What's the name of the deleted Word file in the `C2Proj4.E01` image?

   a. `Employer List.doc`

   b. `Online.docx`

   c. `Rocky Mountain Outline.doc`

   d. None of the above

5. How many SHA-1 hash files were exported to the `C2Proj4 deleted file hashes.csv` file?

   a. 4

   b. 2

   c. 1

   d. None of the above

CHAPTER THREE

DATA ACQUISITION

Labs included in this chapter:

Lab 3.1 Creating a Mini-WinFE Boot CD

Objectives

Bootable forensic tools can be useful when removing a computer or internal hard drives isn't practical because of a connection with networking components or because removing systems could disrupt an organization's business operations. One such tool is Windows Forensic Environment (WinFE), created by Troy Larson at Microsoft. It's based on the Windows Pre-installation Environment (WinPE) that system builders use to image new computers. This bare-bones version of Windows makes it possible to install forensics tools on a boot CD that runs in the RAM of a computer under investigation. Using this boot CD prevents changes to log and OS files as the computer starts. You can also add scripts for installing write-protection, acquisition, and search tools as the CD is being prepared to examine disks in read-only mode, which helps protect evidence from being changed.

Having acquisition tools on a boot CD enables investigators to create forensic images of storage devices or hardware attached to a physical computer or network. Mini-WinFE is a modified version of WinFE that includes several forensics tools and a write-protection tool created by Colin Ramsden, a senior forensic computing analyst with the Royal Military Police. In this lab, you use Mini-WinFE to build a boot CD.

This lab requires a licensed copy of Microsoft Windows 8 or 8.1 Professional Edition (32-bit) to supply the necessary system files.

After completing this lab, you will be able to:

- Prepare a Mini-WinFE boot environment with forensics tools
- Create a Windows boot CD

Materials Required

This lab requires the following:

- The Windows 8 or 8.1 Professional Edition installation disc
- A blank CD
- The `Mini-WinFE.2014.07.03.zip` and `winhex.zip` files on the DVD

Estimated completion time: **30–45 minutes**

Activity

In this lab, you build a Mini-WinFE image that can be burned to a Windows boot CD with forensics tools:

1. Start a Web browser, and go to **http://accessdata.com/product-download.** Download the installation file for FTK Imager 3.1.1, and install this product on your system in the Imager_Lite_3.1.1 folder (creating this folder first, if necessary).

2. In File Explorer, right-click the **Mini-WinFE.2014.07.03.zip** file on the DVD and click **Extract All.** Click to clear the **Show extracted files when complete** check box. Click **Browse,** navigate to and click the **C** drive, click **OK,** and then click **Extract.**

3. Next, copy the **winhex.zip** file on the DVD to the **C:\Mini-WinFE** folder.

4. Right-click the `winhex.zip` file and extract it to the **C:\Mini-WinFE** folder.

5. In the C:\Mini-WinFE folder, create a subfolder named **Windows Installation Files**. Remove the book's DVD, and insert the Windows installation disc. Copy all files on this disc to the Windows Installation Files folder you created.

6. Double-click the `WinBuilder.exe` file in the Windows Installation Files folder. If necessary, click **Yes** in the UAC message box. After WinBuilder starts, expand the **Programs** folder in the left pane, and click the **F.A.U.** and **FTK Imager Lite** check boxes, if necessary. Next to the PATH to "FTK Imager.exe" text box, click the folder icon. In the Open file dialog box, navigate to and double-click the **Imager_Lite_3.1.1** folder, click the **FTK Imager.exe** file, and click **Open**. Verify that the path to the `FTK Imager.exe` file is correct (see Figure 3-1).

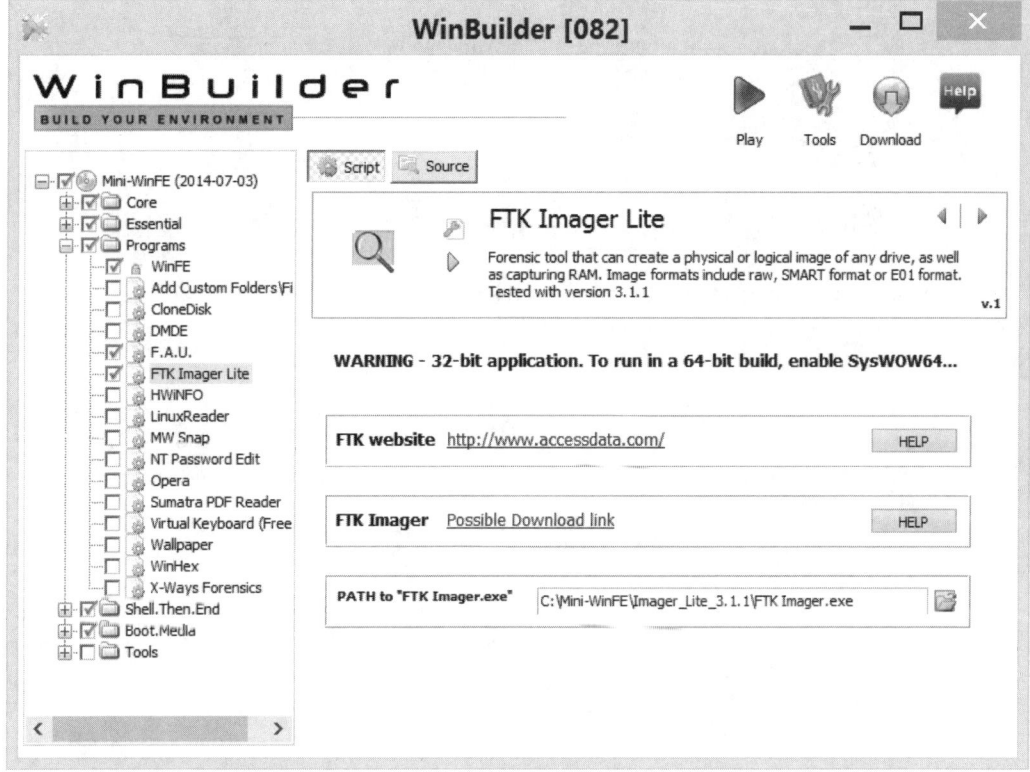

Figure 3-1   Verifying the path to `FTK Imager.exe`

Source: http://winbuilder.net

7. In the left pane, click **WinHex**. Next to the PATH to "winhex.exe" text box, click the folder icon, navigate to and double-click the **winhex** folder, click the **WinHex.exe** file, and click **Open**. Verify that the path to the `WinHex.exe` file is correct (see Figure 3-2).

8. Expand the **Tools** folder, and click the **ADK For Win 8** and **ADK For Win 8.1** check boxes. Click the **Source** button at the top of the right pane. Next to the Source directory text box, click the folder icon. In the Browse For Folder dialog box, navigate to and click the **Windows Installation Files** folder, and then click **OK**. Verify that your window looks like Figure 3-3.

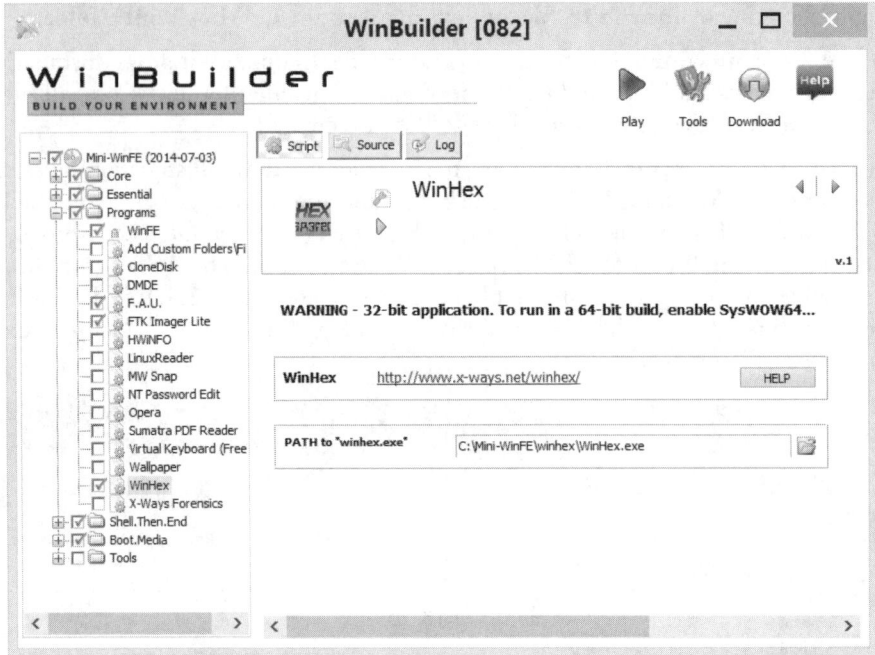

Figure 3-2   Verifying the path to `WinHex.exe`

Source: http://winbuilder.net

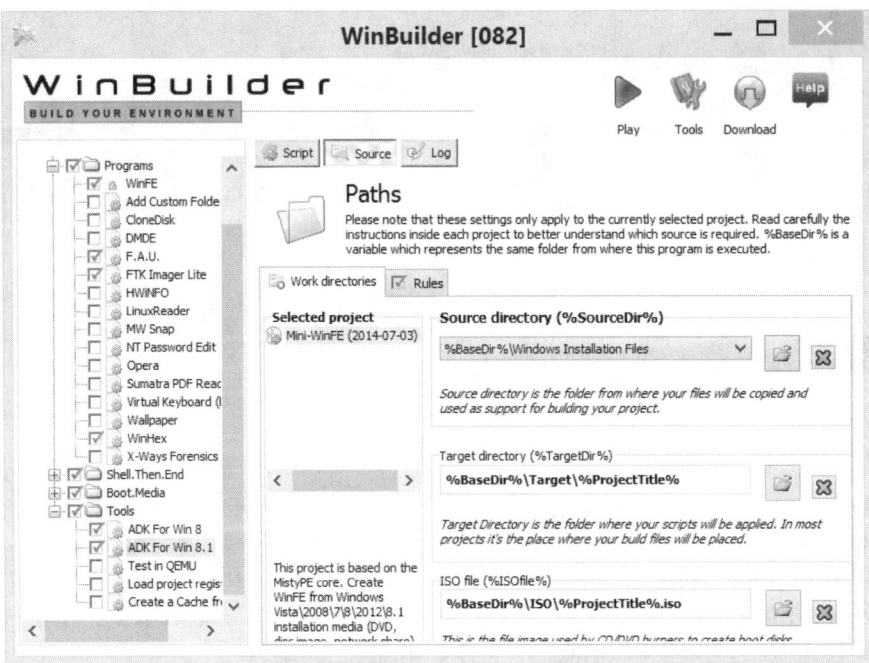

Figure 3-3   Selecting files to include in the boot environment

Source: http://winbuilder.net

9. Click the **Script** button at the top of the right pane, and click the **Play** button at the upper right to build the ISO image. Click **Yes** in the Confirm message box to accept x86 settings, and then WinBuilder processes the scripts and builds an ISO image. If you get an error message, click **OK**. When the process is finished, exit WinBuilder.

10. Insert a blank CD in your CD/DVD drive. In File Explorer, navigate to the **C:\Mini-WinFE** folder, and open the **WinFE.Project.Output** folder. Right-click the `WinPE.iso` file, point to **Burn disc image**, and click **Burn**.

11. After the disc has been created, click **Close**. Eject the CD, and label it **Mini-WinFE Forensic Bootable Disc**. You use this disc in future labs. When you're finished, close all open windows, and leave your computer running for the next lab.

Review Questions

1. WinFE and Mini-WinFE run in Windows on the computer being examined. True or False?

2. Where does a WinFE boot CD run?

   a. On the MFT

   b. In RAM

   c. In the Registry

   d. In unallocated space

3. Examining disks in which mode helps protect evidence from being changed?

   a. Write mode

   b. Safe Boot mode

   c. Read-only mode

   d. Read/write mode

4. With a boot CD, you can create forensic images of which of the following? (Choose all that apply.)

   a. The boot disc

   b. The computer's RAM

   c. Attached hardware

   d. Attached storage devices

5. A computer can be booted by using only an ISO image. True or False?

Lab 3.2 Examining a FAT32 Image

Objectives

FAT32, an improved version of the FAT16 file system, supports disk drives up to 2 terabytes (TB) and filenames up to 255 characters. It's supported by Linux and Mac OS X as well as all versions of Windows except early versions of Windows 95.

After completing this lab, you will be able to:

- Examine a FAT32 dd image in FTK Imager
- Identify a FAT32 file signature

Materials Required

This lab requires the following:

- Windows 8 or 8.1 Professional
- FTK Imager
- WordPad or another text editor
- The C3Proj2.001 file copied from the Chap03 folder on the DVD to your Work\ Labs folder

> Estimated completion time: **15–20 minutes**

Activity

In this lab, you use FTK Imager to examine a FAT32 file structure on a USB device:

1. Double-click the **FTK Imager** desktop icon. If necessary, click **Yes** in the UAC message box.

2. Click **File, Add Evidence Item** from the menu. In the Select Source dialog box, click the **Image File** option button, and then click **Next**.

3. In the Evidence Source Selection dialog box, click **Browse**, navigate to and click your **Work\ Labs** folder, click the **C3Proj2.001** file, and click **Open**. Click **Finish** to load the file.

4. The lower-right pane identifies the file system as MSDOS5.0 FAT32. Expand **C3Proj2.001** and **USBDEVICE [FAT32]** in the Evidence Tree pane, and click **C3Proj2.001** to select it. The Properties pane shows the image type as raw (dd) and the original disk geometry as 512 bytes per sector with a total of 249,341 sectors.

5. Click to expand the [**root**] folder. The File List pane shows the files in the C3Proj2.001 image and their timestamps. The red X next to some files indicates that the user deleted them. Click each file (including the deleted files) to view it.

6. Click the **HEX** toolbar button to display the hexadecimal values for each file. Click the **Bank Location.doc** file, view its hex information, and review its details in the Properties pane (see Figure 3-4). The file signature and file size are the same as in FAT16; however, the start cluster and start sector are different than in FAT16.

7. Click the **interior safe.jpg** file in the File List pane, and notice the JFIF file signature for a JPEG file. Click the **eyeglasses** toolbar button to see the file in the image viewer.

8. Click to expand the **USBDEVICE [FAT32]** folder, if necessary, and examine the FAT32 file structure and all the files in it. Make a screen capture by pressing **Ctrl+Print Screen**, and then start WordPad. Right-click in the empty document and click **Paste**. Save the file in the **Documents** folder with the filename **Structures**, and then exit WordPad.

9. Leave FTK Imager open as you answer the following review questions. When you're finished, exit FTK Imager, and leave your computer running for the next lab.

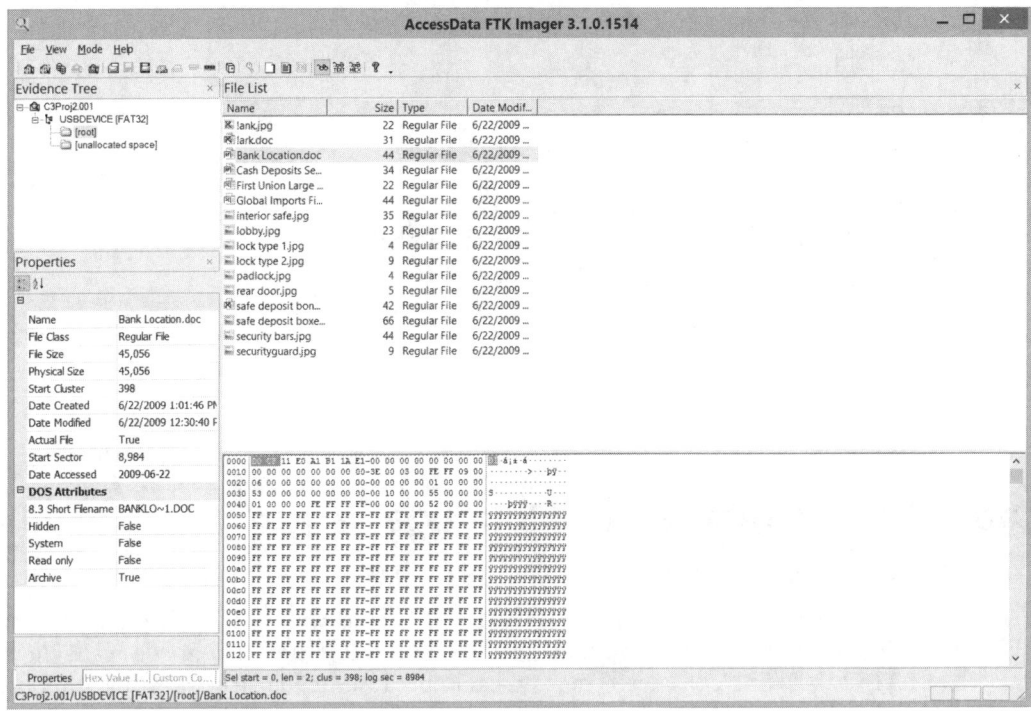

Figure 3-4   Viewing a FAT32 file

Review Questions

1. How many clusters are in the FAT32 image?

   a. 120,229

   b. 120,574

   c. 2048

   d. 8192

2. How many files (existing and deleted) are in the FAT32 image?

   a. 9

   b. 11

   c. 16

   d. 10

3. How many Excel files are in the FAT32 image?

   a. 3

   b. 2

   c. 1

   d. 13

4. What's the start sector of the deleted Excel file?

   a. 214

   b. 8,616

   c. 8,306

   d. 8,262

5. What's the FAT32 drive's volume serial number?

   a. 929E-685C

   b. 2048

   c. 99E-0766

   d. 249,341

Lab 3.3 Examining an NTFS Image

Objectives

NTFS is the default file system in NT 3.51 and later as well as Windows Server OSs because it includes file attributes such as compression and encryption that aren't available in FAT16 or FAT32. NTFS is considered more reliable because of file structures that support redundancy, such as a duplicate Master File Table (MFT) and journaling. NTFS also supports file encryption based on user account information so that multiple users on the same computer can't open each other's encrypted files.

After completing this lab, you will be able to:

- Examine an NTFS dd image in FTK Imager
- Identify an NTFS file signature

Materials Required

This lab requires the following:

- Windows 8 or 8.1 Professional
- FTK Imager
- WordPad or another text editor
- The C3Proj3.001 file copied from the Chap03 folder on the DVD to your Work\ Labs folder

Estimated completion time: **30–40 minutes**

Activity

In this lab, you examine the NTFS file structure and compare it with the FAT32 file structure on a USB storage device:

1. Double-click the **FTK Imager** desktop icon. If necessary, click **Yes** in the UAC message box.

2. Click **File, Add Evidence Item** from the menu. In the Select Source dialog box, click the **Image File** option button, and then click **Next**.

3. In the Evidence Source Selection dialog box, click **Browse**, navigate to and click your **Work\ Labs** folder, click the **C3Proj3.001** file, and click **Open**. Click **Finish** to load the file.

4. The lower-left pane identifies the file system as NTFS. Expand **C3Proj3.001** and **USBDevice [NTFS]** in the Evidence Tree pane, and click **C3Proj3.001** to select it. The Properties pane shows the image type as raw (dd) and the original disk geometry as 512 bytes per sector with a total of 251,904 sectors.

5. Click the **[root]** folder. The File List pane shows the files in the **C3Proj3.001** image and their timestamps. Notice that NTFS has additional hidden folders for bad cluster identification ($BadClus) and two copies of the MFT ($MFT and $MFTMirr), as shown in Figure 3-5.

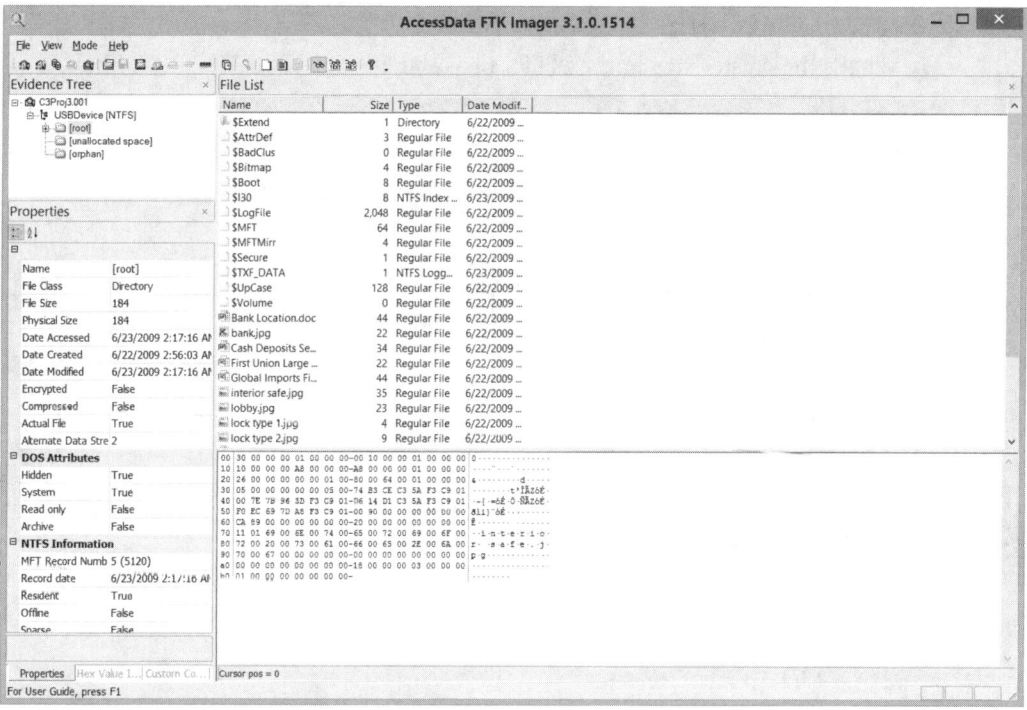

Figure 3-5   Viewing an NTFS image

©2015 AccessData Group, Inc. All Rights Reserved.

6. Click each deleted file (with a red X) to view it. Notice that NTFS uses a Date Accessed field in addition to the Date Created and Date Modified fields.

7. Click the **HEX** toolbar button to display the hexadecimal values for each file. Click the **Bank Location.doc** file, view its hex information, and review its details in the Properties pane. The file signature and file size are the same as in FAT16 and FAT32, but the start locations are different.

8. Click the **interior safe.jpg** file in the File List pane, and notice that the JFIF file signature is the same as the FAT16 and FAT32 file signatures for JPEG files. In addition,

NTFS displays Exif file data with information on a digital camera's model and manufacturer as well as its shutter speed, lens aperture, and ISO speed. This information can be useful to forensics investigators.

9. Notice the complex file structure of the [root] folder, compared with other file systems. Expand all subfolders under [root] to see, for example, the $Secure attribute indexes that support NTFS file permissions and the [orphan] folder used to repair files with broken pointers or corrupted indexes.

10. Make a screen capture, and save it in the WordPad **Structures** document. Exit WordPad.

11. Leave FTK Imager open as you answer the following review questions. When you're finished, exit FTK Imager, and leave your computer running for the next lab.

Review Questions

1. What's the cluster size in the NTFS file system?

    a. 2048

    b. 1024

    c. 4096

    d. 31,487

2. What's the volume serial number of the NTFS image?

    a. E16-566

    b. E6FE-1C5F

    c. 2048

    d. 4096

3. What time was the bank.jpg file deleted?

    a. 2:15:31 a.m.

    b. 4:59:14 p.m.

    c. 12:37:00 p.m.

    d. 12:37:21 p.m.

4. What's the physical size of the deleted mark.doc file?

    a. 31,744

    b. 32,768

    c. 14,808

    d. 118,464

5. What folder in the NTFS image isn't in the FAT32 image?

    a. [unallocated space]

    b. [root]

    c. [orphan]

    d. [encryption]

Lab 3.4 Examining an HFS+ Image

Objectives

HFS+, the file system for Mac OS X 10.4 and later, maintains a journal similar to NTFS to keep track of file changes attempted but not completed because of file errors or hard disk crashes. This journaling feature allows the file system to recover from sudden disk crashes or power losses during a write operation. HFS+ is less susceptible to file corruption caused by broken or missing pointers between blocks of data on a storage device.

After completing this lab, you will be able to:

- Process an HFS+ image in FTK Imager
- Explain the difference between HFS+, FAT32, and NTFS file systems
- Find deleted files

Materials Required

This lab requires the following:

- Windows 8 or 8.1 Professional
- FTK Imager
- WordPad or another text editor
- The `C3Proj4.001` image file copied from the Chap03 folder on the DVD to your Work\Labs folder

Estimated completion time: **10–15 minutes**

Activity

In this lab, you examine the HFS+ file structure and compare it with the FAT32 and NTFS file structures on a USB storage device:

1. Double-click the **FTK Imager** desktop icon. If necessary, click **Yes** in the UAC message box.

2. Click **File, Add Evidence Item** from the menu. In the Select Source dialog box, click the **Image File** option button, and then click **Next**.

3. In the Evidence Source Selection dialog box, click **Browse**, navigate to and click your **Work\Labs** folder, click the **C3Proj4.001** image file, and click **Open**. Click **Finish** to load the image file.

4. Expand **C3Proj4.001** and **USBDevice[HFS+]** in the Evidence Tree pane, and click **C3Proj4.001** to select it. The file properties show the image type as raw (dd) and the original disk geometry as 512 bytes per sector with a total of 249,228 sectors.

5. Expand the **USBDevice** folder in the Evidence Tree pane. The File List pane shows the files in the `C3Proj4.001` image and their timestamps (see Figure 3-6). Notice that there's no [root] folder. Examine the hidden folders (.journal and .journal_info_block) used for journaling file transactions. The Properties pane also shows the UNIX permissions for the USBDevice folder: read, write, delete, and modify.

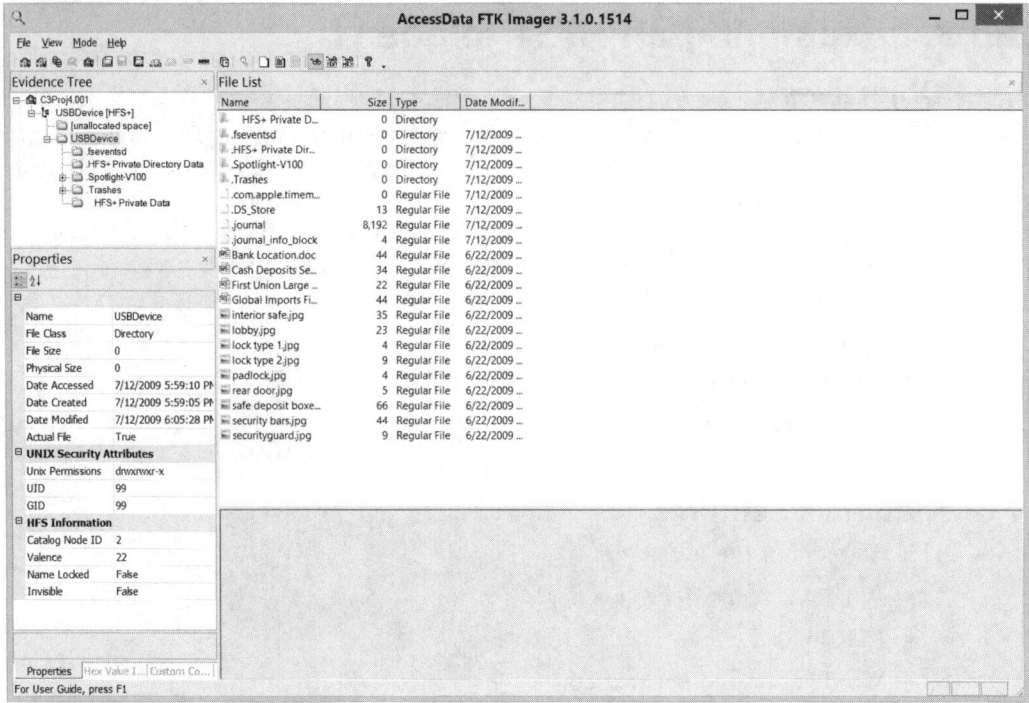

Figure 3-6 Viewing an HFS+ image

©2015 AccessData Group, Inc. All Rights Reserved.

6. Expand the **.Trashes** folder and click the **501** folder. You should see the same deleted files you've seen in previous labs, but HFS+ doesn't add a red X to indicate they were deleted.

7. Click each file with an extension to view its properties and security attributes. The Properties pane lists a Date Accessed field in addition to the Date Created and Date Modified fields.

8. Click the **HEX** toolbar button to display the hexadecimal values for each file. Click the **Bank Location.doc** file, view its hex information, and review its details in the Properties pane. The file signature is the same as in FAT16, FAT32, and NTFS, but the start locations are different in HFS+.

9. Click the **interior safe.jpg** file in the File List pane, and notice that the JFIF file signature is the same as in FAT16 and FAT32. HFS+ also displays Exif file data, as NTFS does.

10. Examine the complex file structure of the USBDevice folder. Make a screen capture, and save it in the WordPad **Structures** document. Exit WordPad.

11. Leave FTK Imager open as you answer the following review questions. When you're finished, exit FTK Imager.

Review Questions

1. What's the cluster size in the HFS+ image?

    a. 1024

    b. 2048

    c. 4096

    d. 3077

2. How many clusters are in the HFS+ image?

    a. 31,153

    b. 21,866

    c. 28,099

    d. 249,228

3. What date was the HFS+ partition created?

    a. 6/22/2009

    b. 7/16/2009

    c. 7/12/2009

    d. 7/14/2009

4. What folder doesn't exist in HFS+ but is found in FAT32 and NTFS?

    a. [encryption]

    b. [USB]

    c. [unallocated space]

    d. [root]

5. In what folder are deleted files stored?

    a. .Trashes

    b. 501

    c. [orphan]

    d. [unallocated space]

CHAPTER FOUR

PROCESSING CRIME AND INCIDENT SCENES

Labs included in this chapter:

- Lab 4.1 Using Mini-WinFE to Boot and Image a Windows Computer
- Lab 4.2 Testing the WinFE Write-Protection Tool
- Lab 4.3 Using DEFT Linux to Boot and Search a Windows Computer
- Lab 4.4 Creating an Image with DEFT

Lab 4.1 Using Mini-WinFE to Boot and Image a Windows Computer

Objectives

Forensics evidence can be located on a local computer, networked computers, servers, or network-attached storage devices. In addition, Windows servers might use hardware RAID drives that can't be imaged without using existing physical hardware and booting into the server's OS, which could alter potential evidence. In Lab 3.1, you created a Mini-WinFE boot CD that includes FTK Imager, WinHex, a write-protection tool, and several Windows tools on a bootable Windows platform. You can use this disc to mount and examine Windows attached storage devices safely and ensure that the chain of custody is preserved. The Write Protect tool is a software write-blocker that can be configured as read-only or read/write without shutting down and restarting the computer. The read-only mode prevents files stored on a hard drive from being changed as they're examined or when the computer starts, and the read/write mode allows writing file changes to the disk. Investigators can connect internal drives to the computer via the hard drive ports on the motherboard or attach external storage devices to facilitate imaging in Mini-WinFE.

Because Mini-WinFE is built on the WinPE environment, many Windows tools, such as File Manager, `diskpart`, `regedit`, and a command prompt window, are available for investigators to use. You can use `diskpart` to list hard drive partitions, create drive partitions, format drives, and examine information about bootable disks during an investigation. Windows Registry is a central repository that stores settings for the Windows environment, including user accounts, passwords, hardware devices, and installed software. You can use `regedit` to extract forensics information from the Registry. In this lab, you use Mini-WinFE to boot and image a Windows computer.

After completing this lab, you will be able to:

- Boot a Windows computer by using Mini-WinFE
- Create an image of a Windows hard drive

Materials Required

This lab requires the following:

- Windows 8 or 8.1 Professional
- The Mini-WinFE boot CD from Lab 3.1
- An additional external or internal hard drive equal to or larger than the Windows bootable hard drive in your computer
- A SATA cable, if necessary

Estimated completion time: **60–180 minutes,** depending on the hard drive's size

Activity

In this activity, you use Mini-WinFE to boot and image a Windows computer:

1. Start your computer, enter the BIOS Setup utility, and change the boot order to check the CD/DVD-ROM drive first. (Ask your instructor if you need help with this task.) Exit the BIOS Setup utility, saving the changes, and shut down the computer.

2. Remove the power supply, and open the computer case. Locate the hard drive, and note its capacity on the hard drive label.

3. Connect a second hard drive (larger than your computer's hard drive, as specified in the Materials Required list), using an unused internal SATA connector on the motherboard. Verify that the power supply and SATA cable on the second hard drive are connected, and position the second hard drive so that it's not resting on a metal surface.

4. Turn on the computer, and insert the Mini-WinFE boot CD created in Lab 3.1 in the CD/DVD-ROM drive. When the computer starts, click **OK** in the warning message, shown in Figure 4-1. The WinFE Write Protect Tool Management Console opens, and you should see two disks listed (see Figure 4-2). Neither disk is mounted, and both are set to read-only mode. In this example, Disk 1 is the original hard drive on your computer, and Disk 0 is the second hard drive that you connected.

4

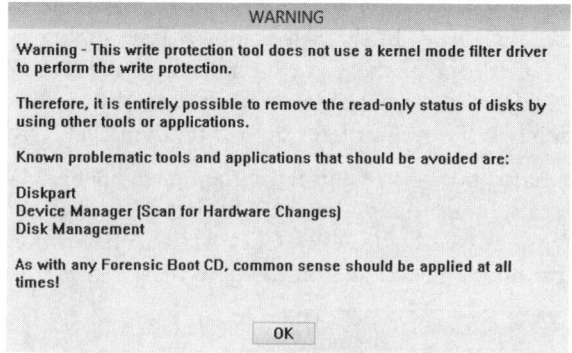

Figure 4-1   The Mini-WinFE warning message

 The settings and sizes might be different on your computer. You need to determine which disk is your boot disk and which one is the second hard drive you connected.

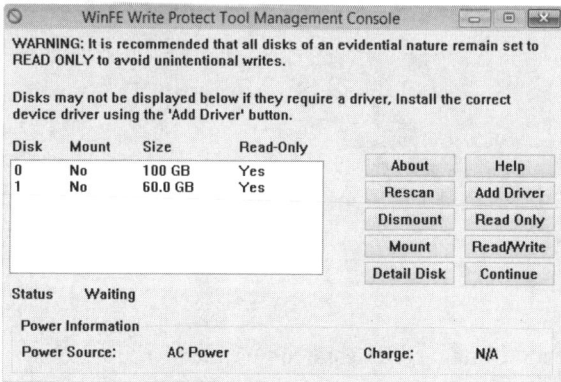

Figure 4-2   Viewing disk settings

5. Click disk **0**, and click the **Read/Write** button on the right. In the Read/Write - Warning message box, click **Yes**. The Read-Only status changes to No, indicating that the disk can now be written to. Click to select disk **0**, if necessary, and click the **Mount** button. In the Mount Disk - Warning message box, click **Yes** to verify that this disk will be connected and ready to receive data.

6. Click disk **1**, and click the **Mount** button. In the Mount Disk - Warning message box, click **Yes**. Click **Continue**.

7. The Windows Forensic Environment desktop is displayed. Note that there's no Start menu, so you select tools by right-clicking the desktop. Right-click the desktop, point to **FORENSIC TOOLS**, and click **FTK Imager**. Click **File**, **Create Disk Image** from the menu. In the Select Source dialog box, click **Next**. In the Select Drive dialog box, click the **Source Drive Selection** list arrow, click the drive containing the Windows partition in the drop-down list, and then click **Finish**.

8. In the Create Image dialog box, click **Add**. In the Select Image Type dialog box, click **E01**, and then click **Next**. Type **C4Proj1** in the Case Number and Evidence Number text boxes, and then click **Next**. Click the **Browse** button next to the Image Destination Folder text box, navigate to and click the second hard drive, and then click **OK**.

9. In the Select Image Destination dialog box, type **C4Proj1** in the Image Filename text box, and then click **Finish**. In the Create Image dialog box, verify that the image source and image destination settings are correct (see Figure 4-3). Click **Start** to begin the imaging process, which could take several hours, depending on the hard drive's size.

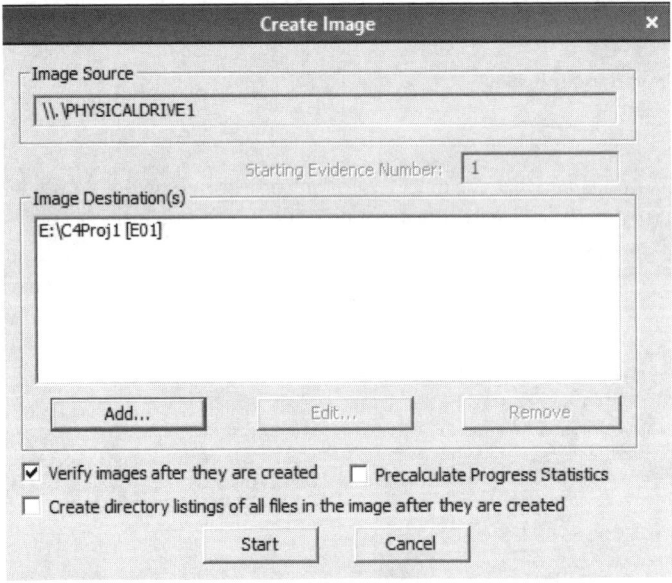

Figure 4-3   Checking settings for imaging

10. When the image is finished, exit FTK Imager, but leave the Windows Forensic Environment desktop open as you answer the following review questions. When you're finished, right-click the desktop, point to **Shutdown**, and click **Shutdown**. Remove the power supply from the computer, remove the second drive, and replace the cover on your computer.

Review Questions

1. The WinFE write-protection tool mounts any hard drive connected to the computer automatically. True or False?

2. Which of the following operations is available in the Write Protect Tool Management Console? (Choose all that apply.)

    a. Mount

    b. Verify Disk

    c. Read Only

    d. Read/Write

3. Which of the following settings prevents making changes to an attached disk?

    a. Rescan

    b. Mount

    c. Read Only

    d. Read/Write

4. To use a boot CD, you must change the boot order in the Windows Safe Mode menu first. True or False?

5. Disks connected to a computer that's booted with Mini-WinFE are displayed automatically in the WinFE Write Protect Tool Management Console. True or False?

Lab 4.2 Testing the WinFE Write-Protection Tool

Objectives

As Windows computers boot or are shut down, changes are made to files and folders that can change dates, log files, and most recently used (MRU) devices recorded in the Windows Registry. Therefore, before you search a live storage device, you must use a write-blocker to prevent any changes that could affect the chain of custody. Write-blocker tools can be hardware or software, and they're designed to allow examining and imaging computer files or OSs without altering potential evidence. They can be used in two modes: read only, which allows forensics tools to search without changing file attributes (such as last modified or last accessed times), and read/write, which allows changes to file attribute dates and log files on live storage devices so that forensics tools can be used. Write-blocker tools aren't needed to search CDs and DVDs because they're read-only devices and don't need to be mounted. In this lab, you test the WinFE write-protection tool.

After completing this lab, you will be able to:

- Verify that the WinFE write-protection tool is working correctly

Materials Required

This lab requires the following:

- Windows 8 or 8.1 Professional
- The Mini-WinFE boot CD from Lab 3.1

Estimated completion time: **15–20 minutes**

Activity

In this lab, you verify that the WinFE write-protection tool is working correctly:

1. Power on your computer, and insert the Mini-WinFE boot CD. Click **OK** in the warning message, and verify that Disk 0 isn't mounted and is set to read-only mode.

2. Click disk **0**, and click the **Mount** button. In the Mount Disk - Warning message box, click **Yes**. Verify that disk 0 is mounted and in read-only mode (see Figure 4-4). Click **Continue**.

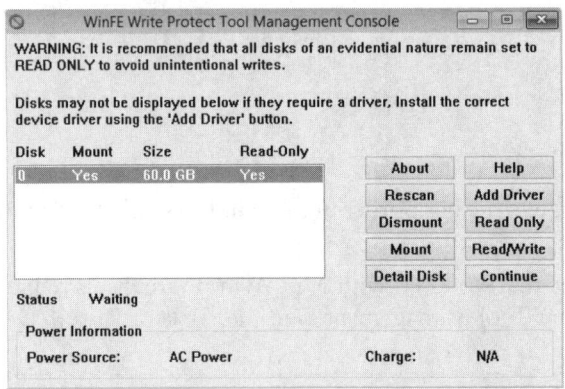

Figure 4-4   Mounting disk 0 and setting it to read-only mode

3. Right-click the Windows Forensic Environment desktop and click **File Manager**. When File Manager opens, right-click **Local Disk** in the left pane and click **Rename**. Type **Test** and press **Enter**. In the error message noting that the disk is write-protected (see Figure 4-5), click **OK**.

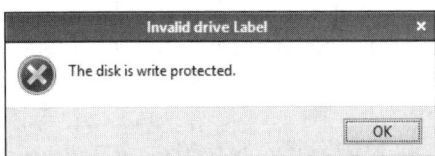

Figure 4-5   Error message about a write-protected disk

4. Close the File Manager window. Right-click the Windows Forensic Environment desktop, point to **FORENSIC TOOLS,** and click **Write Protect Tool.**

5. Click disk 0, and click the **Dismount** button. (You must dismount the disk before changing the mode.) Click the **Read/Write** button, and in the Read/Write - Warning message box, click **Yes.**

6. With disk 0 selected, click the **Mount** button, and then click **Yes** in the warning message. Verify that disk 0 is mounted and set to read-only mode, and then close this console.

7. Right-click the Windows Forensic Environment desktop and click **File Manager.** Right-click **Local Disk** in the left pane and click **Rename.** Type **Test** and press **Enter.** The local disk's name changes to Test.

8. Close File Manager, and then reopen it to confirm that the name change has been saved. Leave File Manager open as you answer the following review questions. When you're finished, close File Manager. Right-click the desktop, point to **Shutdown,** and click **Shutdown.**

Review Questions

1. Why were you unable to change the disk name in Step 3?

    a. Disk 0 was mounted.

    b. Disk 0 had been dismounted.

    c. Disk 0 was in read/write mode.

    d. Disk 0 was in read-only mode.

2. In the WinFE write-protection tool, you can change a disk to read/write mode while it's mounted. True or False?

3. You can search files on a hard drive while it's set to read-only mode in the WinFE write-protection tool. True or False?

4. You can use the WinFE File Manager to do which of the following?

    a. Change the read/write mode of files on the hard drive.

    b. Examine files and folders on storage devices.

    c. Boot the computer's hard drive safely.

    d. Examine the hard drive's physical size.

5. You can't search CDs or DVDs in WinFE File Manager. True or False?

Lab 4.3 Using DEFT Linux to Boot and Search a Windows Computer

Objectives

The Digital Evidence and Forensics Toolkit (DEFT) is a suite of Linux forensics tools available as a free download from the DEFT Association (*www.deftlinux.net*). This tool, widely used by law enforcement agencies around the world, is designed to boot computers without mounting attached storage devices, which prevents any changes from being written and avoids creating swap files. OSs, such as Windows and Linux, create swap files that move between RAM and long-term storage to support virtual memory in the computer, which extends fixed memory capacity and performance.

DEFT can be installed or used in a bootable DVD mode to search storage devices with full write-blocker functions on Windows, Linux, UNIX, and Mac OS X hard disk partitions. It includes many Linux and Windows tools to manage storage devices, connect to network services, browse the Internet, and explore files and folders with a complete suite of forensics tools. In addition, DEFT includes several disk-imaging utilities that support multiple formats and commercial digital forensics tools. In this lab, you create a DEFT boot DVD, mount a volume as read-only, and explore files with Microsoft Office–compatible viewers.

After completing this lab, you will be able to:

- Boot a computer with DEFT and enable the write-protection feature
- Use DEFT to search for and view Microsoft Office files safely

Materials Required

This lab requires the following:

- Windows 8 or 8.1 Professional
- The `deft-8.2.iso` file downloaded from *www.deftlinux.net*

Estimated completion time: **120 minutes**

Activity

In this lab, you create a DEFT boot DVD and use it to boot and search a Windows computer:

1. Start a Web browser, and go to **www.deftlinux.net**. Download the `deft-8.2.iso` file to your **Documents** folder. Insert a blank DVD in your DVD-ROM drive. Right-click the `deft-8.2.iso` file and click **Burn disc image** to create a boot DVD. When the disc has been created, leave it in the drive, and shut down the computer.

2. Start your computer, enter the BIOS Setup utility, and change the boot order to check the CD/DVD-ROM drive first. (Ask your instructor if you need help with this task.) Exit the BIOS Setup utility, saving the changes, and shut down the computer.

3. The computer boots into DEFT Linux and displays menus to choose a language and install options. Allow the disc to load without selecting an option so that the DEFT desktop opens (see Figure 4-6).

4. Double-click the **evidence** folder on the desktop. Right-click **NEW VOLUME** in the left pane and click **Mount in protected mode (Read Only)** (shown in Figure 4-7) to enable the write-protection feature. A green eject arrow is displayed next to the hard drive icon. Close this window.

The volume name might be different, depending on the OS installed on your computer.

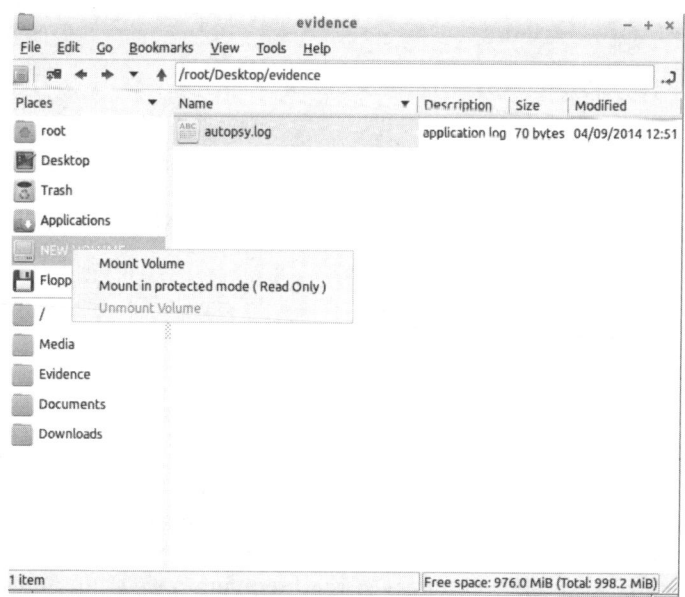

Figure 4-6 The DEFT desktop

Source: DEFT Linux, www.deftlinux.net

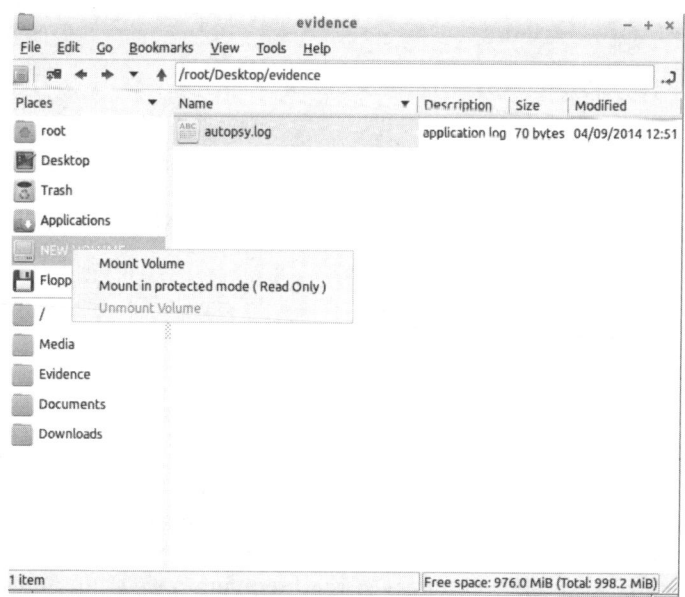

Figure 4-7 Enabling the write-protection feature in DEFT

Source: DEFT Linux, www.deftlinux.net

5. Double-click the **File Manager** icon on the DEFT desktop. Click **NEW VOLUME** in the left pane to view the folders in it. Click the **Users** folder, click a username, and then click **Documents** to view any documents created by this user (see Figure 4-8). (The usernames and stored documents on your system will be different from the ones shown in this figure.)

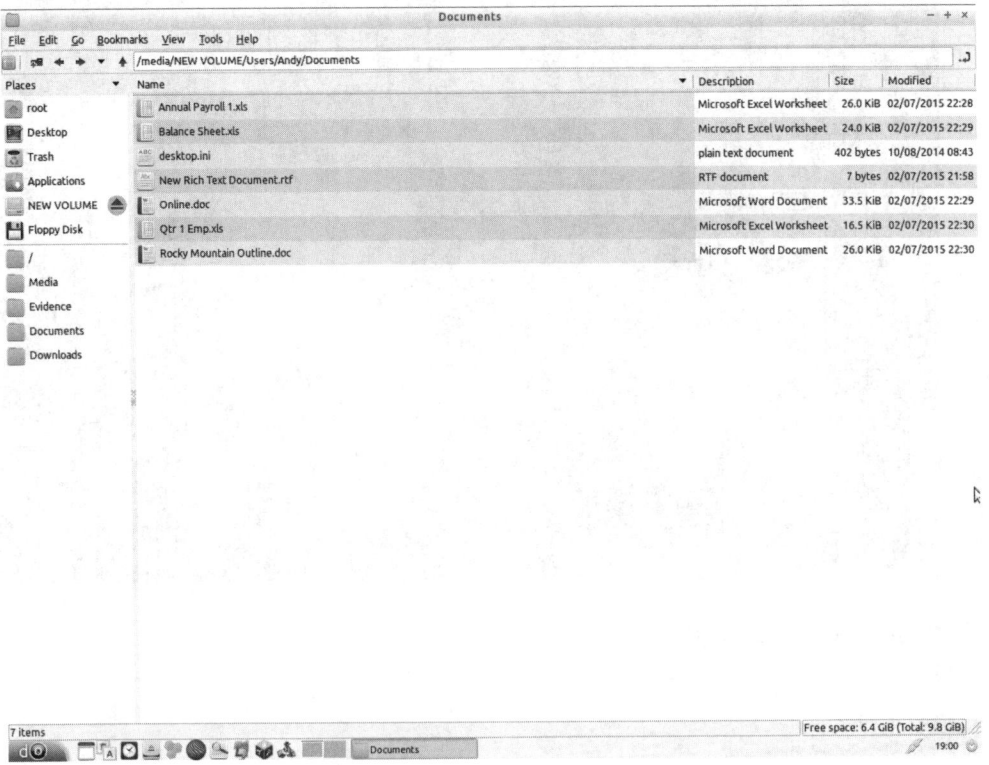

Figure 4-8   Viewing stored documents

Source: DEFT Linux, www.deftlinux.net

6. Double-click any file to open it with the corresponding Microsoft Office viewer. Figure 4-9 shows a Microsoft Excel file open.

7. Try to add text to the file you opened, and then click **File, Save** from the menu to save the changes. An error message informs you that the file is read-only, which confirms the write-protection feature is working.

8. Click **Close** in the error message, close the open file, and click **Discard** to close the file without saving your changes.

9. Close the File Manager window to return to the DEFT desktop. Click **d** at the lower left to view the program menu similar to the Windows listing. Click **DEFT** to view all the installed forensics tools. You use these tools in subsequent labs throughout this book. Leave the DEFT desktop open while you answer the following review questions.

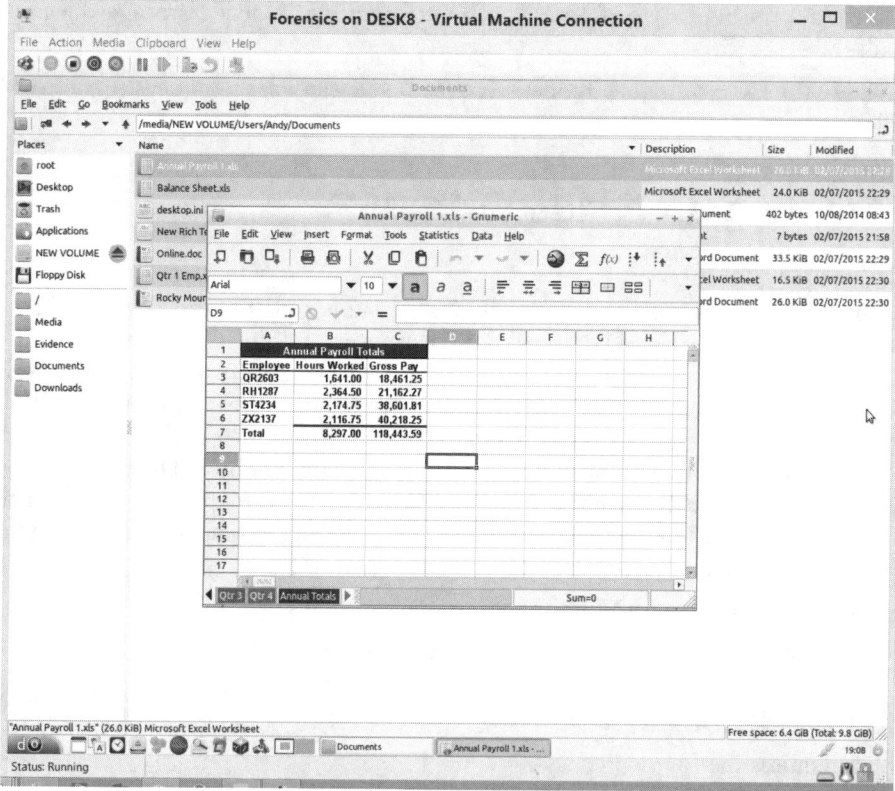

Figure 4-9   Opening a Microsoft Excel file

Source: DEFT Linux, www.deftlinux.net

10. When you're finished, click **d**, point to **Logout**, and then click **Shutdown** to exit DEFT. Power off your computer.

Review Questions

1. DEFT includes only Linux tools. True or False?

2. Which statement about the DEFT write-protection feature isn't true?

   a. It allows mounting storage devices.

   b. It allows unmounting storage devices.

   c. It enables read-only mode.

   d. It enables write-only mode.

3. DEFT includes which of the following features? (Choose all that apply.)

   a. Searching storage devices without causing changes to files

   b. Serving as an alternative word-processing program

   c. Browsing the Internet

   d. Viewing Microsoft Office files

4. DEFT allows booting computers without mounting attached storage devices. True or False?

5. While DEFT's _____ mode is enabled, you can't save changes made to Microsoft files.

Lab 4.4 Creating an Image with DEFT

Objectives

DEFT includes several tools to create disk images in multiple formats supported by commercial forensics suites, such as OSForensics, ProDiscover, and EnCase, and free forensics tools, such as Autopsy. It also has disk-mounting utilities, such as Guymager and MountManager, to view attached storage devices safely. Guymager handles the simultaneous acquisition of multiple mass storage devices in all major image formats and performs integrity checks by generating MD5 or SHA-256 hash values. In this lab, you configure DEFT's write-protection feature to mount your local hard drive in read-only mode to prepare it for imaging and mount an external or internal hard drive in read/write mode to acquire an image.

After completing this lab, you will be able to:

- Capture an image of a Windows computer with DEFT

- Create a disk image on an external or internal hard drive

Materials Required

This lab requires the following:

- Windows 8 or 8.1 Professional

- The DEFT boot DVD from Lab 4.3

- An additional external or internal NTFS-formatted hard drive equal to or larger than the Windows bootable hard drive in your computer

- A SATA cable, if necessary

Estimated completion time: **60–120 minutes,** depending on the hard drive's size

Activity

In this lab, you use DEFT to create an image of the Windows OS on your computer:

1. Start your computer, enter the BIOS Setup utility, and change the boot order to check the CD/DVD-ROM drive first. (Ask your instructor if you need help with this task.) Exit the BIOS Setup utility, saving the changes, and shut down the computer.

2. Remove the power supply, and open the computer case. Locate the hard drive, and note its capacity on the hard drive label.

3. Connect a second NTFS-formatted hard drive larger than your computer's hard drive (as specified in the Materials Required list), using an unused internal SATA connector on the motherboard. Verify that the power supply and SATA cable on the second hard drive are connected, and position the second hard drive so that it's not resting on a metal surface.

4. Turn on the computer, and insert the DEFT boot DVD in the CD/DVD-ROM drive. The computer boots into DEFT Linux and displays menus for choosing a language and installation options. Allow the disc to load without selecting an option so that you boot to the DEFT desktop.

5. Double-click the **evidence** folder on the desktop. Right-click **NEW VOLUME** in the left pane and click **Mount in protected mode (Read Only)** to enable the write-protection feature. Right-click the external or internal hard drive and click **Mount Volume**. Click **Yes** to mount the drive in read/write mode. As shown in Figure 4-10, a green eject arrow is displayed next to the source disk drive (NEW VOLUME, in this example), and a red eject arrow is displayed next to the destination disk (EXTERNAL, in this example). Close this window to return to the DEFT desktop.

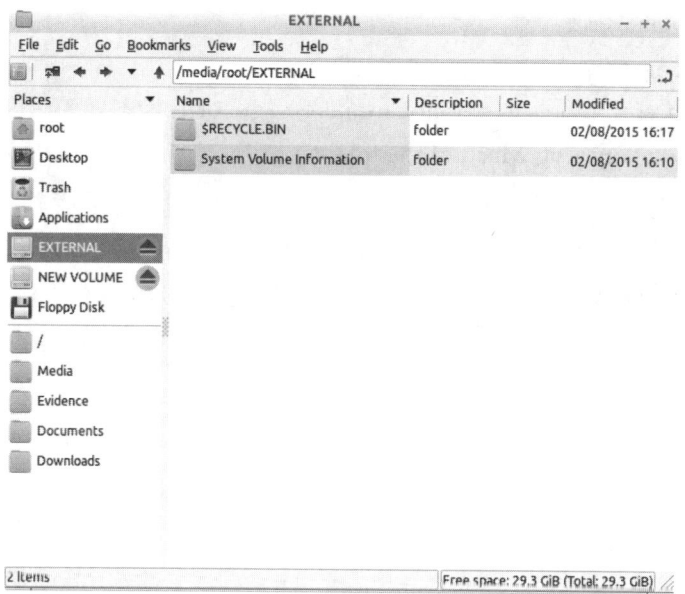

Figure 4-10 Mounting drives in read-only and read/write modes

Source: DEFT Linux, www.deftlinux.net

6. Double-click the **Guymager** desktop icon to open this program. Click to select the **/dev/sda** disk in the Linux device list box, and then right-click it and click **Acquire image**. In the "Acquire image of /dev/sda" dialog box, click the **Linux dd raw image** option button in the "File format" section. Click the **browse** button next to the "Image directory" text box, click the external or internal hard drive where the image will be saved, and enter **C4Proj4** in the second "Image filename (without extension)" text box. Click **Start** to begin the imaging process.

7. When the imaging process is finished, exit Guymager and close all open windows. Leave the DEFT desktop open as you answer the following review questions. When you're finished, exit DEFT, and shut down your computer.

Review Questions

1. Guymager creates disk images that are verified by using which of the following?

   a. Hard disk capacities

   b. MD5 and SHA-256 hash values

   c. Serial ATAs

   d. Linux device characters

2. DEFT doesn't support image formats of free forensics tools. True or False?

3. Attached drives that are read/write are indicated by which of the following in DEFT?

   a. A green eject arrow

   b. A red eject arrow

   c. A listing in File Manager

   d. A listing in Guymager

4. DEFT includes no forensics tools to search hard disks. True or False?

5. Guymager is capable of imaging which of the following?

   a. Only one disk at a time

   b. Multiple storage devices simultaneously

   c. Only dd-formatted images

   d. USB storage devices

Working with Windows and CLI Systems

Labs included in this chapter:

- Lab 5.1 Using DART to Export Windows Registry Files
- Lab 5.2 Examining the SAM Hive
- Lab 5.3 Examining the SYSTEM Hive
- Lab 5.4 Examining the `ntuser.dat` Registry File

Lab 5.1 Using DART to Export Windows Registry Files

Objectives

Investigators often encounter running computers that might contain valuable forensic data in RAM or other disk locations that would be lost if the system were shut down. DART is a collection of Windows tools on the DEFT boot DVD that can be used to examine and image a live Windows computer. It includes imaging, data recovery, forensics, incident response, networking, and password recovery tools as well as tools to view graphics, multimedia, and documents with open-source software. The DART tools can capture the contents of physical RAM on a live computer to yield valuable information, such as open files and cached credentials used to access computer and network resources. DART also includes acquisition tools, such as FTK Imager, HDDRawCopy, and RamCapture, for both 32-bit and 64-bit OSs. Its data recovery tools, such as TestDisk, can recover deleted files on storage devices, recover lost files, and search for FAT, FAT32, NTFS, Ext2, and Ext3 partitions. In this lab, you use the forensics tools in DART, such as FTK Imager, and recover Registry files from your live Windows computer.

After completing this lab, you will be able to:

- Describe the Windows forensics tools included with DART
- Export Registry files with FTK Imager

Materials Required

This lab requires the following:

- Windows 8 or 8.1 Professional
- The DEFT boot DVD from Lab 4.3

> Estimated completion time: **60–90 minutes,** depending on the hard drive's size

Activity

In this lab, you boot a Windows computer and use FTK Imager to export Registry files:

1. Start your computer. Insert the DEFT DVD in the DVD-ROM drive, open File Explorer, and navigate to the **dart.exe** file on the DVD.

2. Right-click the **dart.exe** file and click **Run as administrator**. If necessary, click **Yes** in the UAC message box. Click **Yes** in the DART DISCLAIMER dialog box. DART creates a folder for the log files.

3. Click **Cancel** in the Browse For Folder dialog box, and click **Yes** in the DART DISCLAIMER dialog box to start DART 2.0 without creating a log file. The DART 2.0 console opens.

4. Click the **Acquire** toolbar icon. In the left pane, click to expand **Image**, and then click **FTK Imager** (see Figure 5-1). Click the **START AS ADMIN** button to start FTK Imager.

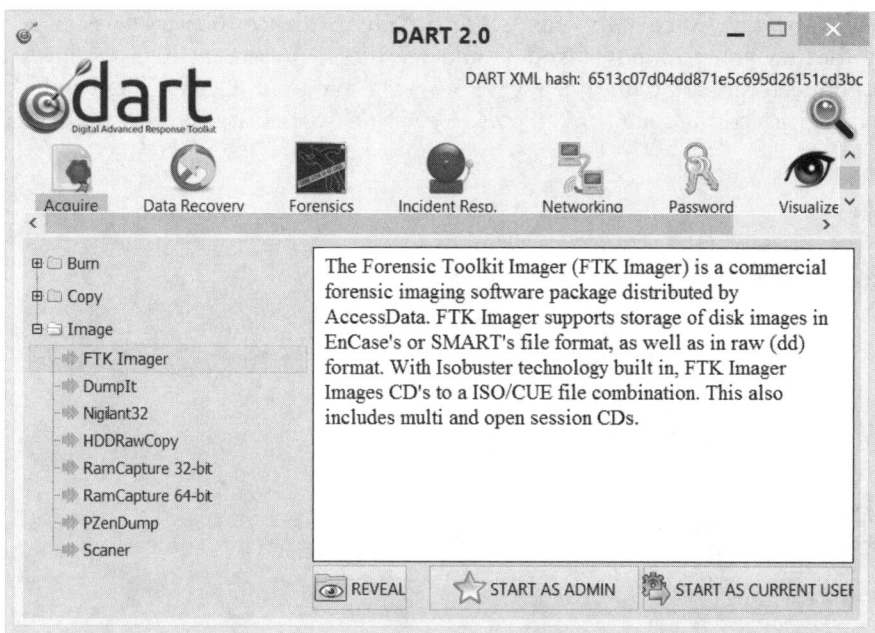

Figure 5-1   Starting FTK Imager via DART

Source: DEFT Linux, www.deftlinux.net

5. Click **File, Obtain Protected Files** from the menu. In the Options section of the Obtain System Files dialog box, click the **Password recovery and all registry files** option button. Click the **Browse** button, navigate to the **C:\Work\Labs\Evidence** folder, click **Make New Folder,** and type **Registry Files** for the new name. Click **OK** to enter this path in the "Destination for obtained files" text box (see Figure 5-2). FTK Imager copies the Windows Registry files to this path.

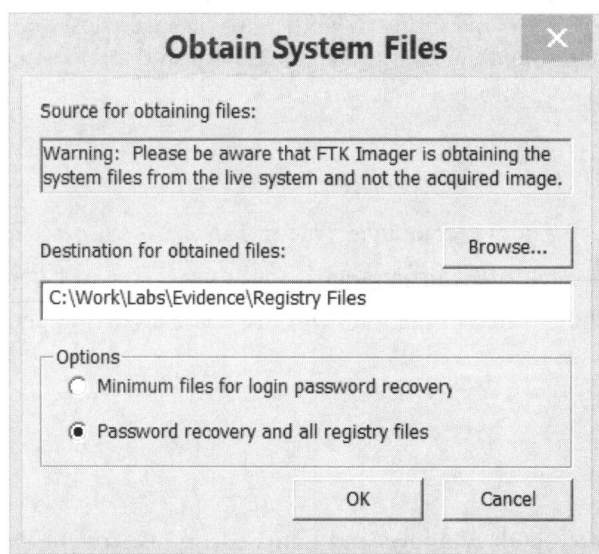

Figure 5-2   Entering a path for copying Registry files

6. In File Explorer, navigate to the **C:\Work\Labs\Evidence\Registry Files** folder to view the files on your computer. You should see files representing Registry hives and user accounts on this computer (see Figure 5-3). The exported Registry files can be viewed in any Registry editor, such as Windows Regedit or AccessData Registry Viewer.

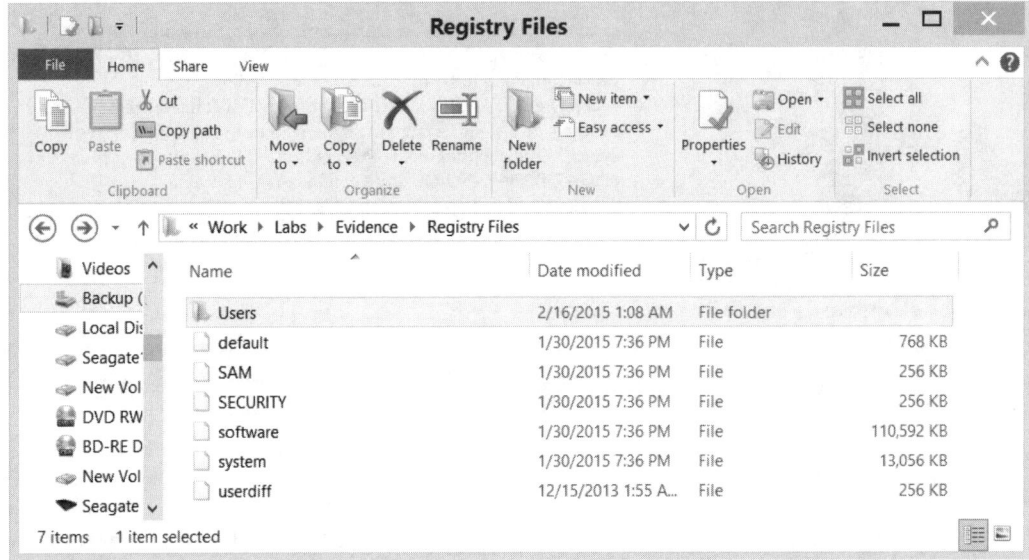

Figure 5-3   Viewing Registry files

7. Exit FTK Imager in DART, and leave the Registry Files folder and DART console open as you answer the following review questions. When you're finished, close the Registry Files folder and the DART console. Remove the DEFT DVD from the DVD-ROM drive and keep it for future labs.

Review Questions

1. DART can be used to boot a Windows computer. True or False?
2. RAM can be captured most safely after a computer is shut down. True or False?
3. DART acquisition tools include which of the following? (Choose all that apply.)
   a. OSForensics
   b. DumpIt
   c. RamCapture
   d. Tcpdump
4. You can use TestDisk to search both Windows and Linux partitions. True or False?
5. DART includes antivirus tools. True or False?

Lab 5.2 Examining the SAM Hive

Objectives

The Registry is the central repository of settings and data for the Windows environment as a computer boots. It's divided into five hives in the C:\Windows\System32\Config folder. Each hive contains specific data, such as passwords, desktop settings, hardware and software configurations, and other valuable forensic information. The Registry files most useful to forensics investigators are the Security Accounts Manager (SAM) and SYSTEM hives and the ntuser.dat file (which is in the C:\Users*username* folder and is unique for each user). The SAM hive stores information on user accounts and their password hashes as well as group definitions and domain associations by using globally unique IDs (GUIDs). In this lab, you copy Registry files from a Windows image with FTK Imager and view the SAM hive with AccessData Registry Viewer.

After completing this lab, you will be able to:

- Examine the SAM hive containing usernames and password hashes
- View Registry files in Registry Viewer

Materials Required

This lab requires the following:

- Windows 8 or 8.1 Professional
- AccessData Registry Viewer
- AccessData FTK Imager
- The InCh05.exe file on the DVD

Estimated completion time: **15–20 minutes**

Activity

In this lab, you examine the SAM hive to determine the user accounts on a seized computer:

1. Copy the **InCh05.exe** file from the DVD to your **C:\Work\Labs\Evidence** folder. In File Explorer, double-click this file and click **Extract** to extract the Windows image to your evidence folder.

2. Right-click the **AccessData FTK Imager** desktop icon and click **Run as administrator**. If necessary, click **Yes** in the UAC message box.

3. Click **File, Add Evidence Item** from the menu. In the Select Source dialog box, click **Image File**, and then click **Next**. In the Select File dialog box, click **Browse**, navigate to and click **C:\Work\Labs\Evidence\InCh05.img**, and then click **OK** to enter this source path (see Figure 5-4). Click **Finish** to open the image in FTK Imager.

4. In the left pane, click to expand **InCh05.img, 6gb [NTFS], [root]**, and **Users**. Click the **Denise** folder, and then right-click the **ntuser.dat** file in the File List pane and click **Export Files**. In the Browse For Folder dialog box, navigate to and click **C:\Work\Labs\ Evidence**, click **Make New Folder**, and type **Chap5** for the new name. Click **OK** to copy the file, and click **OK** in the Export Results message box.

5

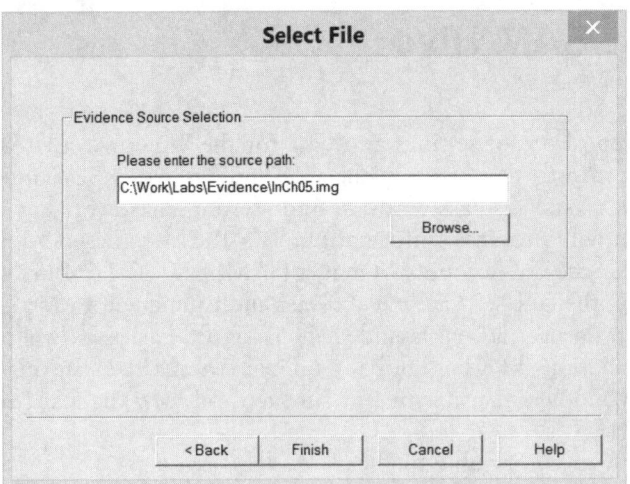

Figure 5-4 Entering a source path for the image

©2015 AccessData Group, Inc. All Rights Reserved.

5. In the left pane, click to expand **Windows** and **System32,** and then click **config.** Ctrl+click **SYSTEM, SOFTWARE, SECURITY, SAM,** and **DEFAULT.** Right-click one of these selected files and click **Export Files.** Navigate to and click **C:\Work\Labs\Evidence\ Chap5,** and click **OK** to copy the files. Click **OK** in the Export Results message box, and then exit FTK Imager.

6. Right-click the **AccessData Registry Viewer** desktop icon and click **Run as administrator.** If necessary, click **Yes** in the UAC message box. Click **Yes** in the ERROR dialog box, click **Cancel** in the Security Device Settings dialog box, and click **OK** in the Registry Viewer dialog box to start Registry Viewer in demo mode.

7. Click **File, Open** from the menu. Navigate to and click **C:\Work\Labs\Evidence\Chap5\ SAM,** and then click **Open.**

8. Click to expand the **SAM, Domains, Account,** and **Users** folders. Click the **000001F4** folder, and drag to enlarge the Key Properties pane at the lower left. Notice the last logon time and the SID unique identifier field, which indicates the type of account and whether it's created automatically when the OS is installed. Values of 500, 501, and 1000 show default accounts (created automatically). This user account is Administrator, and it has been logged on to three times (see Figure 5-5).

9. Click the **000003E9** folder. The jfriday account has been logged on to seven times, and the SID value 1001 indicates that this account was created.

10. Click the **000003EC** folder. The Denise Robinson account, which was created, has never logged on to the computer.

11. Click to expand the **Names** folder, and then click the **jfriday** folder. The Last Written Time entry indicates that this account was accessed on 2/6/2014 when the password was changed.

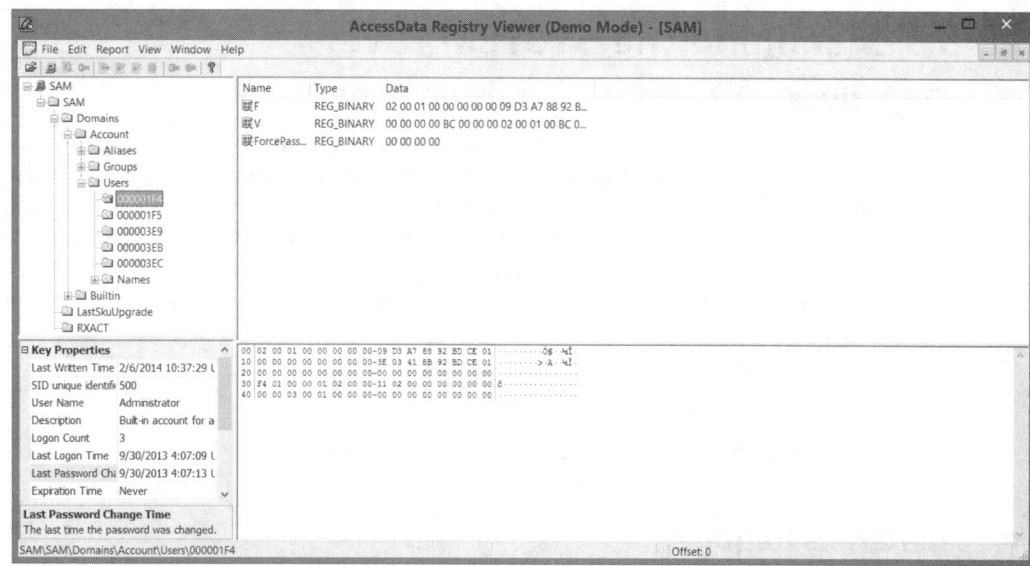

Figure 5-5 Viewing user account information

©2015 AccessData Group, Inc. All Rights Reserved.

12. Leave Registry Viewer open as you answer the following review questions. When you're finished, exit Registry Viewer, and leave your computer running for the next lab.

Review Questions

1. The Registry contains how many hives?

   a. Three

   b. Two

   c. Five

   d. Six

2. How many user accounts are disabled?

   a. Two

   b. Seven

   c. One

   d. Three

3. The SAM hive uses PIDs to store information on user accounts. True or False?

4. Name two SID values that indicate whether an account was created automatically.

5. The Key Properties pane in Registry Viewer shows when user accounts have changed their passwords. True or False?

Lab 5.3 Examining the SYSTEM Hive

Objectives

The SYSTEM Registry hive contains drive letter designations for internal and external storage devices, the system name, and configuration data for the system's hardware and software. This hive is important because it can help identify a computer and any storage devices that might have been mounted in the OS. It also contains information on when the Windows partition was created and activated. The product ID (PID) key in the SYSTEM hive is a unique identifier that can act as an electronic fingerprint to identify a legally activated Windows OS.

After completing this lab, you will be able to:

- View the SYSTEM hive in Registry Viewer
- Look for useful forensic information in the SYSTEM hive

Materials Required

This lab requires the following:

- Windows 8 or 8.1 Professional
- AccessData Registry Viewer
- The SYSTEM hive copied from the DVD's data files to your C:\Work\Labs\Evidence folder

Estimated completion time: **15 minutes**

Activity

In this lab, you examine the SYSTEM hive to determine the user accounts on the seized computer:

1. Right-click the **AccessData Registry Viewer** desktop icon and click **Run as administrator**. If necessary, click **Yes** in the UAC message box. Click **Yes** in the ERROR dialog box, click **Cancel** in the Security Device Settings dialog box, and click **OK** in the Registry Viewer dialog box to start Registry Viewer in demo mode.

2. Click **File, Open** from the menu. Navigate to and click **C:\Work\Labs\Evidence\Chap5\SYSTEM**, and then click **Open**.

3. In the left pane of Registry Viewer, click to expand the **ControlSet001** folder, the **Control** folder, and the **ComputerName** folder, and then click the **ComputerName** folder to display the name at the upper right.

4. Scroll down and click the **TimeZoneInformation** folder to display the computer's time zone information. This information is critical because timestamps for files, folders, and logs are based on the time zone (see Figure 5-6).

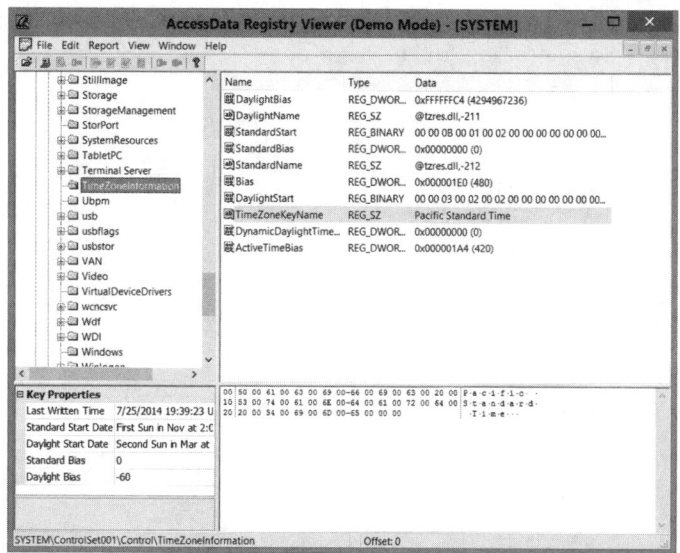

Figure 5-6   Viewing time zone information

©2015 AccessData Group, Inc. All Rights Reserved.

5. Click to expand the **Enum** folder and the **IDE** folder, which contains IDE storage devices, such as the CD/DVD-ROM drive. Click to expand the **USB** folder to see all USB storage devices plugged into the computer. Each storage device has a unique serial number and a Last Written Time entry in the Key Properties pane.

6. Click the **MountedDevices** folder, which lists every storage device that has been mounted in the Windows OS along with its associated drive letter and GUID value (see Figure 5-7). This information can be used to associate hard drives with a Windows computer.

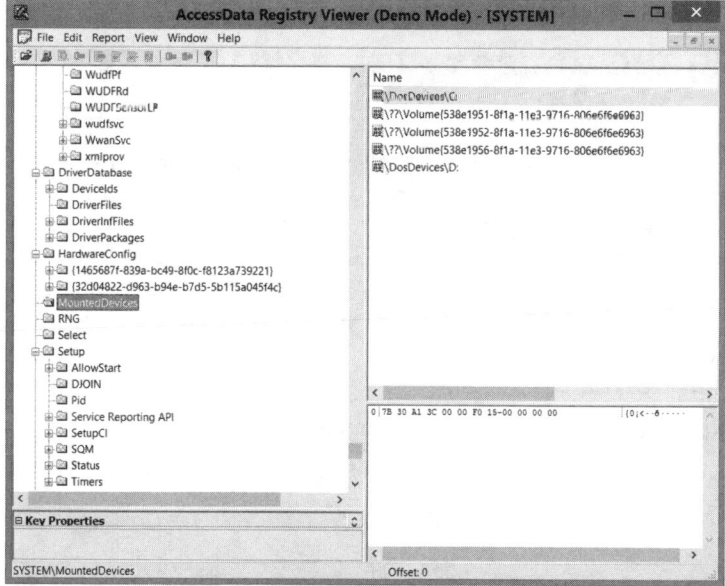

Figure 5-7   Viewing information on mounted devices

©2015 AccessData Group, Inc. All Rights Reserved.

7. Leave Registry Viewer open as you answer the following review questions. When you're finished, leave Registry Viewer running for the next lab.

Review Questions

1. What's the computer name of this system?

   a. mnmsrv

   b. GCFI5E

   c. HAL

   d. MSDTC

2. What's the time zone setting for this computer?

   a. EST

   b. MST

   c. CST

   d. PST

3. How many mounted devices on this system have assigned drive letters?

4. What information is stored in the Enum folder?

   a. User account information

   b. Password information

   c. File locations

   d. Hardware and software values

5. The SYSTEM hive contains configuration data for passwords. True or False?

Lab 5.4 Examining the `ntuser.dat` Registry File

Objectives

The `ntuser.dat` Registry file contains user-specific information, such as personalized settings for the desktop, software, and e-mail accounts, as well as the most recently used (MRU) files and devices. The forensic information in this file can help investigators discover Internet searches and recently used storage devices, for example. The `ntuser.dat` file is in the C:\Users*username* folder, and each account holder in Windows has a separate `ntuser.dat` file. Many password decryption tools require both the `ntuser.dat` file and the SYSTEM Registry hive to retrieve user passwords.

After completing this lab, you will be able to:

- Load a file in Registry Viewer to search for evidence
- Find Windows user account information in the Registry

Materials Required

This lab requires the following:

- Windows 8 or 8.1 Professional
- AccessData Registry Viewer
- The ntuser.dat file extracted in Lab 5.2

Estimated completion time: **15 minutes**

Activity

In this lab, you examine the ntuser.dat file belonging to a suspect's user account for forensics evidence:

1. If necessary, right-click the **AccessData Registry Viewer** desktop icon and click **Run as administrator.** Click **Yes** in the UAC message box. Click **Yes** in the ERROR dialog box, click **Cancel** in the Security Device Settings dialog box, and click **OK** in the Registry Viewer dialog box to start Registry Viewer in demo mode.

2. Click **File, Open** from the menu. Navigate to and click **C:\Work\Labs\Evidence\Chap5\ ntuser.dat,** and click **Open.**

3. Click **Edit, Find** from the menu. In the Find dialog box, type **Denise** and press **Enter.** The first Registry key associated with Denise is displayed at the upper right.

4. Press the **F3** key to search for the next Registry key containing any references to Denise. Notice the GUID associated with the username account information. Press **F3** again to locate the next key, and notice the e-mail account for Denise along with her full name (see Figure 5-8).

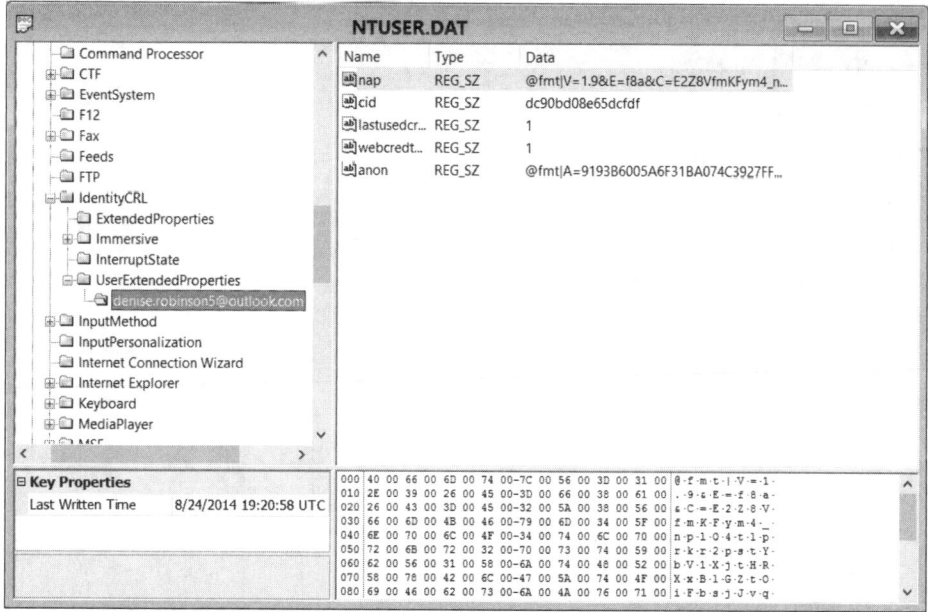

Figure 5-8   Viewing e-mail account information

5. Click **Edit, Find** from the menu. In the Find dialog box, type **jfriday** and press **Enter** to search for any Registry keys associated with this suspect. A message is displayed stating that Registry Viewer couldn't locate any keys associated with this user. This happened because each `ntuser.dat` file is associated with only one user account.

6. Leave Registry Viewer open as you answer the following review questions. When you're finished, close all open windows and shut down the computer.

Review Questions

1. The `ntuser.dat` file contains information on multiple account holders. True or False?

2. What's the e-mail account for the Denise user?

   a. Denise.Robertson@.comcast.net

   b. Denise@AOL.com

   c. denise.robinson5@outlook.com

   d. denise.robinson5@comcast.net

3. The `ntuser.dat` file contains information on which of the following? (Choose all that apply.)

   a. Drive letter designations

   b. Personalized desktop settings

   c. PID key

   d. MRU devices

4. Password decryption tools often need which of the following to retrieve user passwords? (Choose all that apply.)

   a. SYSTEM hive

   b. SAM hive

   c. `ntuser.dat` file

   d. Enum folder

5. The `ntuser.dat` file is in which of the following paths?

   a. C:/Windows/System32/Config

   b. C:/Documents and Settings/Users

   c. C:/Users/*username*

   d. C:/SYSTEM

CURRENT DIGITAL FORENSICS TOOLS

Labs included in this chapter:

- Lab 6.1 Using Autopsy to Search an Image of a Hard Drive
- Lab 6.2 Using OSForensics to Search an Image of a Hard Drive
- Lab 6.3 Using ProDiscover Basic to Search an Image of a Hard Drive

Lab 6.1 Using Autopsy to Search an Image of a Hard Drive

Objectives

Autopsy is a free open-source digital forensics tool that serves as a Web-based interface to Sleuth Kit; it's also available in a version for Windows. It offers features for producing reports and includes timeline analysis, hash filtering, keyword searches, and searches for Web artifacts, such as bookmarks, history, and cookies, in Firefox, Chrome, and Internet Explorer. In addition, Autopsy can recover deleted files and extract Exif information from multimedia files. It produces fast results by running background tasks in parallel processes that can take advantage of multicore processors. In this lab, you examine the `charlie-2009-12-03.E01` image file to look for e-mail evidence containing the keyword "Project2400" and explore the timeline features in Autopsy.

Processing the data file used in this chapter can take quite a long time in Autopsy, depending on your computer's performance and the amount of RAM, so you might want to set it up to take place overnight.

After completing this lab, you will be able to:

- Search an image file in Autopsy
- Use the timeline analysis features in Autopsy

Materials Required

This lab requires the following:

- Windows 8 or 8.1 Professional
- Autopsy 3.1.2 for Windows
- The `charlie-2009-12-03.E01` file

Estimated completion time: **120–240 minutes,** depending on your computer's performance

Activity

In this lab, you use Autopsy to search an image on a Windows computer:

1. Start a Web browser, and go to **http://sourceforge.net/projects/autopsy/files/autopsy/3.1.2/**. Double-click the **.msi** file to download and install Autopsy 3.1.2 for Windows. (*Note*: Choose the 32-bit or 64-bit version, depending on your Windows version.)

2. Next, go to **http://digitalcorpora.org/corp/nps/scenarios/2009-m57-patents/drives-redacted/**, scroll down, and download the `charlie-2009-12-03.E01` file to the **C:\Work\Labs\Evidence** folder on your computer.

3. Double-click the **Autopsy** desktop icon. In the Welcome window, click **Create New Case.**

4. Type **C6Proj1** in the Case Name text box. Click **Browse**, navigate to and click the **C:\Work\Labs\Cases** folder, click **OK** to enter this path in the Base Directory text box (see Figure 6-1), and then click **Next.** Type **C6Proj1** in the Case Number text box and your initials in the Examiner text box, and then click **Finish.**

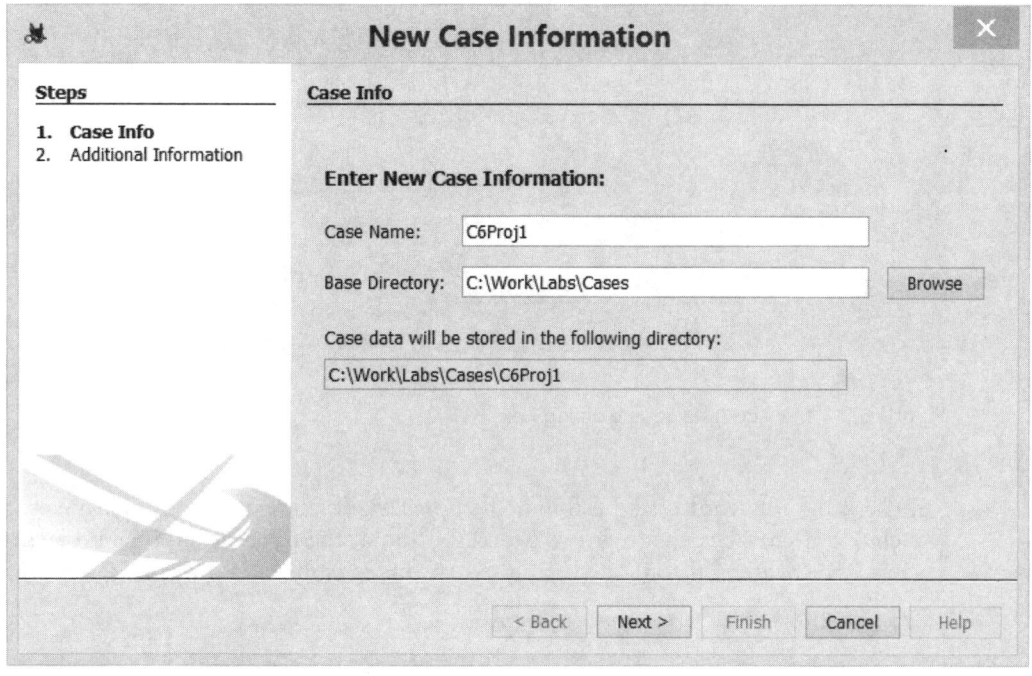

Figure 6-1   Entering new case information

Source: www.sleuthkit.org

5. In the Add Data Source dialog box, click **Browse**, navigate to and click the `charlie-2009-12-03.E01` file you downloaded from the M57 site, click **OK** to enter this path (see Figure 6-2), and then click **Next.** In the Configure Ingest Modules dialog box, click **Next,** and then click **Finish** to start analyzing the evidence. Watch the progress bar in the lower-right corner to determine when the process is finished.

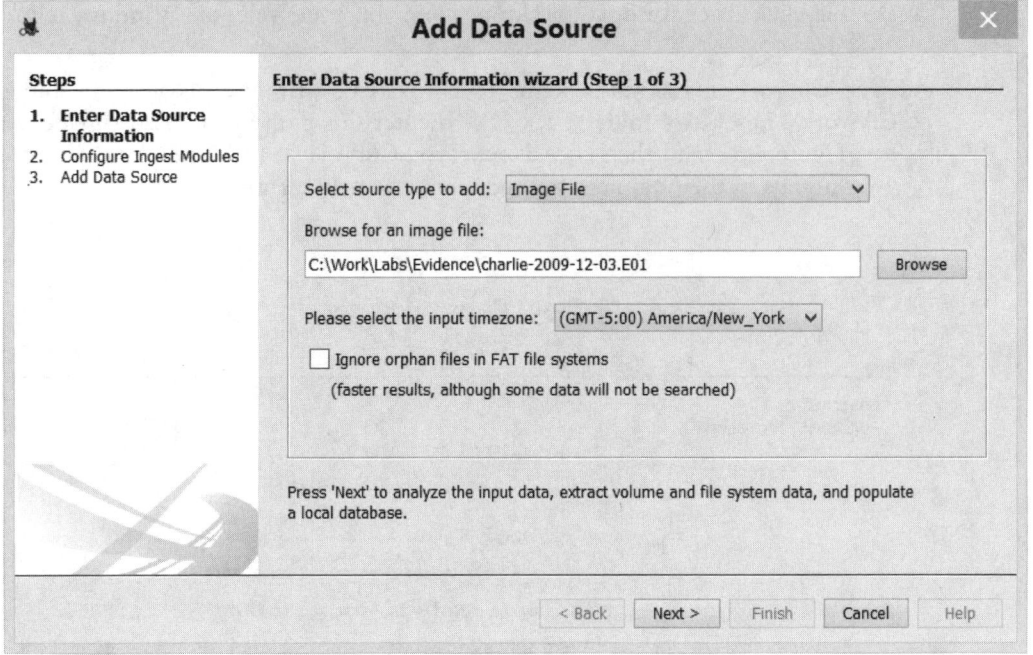

Figure 6-2 The Add Data Source dialog box

Source: www.sleuthkit.org

6. Click the **Keyword Lists** button at the upper right, click all four check boxes, and then click **Search**. Click the **Keyword Search** button at the upper right, type **Project2400**, and click the **Search** button. The search returns nine results, as shown in Figure 6-3.

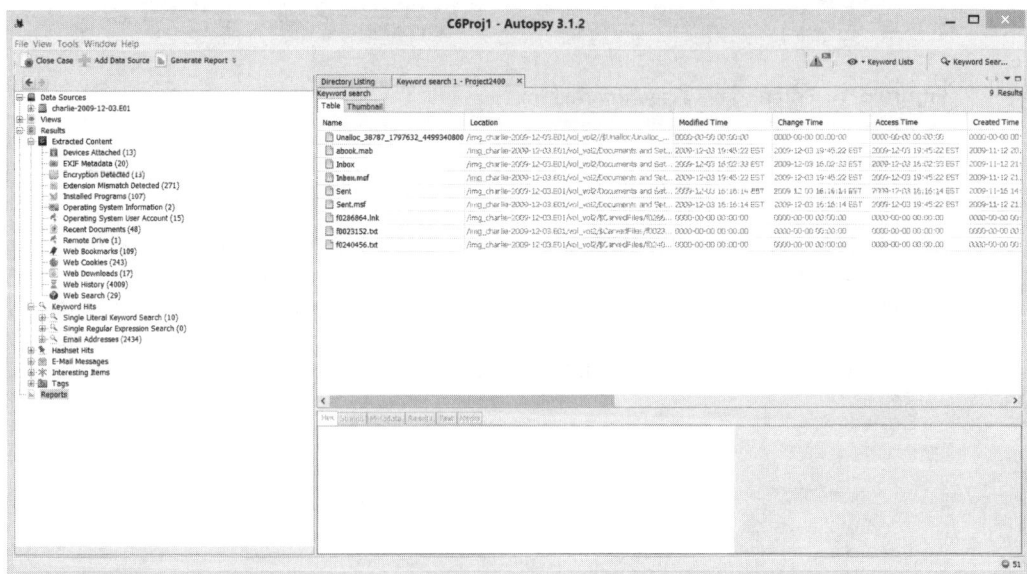

Figure 6-3 Search results displayed in Autopsy

Source: www.sleuthkit.org

7. Click the **Inbox** entry in the right pane, and notice that the Project2400 results are highlighted in yellow. Scroll through the results to find any evidence of Charlie receiving e-mails referencing Project2400. Click the **Sent** entry in the right pane, and look for e-mails sent about Project2400 (see Figure 6-4).

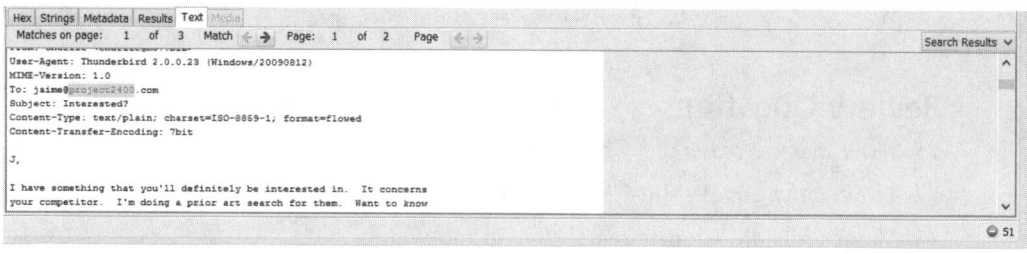

Figure 6-4   Viewing sent e-mails

Source: www.sleuthkit.org

6

8. Click **Tools, Timeline** from the menu. This process takes a few minutes. By default, the timeline is displayed with a large date range. In this case, you're interested in the period between November 16, 2009, and December 9, 2009. In the Timeline Window - Editor dialog box, click the clock icon in the right pane at the lower left, set the date to **November 16, 2009**, and use the sliders under the calendar to set the time to **12:00 AM** (see Figure 6-5). Use the same procedure to enter the end date and time: **December 9, 2009** at **11:59 PM**. Click the **Filters** tab at the lower left, type **Project2400**, click the **Text Filter** check box, and then click the **Apply** button. Click the **Counts** button to see dates with activity involving project2400. These dates are shown by the columns indicating number of hits. Click the **Details** button to see the e-mails for this filename. You can ignore the Updating Counts Graph indicator during processing. Move your mouse pointer over each event to see details. When you're finished, close this dialog box.

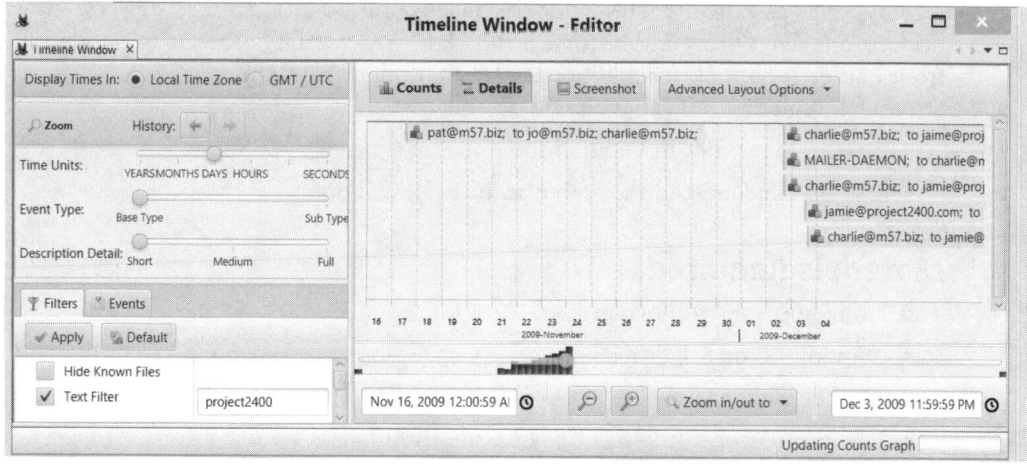

Figure 6-5   Entering timeline settings

Source: www.sleuthkit.org

9. Click **Tools, Generate Report** from the menu. In the Generate Report dialog box, click **Results - HTML**, and then click **Next**. Click **All Results**, and then click **Finish**.

10. When the green check mark is displayed, click the **Results - HTML** link, and leave the report open as you answer the following review questions. When you're finished, exit the Web browser and Autopsy. Save the case, if prompted.

Review Questions

1. How many e-mails did Charlie get?

2. How many e-mails did Charlie send?

3. What tools did Charlie search for on the Web?

4. Did Charlie install any tools on this computer?

5. How many cameras can be identified by checking the Exif information?

    a. 20

    b. 26

    c. 10

    d. 5

Lab 6.2 Using OSForensics to Search an Image of a Hard Drive

Objectives

OSForensics can perform searches quickly and is capable of sorting date ranges. Investigators can search for exact phrases, documents, graphics, multimedia files, wildcards, and exclusion files. OSForensics also includes a timeline viewer similar to Autopsy's that can reveal recent activity, such as e-mail correspondence, deleted files, MRU storage devices, attached USB devices, and Web browsing history. In this lab, you use OSForensics to validate the results from Lab 6.1 and look for additional data that might be useful.

After completing this lab, you will be able to:

- Search image files in OSForensics
- Use the timeline and file search features in OSForensics

Materials Required

This lab requires the following:

- Windows 8 or 8.1 Professional
- OSForensics
- The `charlie-2009-12-03.E01` file from Lab 6.1

Estimated completion time: **180–240 minutes,** depending on your computer's performance

Activity

In this lab, you use OSForensics to search an image on a Windows computer:

1. Start OSForensics. If necessary, click **Continue Using Free Version**. Click **Start** in the left pane, and click **Create Case** in the right pane.

2. In the New Case dialog box, type **C6Proj2** in the Case Name text box, enter your initials in the Investigator text box, and click the **Investigate Disk(s) from Another Machine** option button for the acquisition type. Click **Custom Location** for the case folder. Click the **Browse** button, navigate to and click the **C:\Work\Labs\Cases** folder, click the **Make New Folder** button, type **C6Proj2**, and click **OK** twice.

3. Click the **Add Device** button, click the **Image File** option button, navigate to C:\Work\Labs\Evidence\charlie-2009-12-03.E01, and click **Open**. Click **Partition 0** in the "Select a partition in the image" dialog box, and then click **OK** twice.

4. Click the **Create Index** button in the left pane. In the Step 1 of 5 window, click the **Use Pre-defined File Types** option button, click to select all the file types listed, and click **Next**. In the Step 2 of 5 window, click the **Add** button. In the Add Start Location dialog box, verify that the **Whole Drive** option button is selected and then click **OK**. Click **Next**, and in the Step 3 of 5 window, click **Start Indexing**. When OSForensics finishes indexing (which might take more than 4 hours), click **OK** in the message box about the file limit, and then click **OK** again.

5. Click the **Search Index** button in the left pane, type **project2400** in the Enter Search Words text box, and click **Search** in the right pane. Figure 6-6 shows the results. Right-click the file, point to **Bookmark**, and click **Red**.

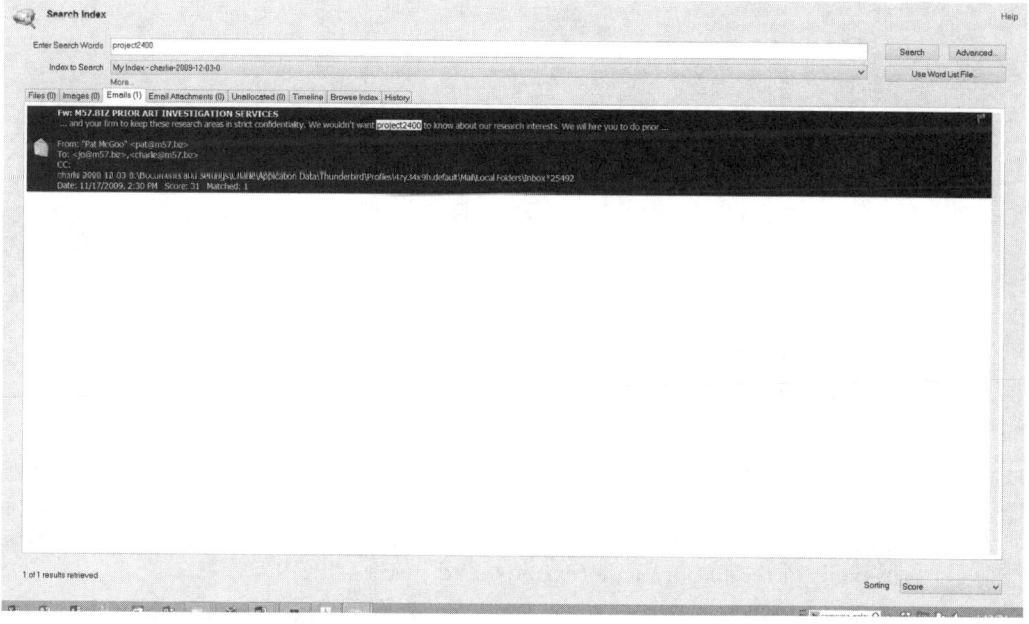

Figure 6-6 Viewing the search results

Source: PassMark Software, www.osforensics.com

6. Right-click the blue highlighted e-mail in the Search Index dialog box and click **Open** to view the other e-mail correspondence in this image. The e-mail about project2400 opens and displays the message and associated e-mail addresses. Use the scroll bar to view all the other e-mails.

7. Click to select the first e-mail, hold down **Shift**, scroll down to the last e-mail, and click it to select all highlighted e-mails. Right-click the highlighted e-mails and click **Export List of Selected E-mail to**. Click **html** for the report format, type **E-mail Correspondence**, and click **Save** to save it to the Cases folder. Right-click the highlighted e-mails, point to **Bookmark**, and click **Red** to add the e-mail evidence.

8. Click **File, Close** from the menu. Click **Start** in the left pane, and click **Generate Report**. Click the **Copy files to report location** option button, and click **OK**. If necesssary, click **OK** in the error message. If the report doesn't open automatically, start a Web browser, and open the **C:\Work\Labs\Cases\C6Proj2\Case Report\report.html** file.

9. Click the **Recent Activity** button in the left pane. In the Recent Activity pane, click the **Scan Drive** option button at the upper left to select the current evidence image, click the **Config** button at the upper right, click the **Search date range only** option button, click **November 16, 2009** in the From drop-down list, click **December 3, 2009** in the To drop-down list, click **OK**, and then click **Scan**. In the Recent Activity - Summary report displaying the list of hits (see Figure 6-7), click **OK**. Click the **Timeline** tab to display the timeline of events occurring during the period you configured.

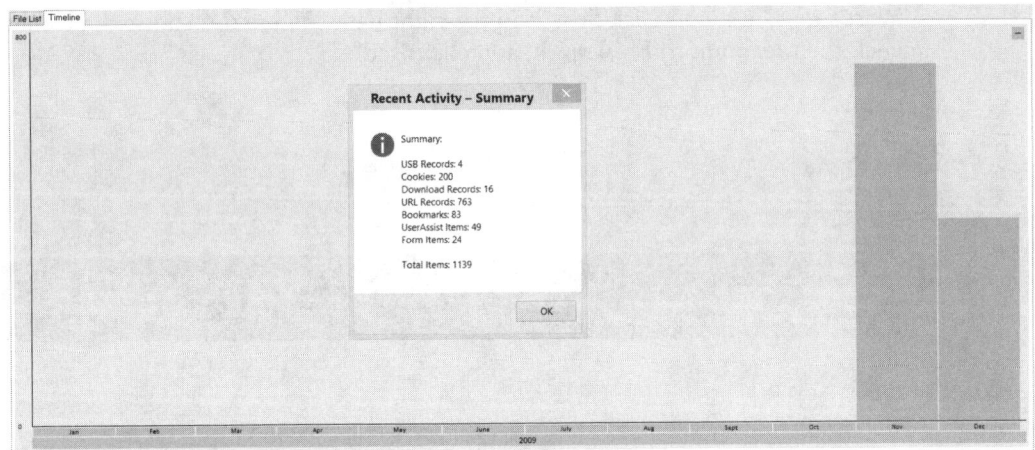

Figure 6-7   Viewing the summary report
Source: PassMark Software, www.osforensics.com

10. Click the **File List** tab to display the files recovered, Web sites visited, and programs that ran during the timeline. Scroll down the list, and then Shift+click to select the first and last e-mails Charlie received. Right-click the selected files and click **Add to Case**. Click **List of Selected Items**. In the Please Enter New Case Item Details window, type **Charlie E-mails** in the Export Title text box, and then click **OK**.

11. Leave the File List pane open as you answer the following review questions. When you're finished, exit OSForensics.

Review Questions

1. How many e-mails did Charlie get?

2. What browsers were used during the specified time period?

3. OSForensics can reveal Web browsing history. True or False?

4. How many USB devices were connected to Charlie's computer during the specified time?

5. The search didn't reveal any software installed on Charlie's computer. True or False?

Lab 6.3 Using ProDiscover Basic to Search an Image of a Hard Drive

Objectives

ProDiscover Basic was recently sold to the ARC Group and is no longer offered free. The version included with this book has many of the same features as the commercial product, however, including file search capabilities on all Windows file systems, such as FAT12, FAT16, FAT32, and NTFS, as well as Sun Solaris Unix File Systems, including Linux Ext2, Ext3, and Ext4. In addition, ProDiscover supports disk imaging and analysis of local and network-attached storage devices, using TCP/IP with full reporting capabilities. In this lab, you examine an image to search for references to "Project2400."

After completing this lab, you will be able to:

- Search an image file in ProDiscover
- Use ProDiscover to search for e-mails

Materials Required

This lab requires the following:

- Windows 8 or 8.1 Professional
- ProDiscover Basic
- The `charlie-2009-12-03.E01` file from Lab 6.1

Estimated completion time: **180–240 minutes,** depending on your computer's performance

Activity

In this lab, you use ProDiscover Basic to search an image on a Windows computer:

1. Double-click the **ProDiscover Basic** desktop icon. In the Launch Dialog dialog box, click the **New Project** tab, if necessary. Type **C6Proj3** in the Project Number and Project File Name text boxes, and then click **Open**.

2. In the tree view, click to expand **Add**, and click **Image File**. In the Open dialog box, navigate to and click **C:\Work\Labs\Evidence\charlie-2009-12-03.E01**, and then click **Open**.

3. In the tree view, click to expand **Content View**, if necessary, and then expand **Images**, **C:\Work\Labs\Evidence\charlie-2009-12-03.E01**, and the C drive, and click **All Files**. If necessary, click **Yes** in the ProDiscover message box that opens. ProDiscover starts processing records, which might take some time.

4. Click the **Search** toolbar button, and click the **Content Search** tab, if necessary. Type **Project2400** in the Search for the pattern(s) text box, and under Select the Disk(s)/ Image(s) you want to search in, click **C:\Work\Labs\Evidence\charlie-2009-12-03.E01\C:** (see Figure 6-8). Click **OK**.

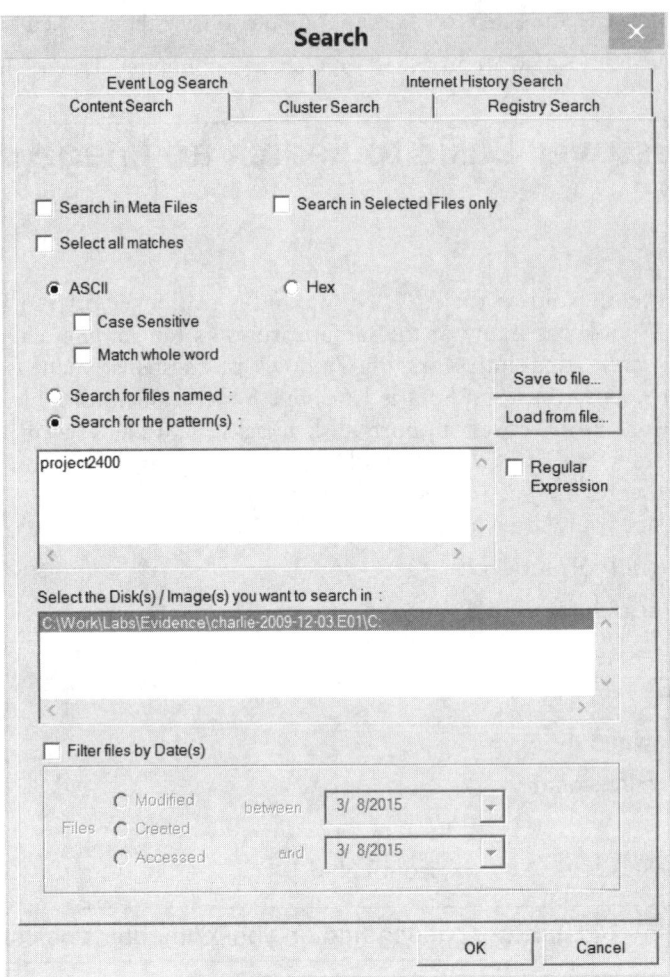

Figure 6-8 Entering search parameters

5. In the Search 1 tab of the search results (see Figure 6-9), click the **Filter** button, and then click **Project2400**. Click the **Selection** button, and click **Select All**. Type **E-mail 12-03-2009 image** in the Investigator comments text box, click the **Apply to all items** check box, and click **OK**. Click **Add to Report**.

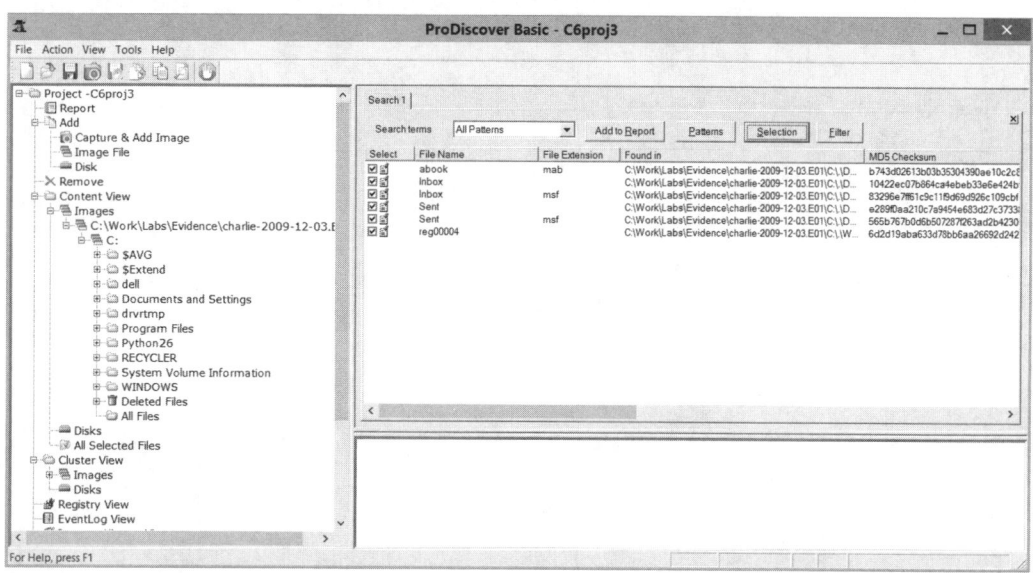

Figure 6-9 Viewing recovered e-mails

©2015 The ARC Group of NY, www.arcgroupny.com

6. Click the first **Inbox** item in the results, and scroll through all the messages Charlie received to view the header information, including e-mail addresses, timestamps, and IP addresses. Notice the highlighted references to Project2400 in the messages.

7. Click the first **Sent** item in the results to view all the e-mails Charlie sent, including e-mail addresses, timestamps, and highlighted references to Project2400.

8. Click **Report** in the tree view to display the evidence report for the project, and leave it open as you answer the following review questions. When you're finished, click **File, Save Project**. In the Save As dialog box, navigate to and click the **C:\Work\Labs\Cases** folder, and then click **Save**. Click **File, Exit** to exit ProDiscover Basic. (*Note:* If you want to open this case again in the future, click **File, Open Project** from the menu, navigate to and click **C:\Work\Labs\Cases\C6Proj3.dft**, and click **Open**.)

Review Questions

1. ProDiscover can analyze only local storage devices. True or False?

2. How many e-mails did Charlie get containing references to Project2400?

3. How many e-mails did Charlie send with references to Project2400?

4. What time zone was this computer set to?

   a. Pacific time

   b. Mountain time

   c. Central time

   d. Eastern time

5. ProDiscover Basic can search both Windows and Linux file systems. True or False?

LINUX AND MACINTOSH FILE SYSTEMS

Labs included in this chapter:

- Lab 7.1 Using Autopsy to Process a Mac OS X Image
- Lab 7.2 Using Autopsy to Process a Mac OS 9 Image
- Lab 7.3 Using Autopsy to Process a Linux Image

Lab 7.1 Using Autopsy to Process a Mac OS X Image

Objectives

The Windows version of Autopsy features the Android Analyzer, which can extract SMS and MMS text messages, call logs, contact information, and GPS data from Google Maps used on Android mobile devices. In Autopsy 3, you can analyze `.E01` and `.dd` images from Linux, UNIX, Mac OS, and Windows file systems. The HFS+ or Mac OS Extended file system was introduced with OS X 10.3 and is used in the current 10.10.2 version, known as Yosemite. This improved version of HFS supports the large disk sizes in current computers. In this lab, you import an OS X image into Autopsy and process it to look for potential evidence.

After completing this lab, you will be able to:

- Import an OS X image into Autopsy
- Use Autopsy to search for evidence in an OS X image

Materials Required

This lab requires the following:

- Windows 8 or 8.1 Professional
- Autopsy for Windows
- The `GCFI-OSX.zip` file on the DVD

This file might take several hours to process, depending on your computer's performance.

Estimated completion time: **180–240 minutes**

Activity

In this lab, you import an OS X image into Autopsy to process evidence:

1. Extract the **GCFI-OSX.zip** file to your **C:\Work\Labs\Evidence** folder. (This process might take a few minutes.) Start Autopsy for Windows. In the Welcome window, click **Create New Case**. Type **C7Proj1** in the Case Name text box, verify that **C:\Work\Labs\Cases** is displayed in the Base Directory text box, and then click **Next**.

2. In the New Case Information dialog box, type **C7Proj1** in the Case Number text box and your initials in the Examiner text box, and then click **Finish**.

3. In the Add Data Source dialog box, click **Browse**, navigate to the **C:\Work\Labs\Evidence\OSX** folder, click the **GCFI-OSX.001** file, and then click **Open**. Click **Next**.

4. Click **Next** to accept the ingest modules, and then click **Finish** to start analyzing the evidence, which could take a while. Figure 7-1 shows the results.

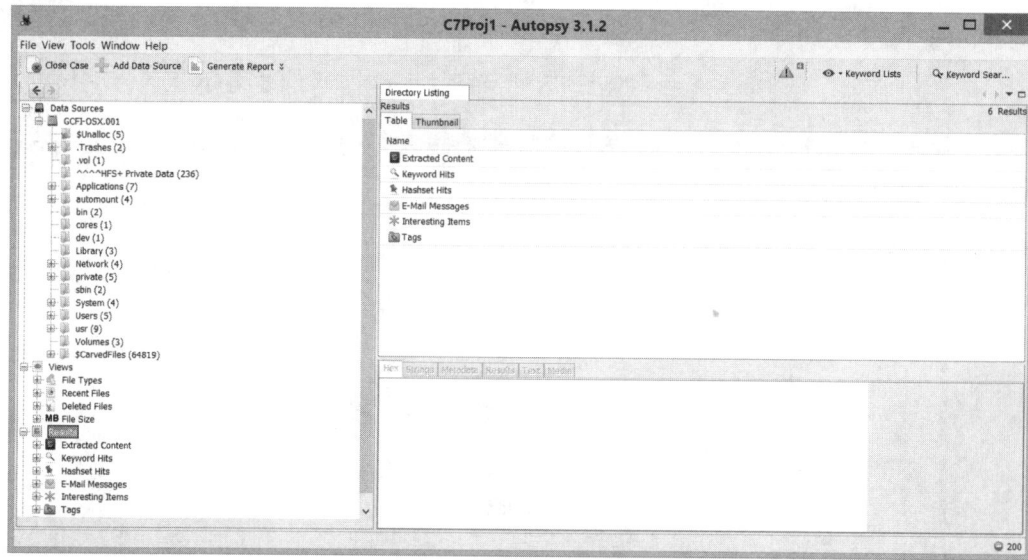

Figure 7-1   Viewing the results in Autopsy

Source: www.sleuthkit.org

5. Click the **Keyword Lists** button at the upper right. Click the **Phone Numbers, IP Addresses, Email Addresses,** and **URLs** check boxes, and then click the **Search** button. Autopsy begins searching the image, which could take some time.

6. Click the **Keyword Search** button, type **Jim Shu** in the text box, and click **Search.** When the search is finished, click the **Keyword search 2** tab, if necessary. The first section of files consists of unallocated and carved files that might have been deleted or cache files. Click the **Table** tab, if necessary, and then click the second unallocated space from the top to display the text associated with search results for Jim Shu.

7. Scroll to the right to display all the file attributes, such as location, timestamps, size, file types, MD5 hash sets, and keyword previews (see Figure 7-2).

8. In the left pane, expand **GCFI-OSX.001** to view the file system folders in the image along with the number of files or folders in each folder. Next, expand **Views** and **File Types** and then click **Images** to see all the graphics files (which might take some time). Click the **Thumbnail** tab to see the graphics.

9. In the left pane, expand **Documents** to view the file types and the number of hits. Click **Office** and then click the **Table** tab, if necessary, to see the Word documents. Click a document to view it in the lower-right pane.

10. In the left pane, expand **Keyword Hits**, if necessary, and then expand **Phone Numbers, IP Addresses, Email Addresses,** and **URLs** to see the search results. Expand **E-Mail Messages** to view correspondence with Jim Shu, including sent messages, deleted messages, the inbox, and so forth.

11. Leave Autopsy open as you answer the following review questions. When you're finished, exit Autopsy, but leave your computer running for the next lab.

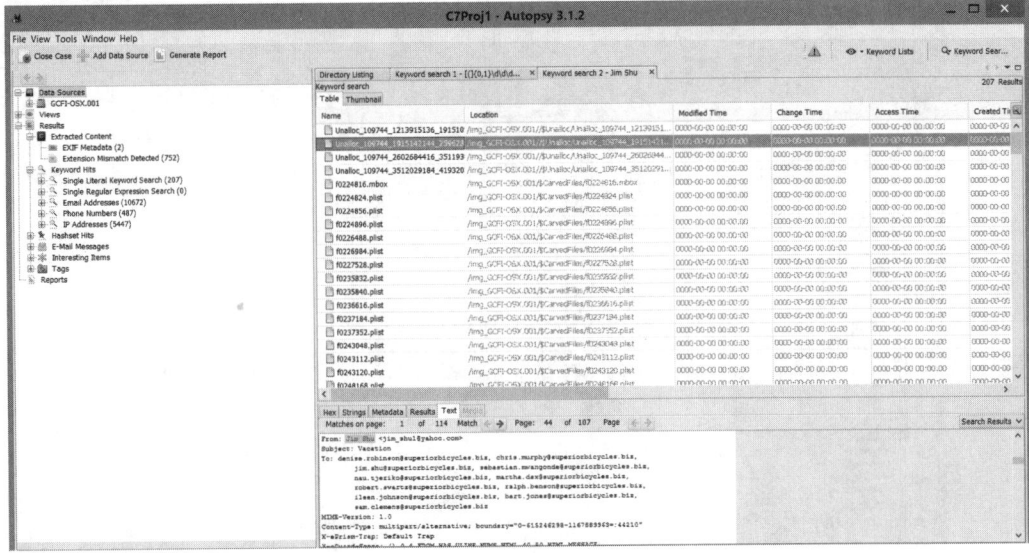

Figure 7-2 Viewing file attributes

Source: www.sleuthkit.org

Review Questions

1. How many Word files are in the image?

2. What or who is the subject of the first message from Jim Shu?

   a. Sebastian

   b. Jim Shu

   c. Superior Bicycles

   d. Free tools

3. What phone number had the most search results?

   a. 602-839-2763

   b. 800-810-0595

   c. 662-656-5045

   d. 859-232-2380

4. The Ext3 file system is used in Mac OS X. True or False?

5. Who sent the last e-mail to Jim Shu?

   a. Martha Dax

   b. Sebastian Mwangonde

   c. Nau Tjeriko

   d. Bart Johnson

Lab 7.2 Using Autopsy to Process a Mac OS 9 Image

Objectives

Mac OS 9 is also known as Apple's "classic Mac" OS. This OS, introduced in 1997, lacks many of the features in today's file systems, such as protected memory and preemptive multitasking. In 2002, Apple officially discontinued OS 9 and developed the current line of OS X operating systems. However, forensics investigators might still encounter OS 9 images on older Apple hardware. In this lab, you use Autopsy to examine an OS 9 image file and search for potential evidence.

After completing this lab, you will be able to:

- Import an OS 9 image into Autopsy
- Use Autopsy to search for evidence in an OS 9 image

Materials Required

This lab requires the following:

- Windows 8 or 8.1 Professional
- Autopsy for Windows
- The GCFI-OS9.zip file on the DVD

NOTE

This file might take several hours to process, depending on your computer's performance.

Estimated completion time: **120–180 minutes**

Activity

In this lab, you import an OS 9 image into Autopsy to process evidence:

1. Extract the **GCFI-OS9.zip** file to your **C:\Work\Labs\Evidence** folder, which might take a few minutes. Start Autopsy. In the Welcome window, click **Create New Case**. Type **C7Proj2** in the Case Name text box, verify that **C:\Work\Labs\Cases** is displayed in the Base Directory text box, and then click **Next**.

2. In the New Case Information dialog box, type **C7Proj2** in the Case Number text box and your initials in the Examiner text box, and then click **Finish**.

3. In the Add Data Source dialog box, click **Browse**, navigate to the **C:\Work\Labs\Evidence\OS9** folder, click the **GCFI-OS9.001** file, and then click **Open**. Click **Next**.

4. Click **Next** to accept the ingest modules, and then click **Finish** to start analyzing the evidence, which could take a while. The progress bar shows 100% when the processing is finished.

5. Click the **Keyword Lists** button at the upper right. Click the **Phone Numbers, IP Addresses, Email Addresses,** and **URLs** check boxes, and then click the **Search** button. Autopsy begins searching the image, which could take some time.

6. In the left pane, expand **Keyword Hits,** if necessary, and then expand **Phone Numbers, IP Addresses, Email Addresses,** and **URLs** to see the search results. Examine the e-mail address results for details such as timestamps and the text of messages (see Figure 7-3).

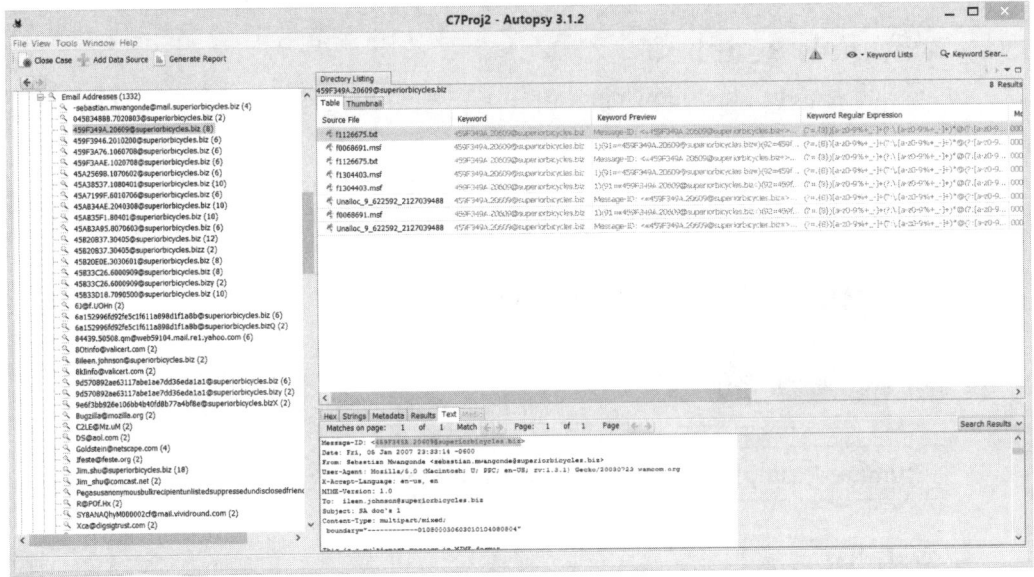

Figure 7-3   Viewing the results of an e-mail search

Source: www.sleuthkit.org

7. In the left pane, expand **Views** and **File Types,** and then click **Images** to view graphics files. To view the data for a file, click the file in the left pane to see it in the lower-right pane, or click the **Thumbnail** tab to see just the image with its filename. Repeat this process for the **Videos** and **Audio** folders.

8. In the left pane, expand `GCFI-OS9.001` to view its partitions. Click **vol8** to view the HFS partition and its folders (see Figure 7-4).

9. Leave Autopsy open as you answer the following review questions. When you're finished, exit Autopsy, but leave your computer running for the next lab.

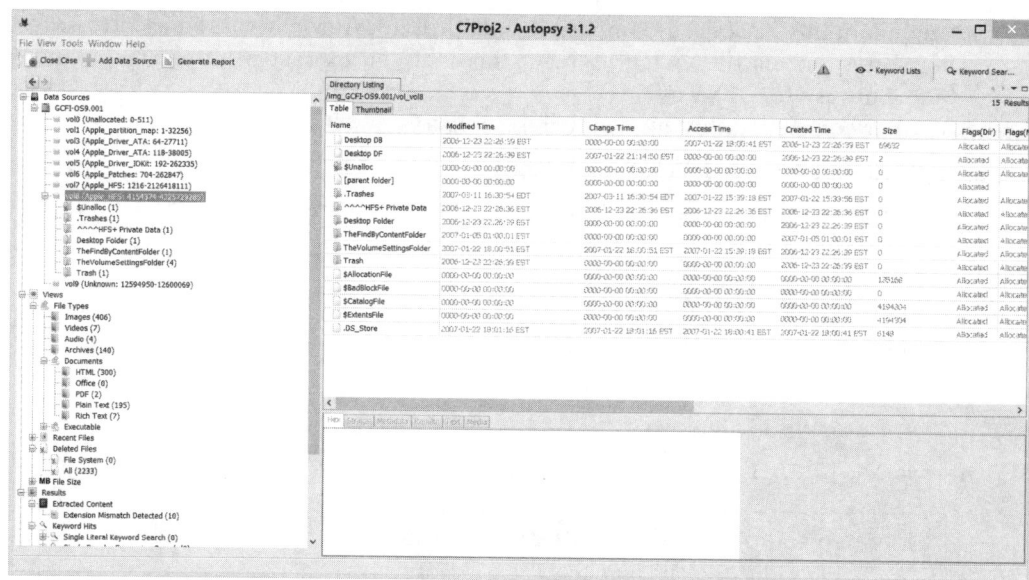

Figure 7-4 Viewing files in the HFS partition

Source: www.sleuthkit.org

Review Questions

1. Viewing timestamps of e-mails isn't possible in OS 9. True or False?

2. How many videos are in the image?

3. Executable files were found in this image. True or False?

4. Which phone number was dialed most often?

    a. 847-718-0400

    b. 770-488-4902

    c. 831-761-6200

    d. 252-227-7013

5. In what file system is the vol8 partition formatted?

Lab 7.3 Using Autopsy to Process a Linux Image

Objectives

The Ext3 file system, used in many Linux distributions, added a journaling capability, which has a built-in file recovery mechanism used after a crash. With the increasing popularity of open-source office suites, such as Star Office and Open Office, forensics investigators are likely to find systems formatted in Ext3. Ext4, the most recent file system, is included in the Linux 2.6.28 kernel. It improves performance and reliability and maintains backward-compatibility with Ext3. Autopsy can be used to search images formatted in this file system, too. In this lab, you extract a Linux image and import it into Autopsy for analysis.

After completing this lab, you will be able to:

- Import a Linux image into Autopsy
- Use Autopsy to search for evidence on a Linux partition

Materials Required

This lab requires the following:

- Windows 8 or 8.1 Professional
- Autopsy for Windows
- The GCFI-LX.xxx.exe file on the DVD

> Estimated completion time: **180–240 minutes**

Activity

In this lab, you import a Linux image into Autopsy to process evidence:

1. Extract the **GCFI-LX.xxx.exe** file to your **C:\Work\Labs\Evidence** folder, which might take a few minutes. Start Autopsy for Windows. In the Welcome window, click **Create New Case**. Type **C7Proj3** in the Case Name text box, verify that **C:\Work\Labs\ Cases** is displayed in the Base Directory text box, and then click **Next**.

2. In the New Case Information dialog box, type **C7Proj3** in the Case Number text box and your initials in the Examiner text box, and then click **Finish**.

3. In the Add Data Source dialog box, click **Browse**, navigate to the **C:\Work\Labs\ Evidence** folder, click the **GCFI-LX.001** file, and then click **Open**. Click **Next**.

4. Click **Next** to accept the ingest modules, and then click **Finish** to start analyzing the evidence, which could take a few hours, depending on your computer's performance. The progress bar shows 100% when the processing is finished.

5. In the left pane, expand **GCFI-LX.001** to view the folder structure (see Figure 7-5). This structure is common in many Linux distributions. Right-click **GCFI-LX.001** to see these available options: Image Details, Extract Unallocated Space to Single Files, Open File Search by Attributes, and Run Ingest Modules (used to process the image again).

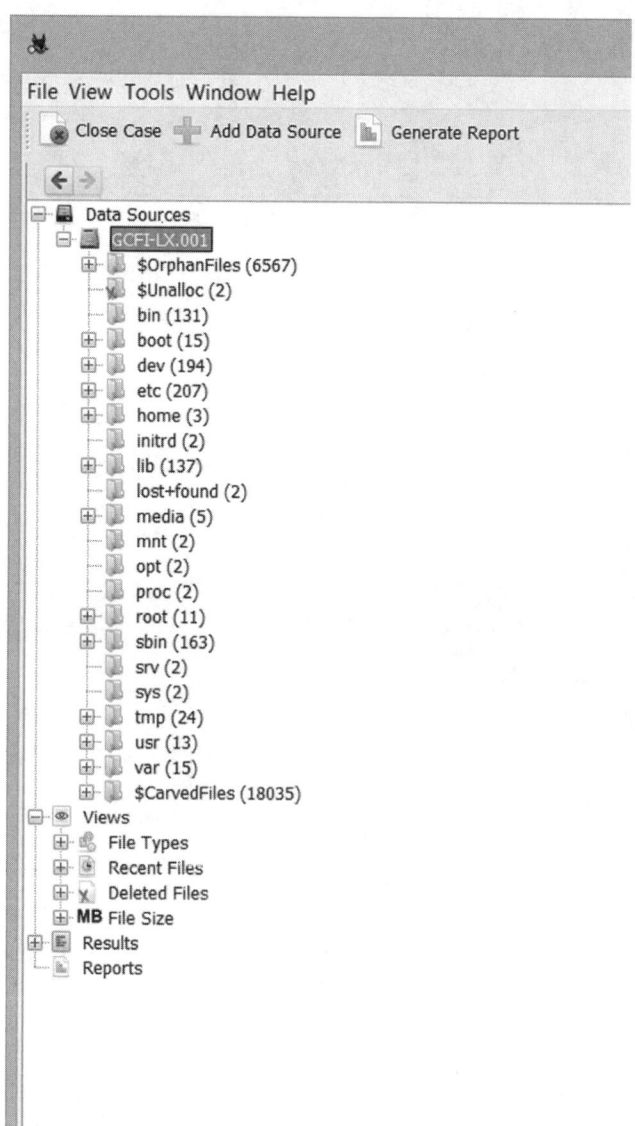

Figure 7-5   Viewing the folder structure

Source: www.sleuthkit.org

6. Click the **Keyword Search** button, type **martha** in the text box, and click **Search**. In the right pane, click the **Keyword search 1 - martha** tab, if necessary, to view all the search results. Click the **Sent** entry to view the e-mail Martha Dax sent to Chris Murphy (see Figure 7-6).

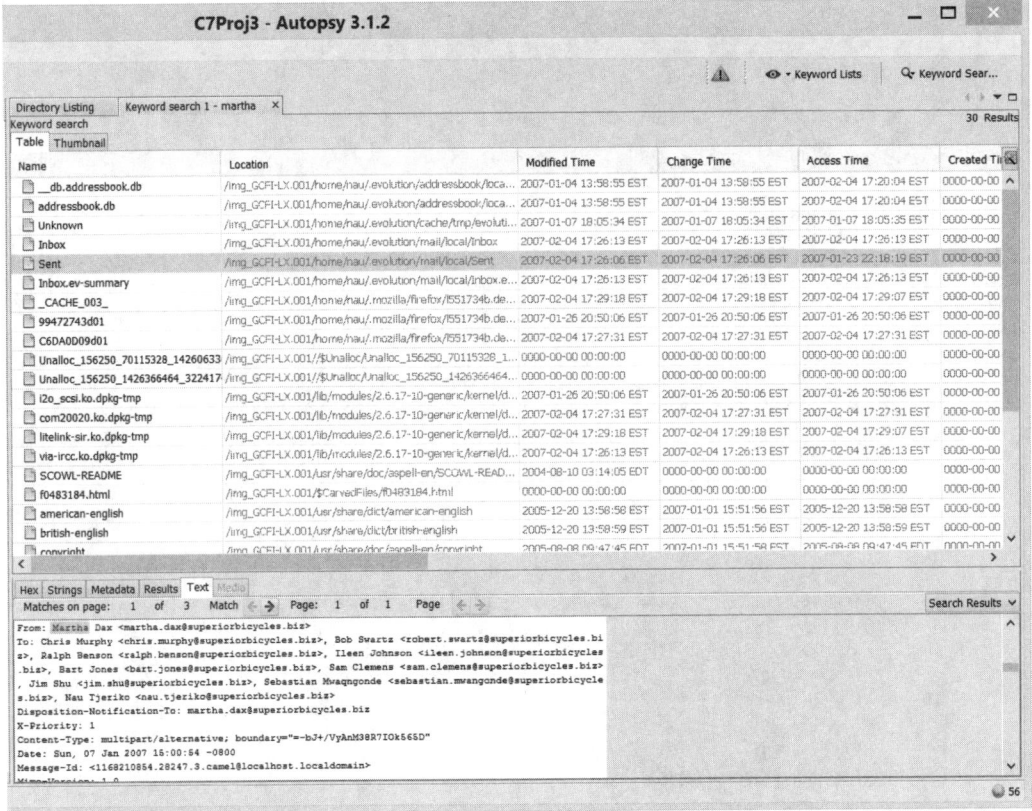

Figure 7-6 Viewing sent e-mails

Source: www.sleuthkit.org

7. Click the **Keyword Search** button, type **Chris Murphy** in the text box, and click **Search**. Click the **Keyword search 2 - Chris Murphy** tab, if necessary. In the left pane, click to expand **E-Mail Messages**, and then click the **Default** folder under the first [Default] icon to see all e-mail correspondence.

8. In the left pane, expand **Results**, if necessary, and **Extracted Content**, and then click **Extension Mismatch Detected** to view file extensions that don't match their file types. This information might reveal files that have been altered to keep them hidden.

9. Leave Autopsy open as you answer the following review questions. When you're finished, exit Autopsy, and shut down your computer.

Review Questions

1. How many e-mails were recovered from the inbox?

2. How many Word and Excel files were recovered in this image?

3. Martha communicated via e-mail only with Chris Murphy. True or False?

4. What executable file was recovered in this image?

5. How many matches were found for the Martha keyword?

RECOVERING GRAPHICS FILES

Labs included in this chapter:

- Lab 8.1 Using Autopsy to Search an Image for Multimedia Files
- Lab 8.2 Using OSForensics to Search an Image for Multimedia Files
- Lab 8.3 Using ProDiscover Basic to Search an Image for Multimedia Files

Lab 8.1 Using Autopsy to Search an Image for Multimedia Files

Objectives

Autopsy has tools that can recognize graphics files in images and extract Exif information. Additional features include finding other multimedia files, such as video and audio files, and recovering deleted files from unallocated space. Autopsy also provides graphics information, such as timestamps, MD5 hash values, and file size. In this lab, you search an image for multimedia files.

After completing this lab, you will be able to:

- Use Autopsy to search for multimedia files
- Identify deleted graphics or video files in evidence

Materials Required

This lab requires the following:

- Windows 8 or 8.1 Professional
- Autopsy 3.1.2 for Windows
- The `jo-favorites-usb-2009-12-11.E01` file downloaded in Step 1

> Estimated completion time: **30–60 minutes,** depending on your computer's performance

Activity

In this lab, you search the `jo-favorites-usb-2009-12-11.E01` file with Autopsy:

1. Start a Web browser, and go to **http://digitalcorpora.org/corp/nps/scenarios/2009-m57-patents/usb/**. Download the **`jo-favorites-usb-2009-12-11.E01`** file to the **C:\Work\Labs\Evidence** folder on your computer.

2. Start Autopsy. In the Welcome window, click **Create New Case**.

3. Type **C8Proj1** in the Case Name text box. Click **Browse**, navigate to and click the **C:\Work\Labs\Cases** folder, click **OK** to enter this path in the Base Directory text box, and then click **Next**. Type **C8Proj1** in the Case Number text box and your initials in the Examiner text box, and then click **Finish**.

4. In the Add Data Source dialog box, click **Browse**, navigate to the **C:\Work\Labs\Evidence** folder, click the **`jo-favorites-usb-2009-12-11.E01`** file, and click **Open**. Click **Next** twice, and then click **Finish**. Autopsy begins analyzing the evidence, which might take a few minutes. The progress bar at the lower right shows when the process is finished.

5. In the left pane, expand **Views** and **File Types** to see the files found on this USB device (see Figure 8-1).

6. Expand **Results** and **Extracted Content**, if necessary, and click **EXIF Metadata** to view the graphics files in the Directory Listing pane on the right. Click the first **JPG** file, and click the **Text** tab in the bottom pane to view Exif metadata (see Figure 8-2). Click the **Media** tab to view the picture.

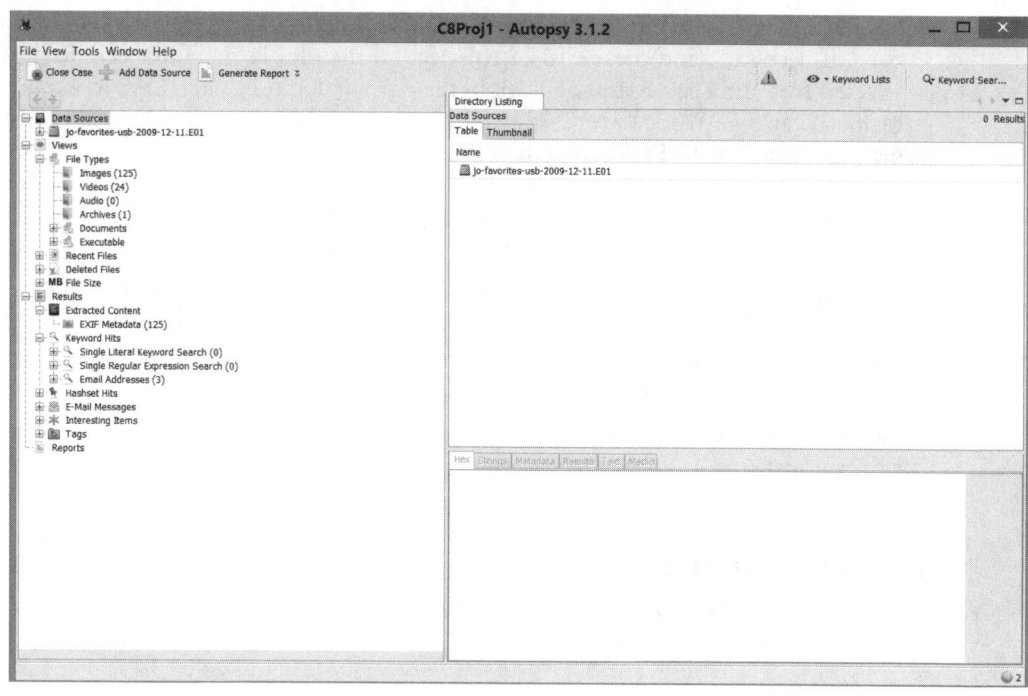

Figure 8-1 Viewing files found in an image

Source: www.sleuthkit.org

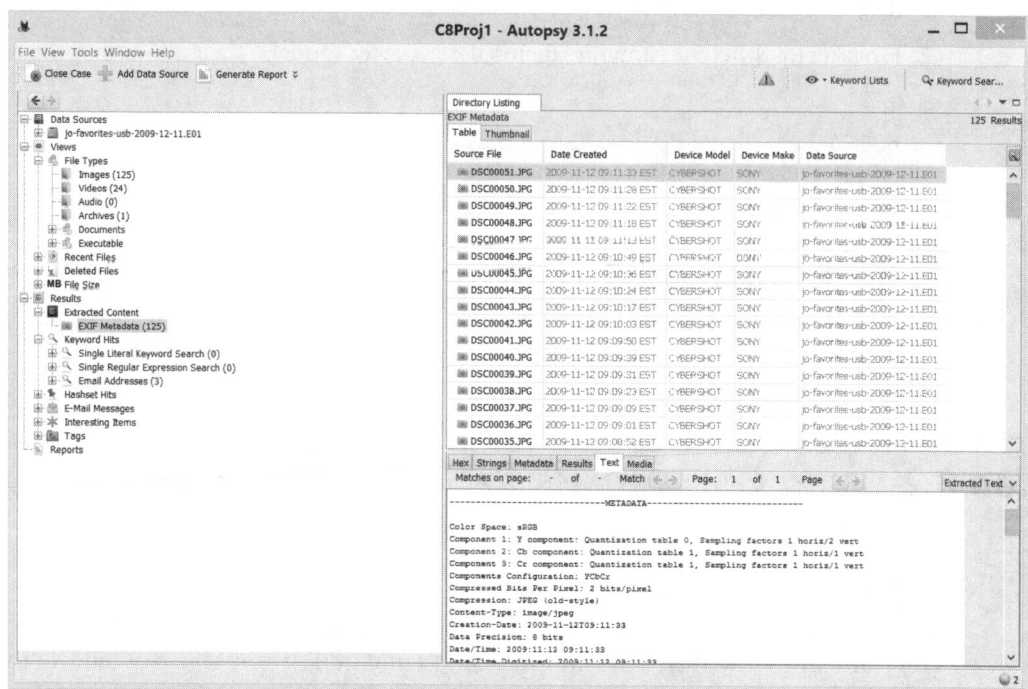

Figure 8-2 Viewing Exif metadata

Source: www.sleuthkit.org

7. Click the **Hex** tab to view the Exif file header information. Click the first **JPG** file in the top pane, if necessary, and press **Ctrl+A** to select all the files in the Table tab. Right-click the selected files and click **Extract File(s)**. In the Save dialog box, click **Save** to export the files to the default **C:\Work\Labs\Cases\C8Proj1\Export** folder. Click **OK** in the Information message box. The NTFS file system in Windows has a built-in Exif viewer. To use this tool, navigate to the **C:\Work\Labs\Cases\C8Proj1\Export** folder in File Explorer. Right-click any graphics file and click **Properties**. Click the **Details** tab to see the Exif information.

8. In the left pane of Autopsy, click **Videos** under File Types to see the video files in this image. Deleted files are indicated by a red ×. Scroll to view all the file attributes, such as timestamps and MD5 hash values, and then scroll to the top of the file list in the Table tab. Right-click the **KittyMontage.mov** file and click **Open in External Viewer** to see the video in Windows Media Player or the QuickTime viewer.

9. Leave Autopsy open as you answer the following review questions. When you're finished, exit Autopsy.

Review Questions

1. How many deleted files were in the Videos folder?

   a. 24

   b. 14

   c. 12

   d. 8

2. How many different cameras (denoted as "device models") were found in the evidence?

   a. 2

   b. 125

   c. 14

   d. 84

3. What file system was used in the `jo-favorites-usb-2009-12-11.E01` image?

4. Autopsy doesn't provide camera information, such as exposure time or flash use. True or False?

5. Autopsy displays hash values for video files. True or False?

Lab 8.2 Using OSForensics to Search an Image for Multimedia Files

Objectives

OSForensics has a built-in graphics viewer that can open BMP (bitmap), JPG, GIF, PNG, and TIFF files and show their Exif information. In addition, it can search Windows thumbnail cache folders to look for evidence of graphics files that were deleted. OSForensics doesn't include an audio or video player; instead, it opens these files in Windows Media Player. In this lab, you use OSForensics to search an image for multimedia files.

After completing this lab, you will be able to:

- Use OSForensics to search for multimedia files
- Use the OSForensics built-in graphics analysis tools

Materials Required

This lab requires the following:

- Windows 8 or 8.1 Professional
- OSForensics
- The `jo-favorites-usb-2009-12-11.E01` file downloaded in Lab 8.1

Estimated completion time: **30–60 minutes**

Activity

In this lab, you search the `jo-favorites-usb-2009-12-11.E01` file with OSForensics:

1. Start OSForensics. Click **Start** in the left pane, if necessary, and click **Create Case** in the right pane.

2. In the New Case dialog box, type **C8Proj2** in the Case Name text box, enter your initials in the Investigator text box, and click the **Investigate Disk(s) from Another Machine** option button for the acquisition type. Click **Custom Location** for the case folder. Click the **Browse** button, navigate to and click the **C:\Work\Labs\Cases** folder, click the **Make New Folder** button, type **C8Proj2**, and click **OK** twice.

3. Click the **Add Device** button, click the **Image File** option button, navigate to and click the **C:\Work\Labs\Evidence** folder, click the `jo-favorites-usb-2009-12-11.E01` file, and click **Open**. In the "Select a partition in the image" dialog box, click **Partition 0**, and then click **OK** twice.

4. Click the **Create Index** button in the left pane. In the Step 1 of 5 window, click the **Use Pre-defined File Types** option button, if necessary. Click to select all the file types listed, and click **Next**. In the Step 2 of 5 window, click the **Add** button. In the Add Start Location dialog box, verify that the **Whole Drive** option button is selected, and then click **OK**. Click **Next**, and in the Step 3 of 5 window, click **Start Indexing**. When OSForensics finishes indexing the image (which might take a few minutes), click **OK** in the message box about the file limit, if prompted.

5. Click the **Search Index** button in the left pane, click **Search** in the right pane, and click the **Images** tab, if necessary, to view the graphics files (see Figure 8-3).

6. Click **Start** in the left pane, and then click **File and Hex Viewer**. In the "Select a file to open" dialog box, click `jo-favorites-usb-2009-12-11-:` in the left pane, click the **DSC00009.JPG** file, and then click **Open** to see the file in the graphics viewer.

7. Click the **Hex/String Viewer** tab to see the file header hex values, and then click the **Metadata** tab to see the Exif information (see Figure 8-4). Click the **File Info** tab to see the timestamps, file size, and other attributes.

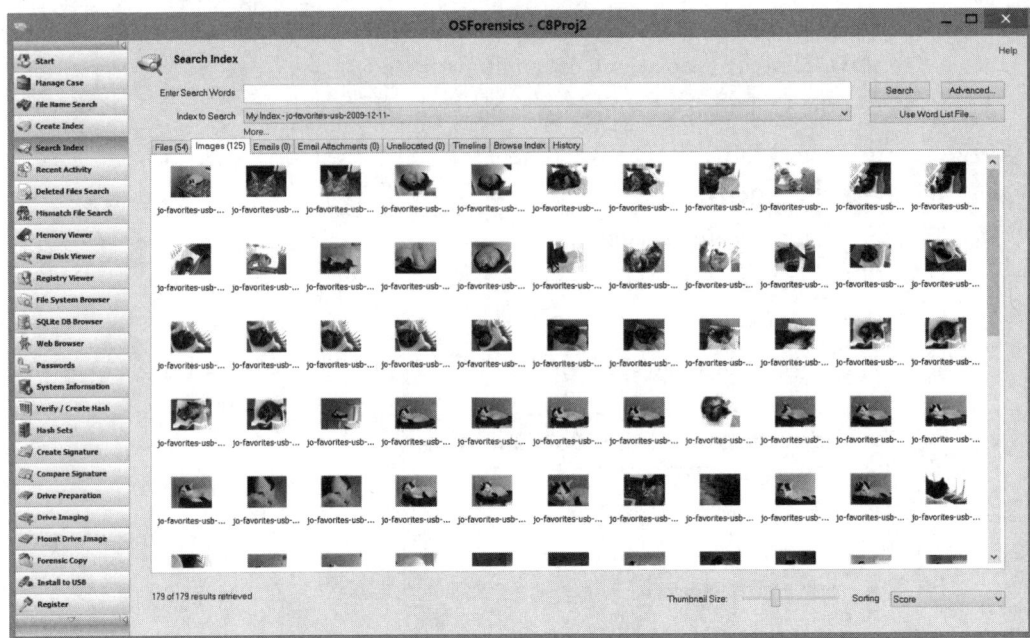

Figure 8-3 Viewing graphics files in OSForensics

Source: PassMark Software, www.osforensics.com

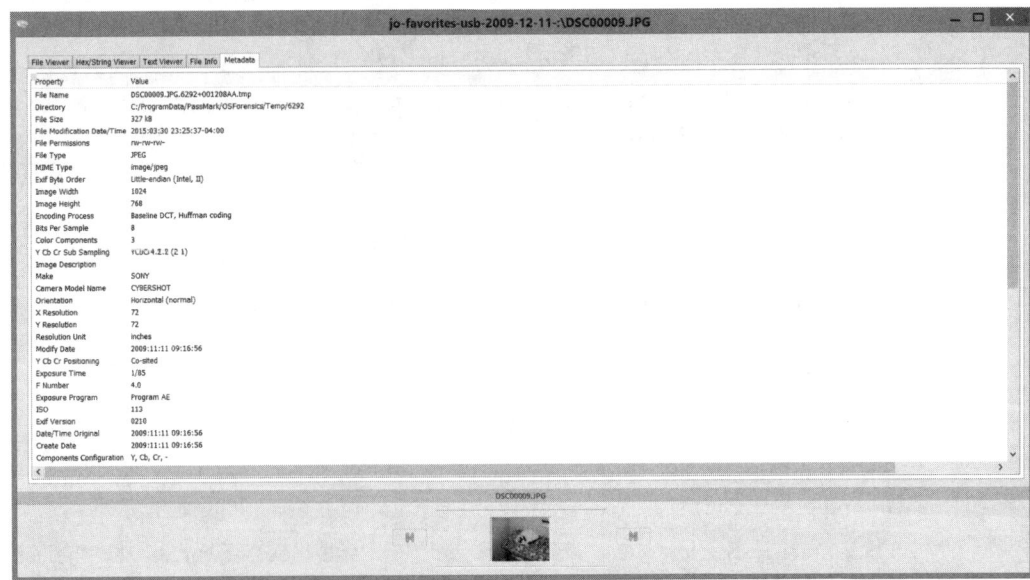

Figure 8-4 Viewing Exif information in OSForensics

Source: PassMark Software, www.osforensics.com

8. Close the File and Hex Viewer, and click **File System Browser** in the left pane. Click **jo-favorites-usb-2009-12-11-:**, and then Shift+click the first JPG file, scroll to the bottom of the list, and click the last JPG file. Right-click the selected files and click **Add Selected File(s) to Case**. In the Please Enter Case Export Details window, type **Pictures** in the Export Title text box, click the **Use same details for all** check box, and then click **Add**.

9. Click the **Videos** folder in the File System Browser to view the video files. (Filenames beginning with **._** are resource forks containing file attributes, not the actual files.) Right-click **MontereyKitty.m4v**, point to **Open With**, and double-click **Windows Media Player** (because OSForensics doesn't have a built-in video player). After viewing the video, exit Windows Media Player. Right-click the **MontereyKitty.m4v** file again, point to **Hash**, and then click **Calculate hash**. In the Verify/Create Hash dialog box, click **Calculate** to determine the SHA-1 hash value, which is displayed in the Calculated Hash text box. Click the **Hash Function** list arrow to view other options supported by OSForensics, click **MD5** in the drop-down list, and click **Calculate** to view the hash value. Close the File System Browser.

10. Click **Start** in the left pane, and then click **Generate Report** in the right pane. Click the **Copy files to report location** option button, click **Browse**, navigate to and click the **C:\Work\Labs\Cases\C8Proj2** folder, and click **OK**. Click **OK** in the Export Report dialog box. If an error message is displayed, click **OK**.

11. Leave OSForensics open as you answer the following review questions. When you're finished, exit OSForensics.

Review Questions

1. What date was the first video created?

2. How many QuickTime videos were recovered from the USB image?

3. OSForensics has no built-in viewer for playing video files. True or False?

4. How many hash generator options does OSForensics support?

   a. 2

   b. 4

   c. 1

   d. 0

5. What's the SHA-256 hash value for the MontereyKitty.m4v file?

Lab 8.3 Using ProDiscover Basic to Search an Image for Multimedia Files

Objectives

ProDiscover Basic doesn't include an internal video viewer; it relies on Windows Media Player to view video files. However, it does have a powerful search engine so that you can find multimedia files quickly. Additionally, ProDiscover provides Exif information, hash values, and other attributes to validate files you recover and has a detailed reporting function, similar to the one in Autopsy and OSForensics. In this lab, you use ProDiscover to search an image for multimedia files.

After completing this lab, you will be able to:

- Use ProDiscover to search for multimedia files

Materials Required

This lab requires the following:

- Windows 8 or 8.1 Professional
- ProDiscover Basic
- The `jo-favorites-usb-2009-12-11.E01` file downloaded in Lab 8.1

> Estimated completion time: **30–60 minutes**

Activity

In this lab, you search the `jo-favorites-usb-2009-12-11.E01` file with ProDiscover Basic:

1. Double-click the **ProDiscover Basic** desktop icon, and click the **New Project** toolbar button. Type **C8Proj3** in the Project Number and Project File Name text boxes, and then click **OK**.

2. In the tree view, click to expand **Add**, and click **Image File**. In the Open dialog box, navigate to and click the **C:\Work\Labs\Evidence** folder, click the **jo-favorites-usb-2009-12-11.E01** file, and then click **Open**.

3. In the tree view, click to expand **Content View**, if necessary. Expand **Images, C:\Work\Labs\Evidence\jo-favorites-usb-2009-12-11.E01**, and the C drive, and click **All Files**. If necessary, click **Yes** in the ProDiscover message box that opens. All the files in this USB image are displayed in the right pane with their file attributes.

4. Right-click the **DSC00012** file and click **View** to open it in Windows Photo Viewer (or your computer's default graphics viewer). When you're finished, close Windows Photo Viewer. Right-click the **DSC00012** file again and click **View EXIF Data** to see the Exif information (see Figure 8-5). Click **OK** when you're finished.

5. Click the **Search** toolbar icon, and click the **Content Search** tab, if necessary. Click the **Search for files named** option button, type **jpg**, and press **Enter**. Type **mov** in the text box, click the default disk listed under "Select the Disk(s)/Image(s) you want to search in," and click **OK**. The search results in the Search 1 tab include MD5 hash values (see Figure 8-6). Click the **Selection** button, click **Select All**, click the **Apply to all items** check box, and click **OK**. Each file is displayed with a check mark (which might take a few minutes). When all the files have been selected, click the **Add to Report** button.

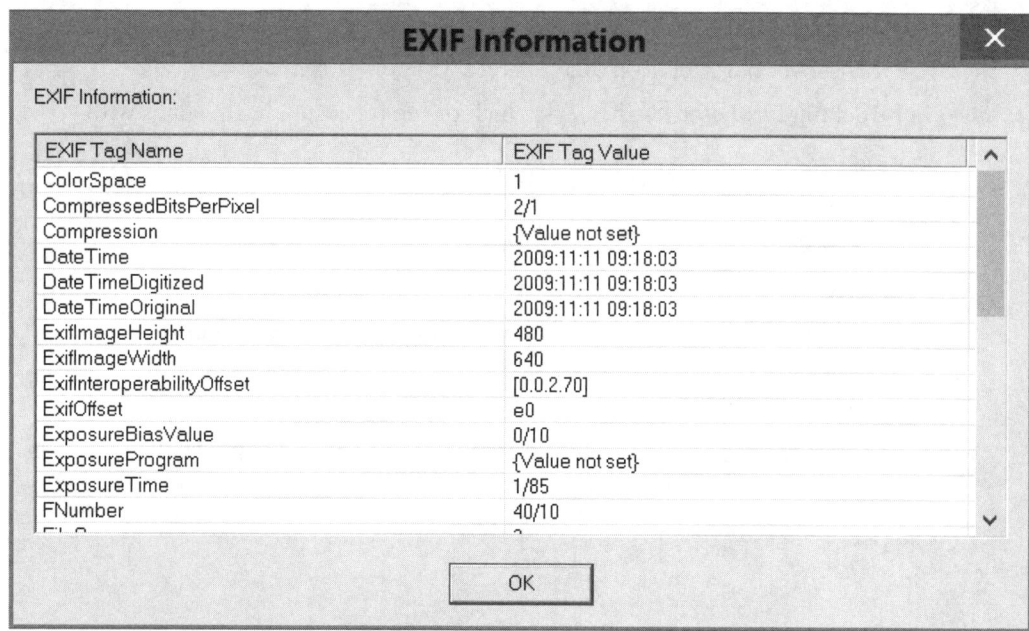

Figure 8-5   Viewing Exif information in ProDiscover

© 2015 The ARC Group of NY, www.arcgroupny.com

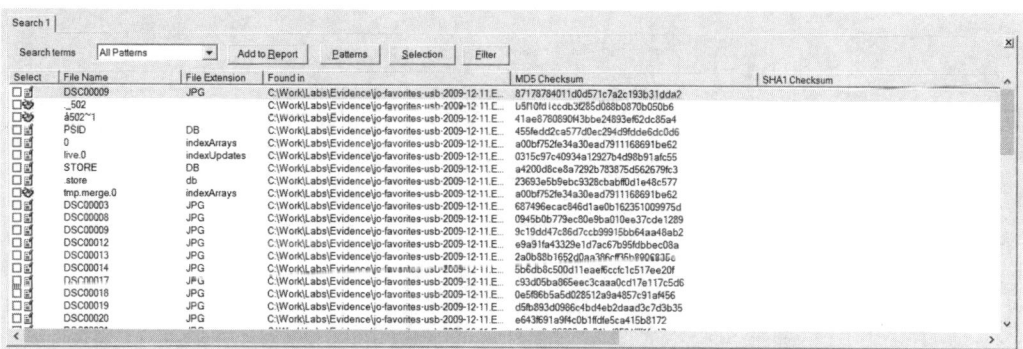

Figure 8-6   Viewing search results

© 2015 The ARC Group of NY, www.arcgroupny.com

6. Click **Videos** in the left pane. Right-click the `KittyMontage.mov` file in the upper-right pane and click **View** to see the video. ProDiscover uses an external player for video files.

7. Click **Report** in the tree view to display the evidence report, and leave it open as you answer the following review questions. When you're finished, exit ProDiscover, clicking **Yes** to save the case in the **C:\Work\Labs\Cases** folder.

Review Questions

1. ProDiscover has a built-in video player. True or False?

2. By default, ProDiscover displays which of the following hash values with search results?

   a. SHA-1

   b. MD5

   c. SHA-256

   d. CRC

3. How many evidence items were recovered from the USB image?

4. All the files recovered from the USB device were last accessed on the same date. True or False?

5. The ProDiscover report includes the location of each file in the USB image. True or False?

CHAPTER NINE

DIGITAL FORENSICS ANALYSIS AND VALIDATION

Labs included in this chapter:

Lab 9.1 Using Autopsy to Search for Keywords in an Image

Objectives

As you've seen, you can use Autopsy to search for keywords in images and locate full or partial matches with words or phrases in files and folders. Search results show file attributes, including hash values. In this lab, you search an image for any references to the keyword "project" and extract the hash values for each file.

After completing this lab, you will be able to:

- Use the keyword search tools in Autopsy
- Determine hash values for files recovered with search tools

Materials Required

This lab requires the following:

- Windows 8 or 8.1 Professional
- Autopsy 3.1.2 for Windows
- The gcfi-ntfs-dd.exe file on the DVD

Estimated completion time: **120–180 minutes,** depending on your computer's performance

Activity

In this lab, you use Autopsy to search for references to the keyword "project":

1. In File Explorer, double-click the **gcfi-ntfs-dd.exe** file on the DVD, and extract it to the **C:\Work\Labs\Evidence** folder.

2. Start Autopsy. In the Welcome window, click **Create New Case**.

3. Type **C9Proj1** in the Case Name text box. Click **Browse**, navigate to and click the **C:\Work\Labs\Cases** folder, click **OK** to enter this path in the Base Directory text box, if necessary, and then click **Next**. Type **C9Proj1** in the Case Number text box and your initials in the Examiner text box, and then click **Finish**.

4. In the Add Data Source dialog box, click **Browse**, navigate to and click the **gcfi-ntfs.dd** file you extracted, click **Open**, and then click **Next**. Click **Next** to accept the ingest modules, and then click **Finish** to start analyzing the evidence, which could take a while. Watch the progress bar in the lower-right corner to determine when the process is finished.

5. Click the **Keyword Lists** button at the upper right, click all four check boxes, and click **Search**. Click the **Keyword Search** button, type **project** in the text box, click the **Substring Match** option button, and click **Search**. The results aren't highlighted; if you select one and then click the **Text** tab in the lower pane, a message states that there are no keyword

hits on this page. Substring searches can occasionally reveal matches in filenames, deleted or modified files, and slack or carved disk space. As Figure 9-1 shows, there seem to be no substring matches in the 642 search results.

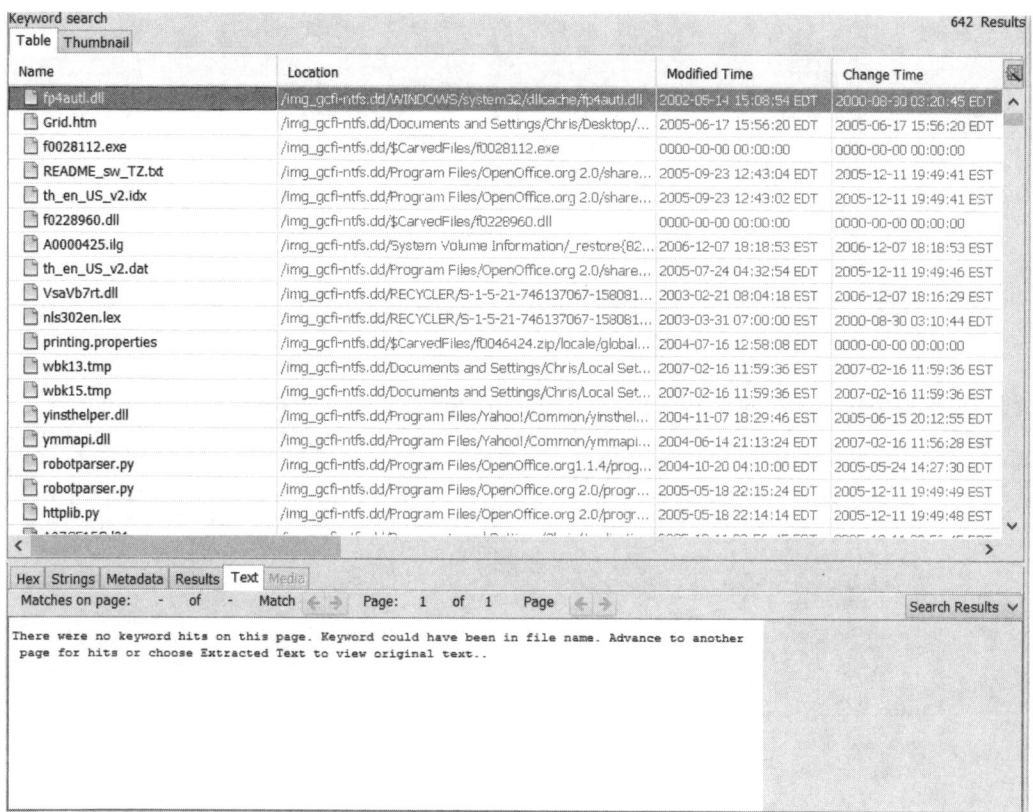

Figure 9-1   Viewing substring matches in the search results

Source: www.sleuthkit.org

6. Click the **Keyword Search** button, click the **Exact Match** option button (if necessary), type **project,** and click **Search**. The search returns 371 results (see Figure 9-2). Click the **Keyword search 3 - project** tab, and click the **Name** header to sort the results alphabetically by name. Scroll down and click the **CREDITS.txt** file to view its contents in the lower pane. Notice the yellow highlighted hits for the keyword "project." Slide the horizontal scroll bar to the right to see the attributes for this file, including the MD5 hash.

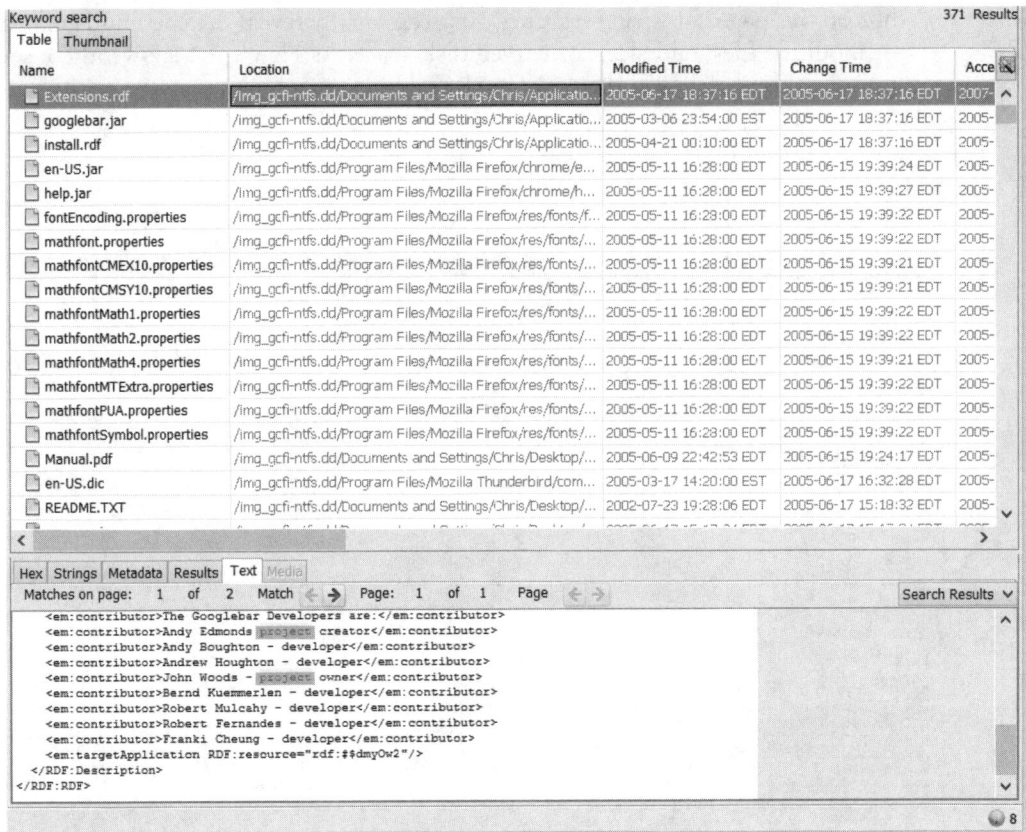

Figure 9-2   Viewing exact matches in the search results

Source: www.sleuthkit.org

7. Right-click the **CREDITS.txt** file, if necessary, and click **Extract File(s)**. Click **Save** to save the files in the Export folder, and click **OK** in the Information message box. This process is used to export evidence that might need further analysis.

8. In the left pane, expand **Keyword Hits**, if necessary. Expand **Single Regular Expression Search**, and then click **project** to see the collective search results for the keyword "project." Click the first result in the **Table** tab, and view its text content in the lower pane, as shown in Figure 9-3. Although you should search all results for potential evidence, some matches might not be relevant to your investigation.

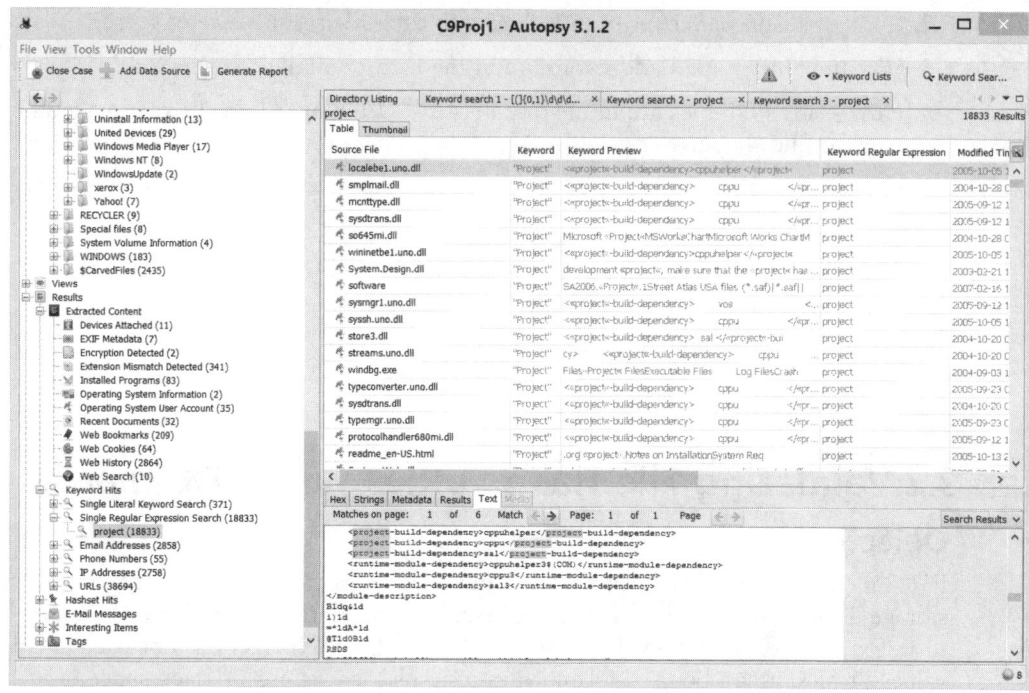

Figure 9-3   Viewing the collective search results

Source: www.sleuthkit.org

9. In the left pane, expand **Single Literal Keyword Search**, and click **project**. Click the **Source File** header to sort the list alphabetically. Scroll down and click the `Inbox.dbx` file, which is the e-mail inbox, to see the e-mails with references to "project" highlighted in yellow.

10. Right-click the `HISTORY.txt` file and click **Extract File(s)**. Click **Save** to save the files in the Export folder, and then click **OK** in the Information message box. Repeat this process for the `LFG.pdf` file, the first `Manual.pdf` file, and the first `README.TXT` file.

11. Leave Autopsy open as you answer the following review questions. When you're finished, leave Autopsy running for Lab 9.2.

Review Questions

1. How many exact matches were found for the keyword "project"?

   a. 371

   b. 18,833

   c. 55

   d. 2758

2. Autopsy displays SHA-1 hash values with each file result. True or False?

3. Was Jim Shu's e-mail address found in the list of e-mail addresses?

4. How many PDF files are in the `gcfi-ntfs.dd` image? (*Hint*: Expand Views in the left pane to find the answer.)

5. In Autopsy, substring searches can reveal matches in which of the following? (Choose all that apply.)

   a. Filenames

   b. Unformatted disks

   c. Deleted or modified files

   d. Slack space

Lab 9.2 Validating File Hash Values with FTK Imager

Objectives

FTK Imager can calculate hash values in physical and logical hard drive partitions, images of storage devices, and files in folders. The results of calculating file hash values can be exported to an Excel file for use as a validation tool. Although FTK Imager can't be used to edit the hex values of files, it can be used to find files in hidden partitions or slack space on disk drives. In this lab, you use FTK Imager to validate hash values of the files you exported in Lab 9.1.

After completing this lab, you will be able to:

- Calculate MD5 hash values in FTK Imager
- Export file hashes to an Excel file for analysis

Materials Required

This lab requires the following:

- Windows 8 or 8.1 Professional
- AccessData FTK Imager
- Autopsy 3.1.2 for Windows
- Microsoft Excel

Estimated completion time: **15–20 minutes**

Activity

In this lab, you use FTK Imager to calculate the MD5 hash values for the files exported in Lab 9.1:

1. Start FTK Imager, clicking **Yes** in the User Account Control message box, if necessary.

2. Click **File**, **Add Evidence Item** from the menu. In the Select Source dialog box, click the **Contents of a Folder** option button, and then click **Next**. In the Select File dialog box, click **Browse**, type **C:\Work\Labs\Cases\C9Proj1\Export** in the Folder text box, and click **OK**. Click **Finish** to add the files to the Export folder.

3. Expand **Export** in the Evidence Tree. Right-click **C:\Work\Labs\Cases\C9Proj1\Export** and click **Export File Hash List**.

4. In the Save As dialog box, type **C9Proj1 Exported Files** in the "File name" text box, verify that the path is **C:\Work\Labs\Evidence**, and click **Save**.

5. Click the **eyeglass** toolbar icon, and click the **CREDITS.txt** file to view it. Click the **Manual.pdf** file to open it in the built-in viewer. The file size is displayed in the File List pane, and the image file's size, which includes slack space, is shown in the Properties pane under the Evidence Tree (see Figure 9-4). Click the **eyeglass "HEX"** toolbar icon to view the file's hex values in the lower-right pane. The hex values are read-only, so they can't be edited.

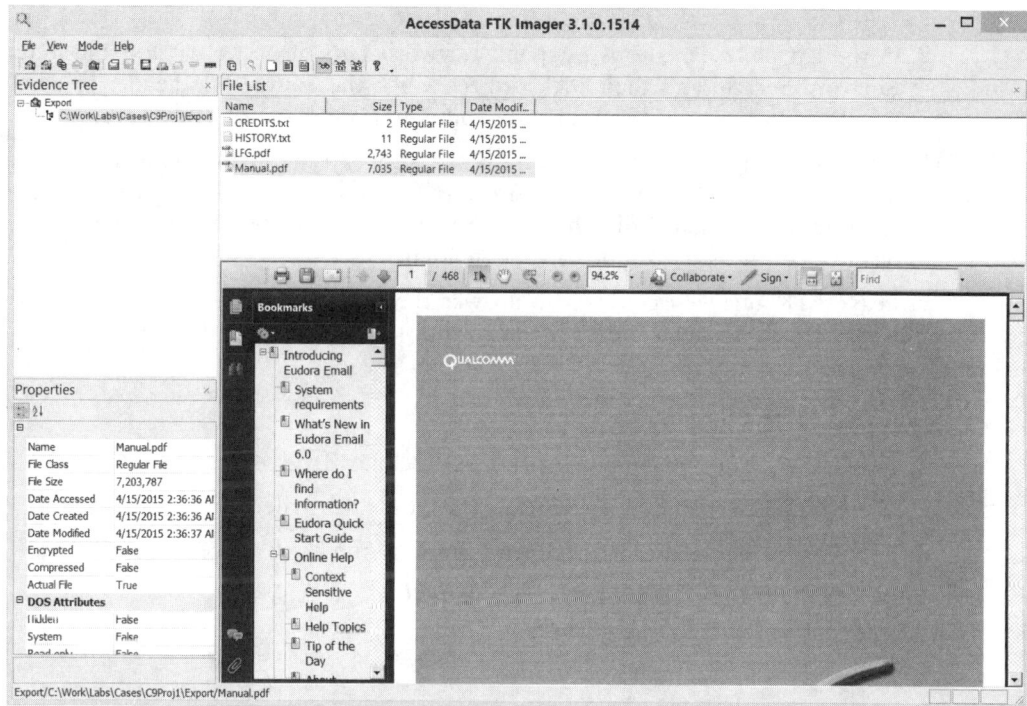

Figure 9-4   Using FTK Imager's built-in file viewer

6. In File Explorer, navigate to the **C:\Work\Labs\Evidence** folder, and double-click the **C9Proj1 Exported Files.csv** file to open it in Microsoft Excel. Increase the width of columns A and B to view the MD5 and SHA-1 hash values for each file (see Figure 9-5).

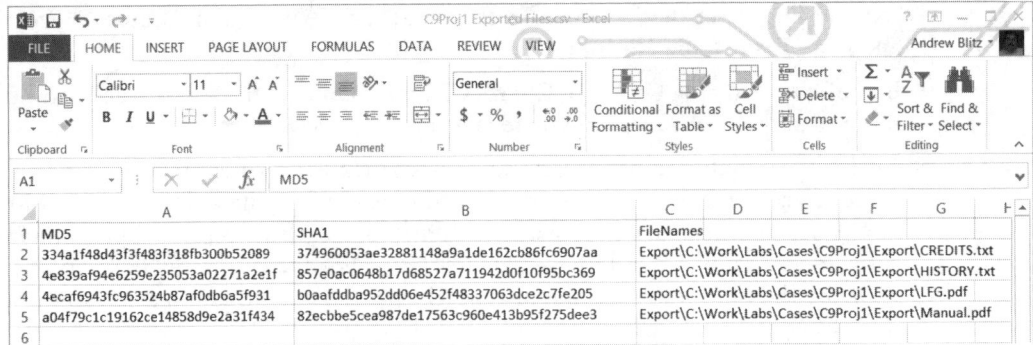

Figure 9-5   Viewing file hashes in Excel

7. In the left pane of Autopsy, expand **Keyword Hits**, if necessary. Expand **Single Literal Keyword Search**, and then click **project**. Click the **Source File** header to sort the files, scroll down the list in the Table tab, and double-click the **CREDITS.txt** file.

8. Scroll to the right until the MD5 hash value appears, and compare it with the hash value in the **C9Proj1 Exported Files.csv** file. If the MD5 hash values in Autopsy match the values in the Excel file, the evidence has been validated. Repeat Step 7 for the other hash values in the Excel file to validate them.

9. Leave FTK Imager open as you answer the following review questions. When you're finished, exit Autopsy and FTK Imager, but leave Excel open for Lab 9.3.

Review Questions

1. FTK Imager can calculate only MD5 hash values. True or False?

2. What's the SHA-1 hash value for the HISTORY.txt file?

3. FTK Imager can find files in hidden partitions and slack space. True or False?

4. What's the file size of the LFG.pdf file *without* slack space?

    a. 2,808,031

    b. 1718

    c. 2743

    d. 7,203,787

5. FTK Imager can't be used to edit hex values. True or False?

Lab 9.3 Validating File Hash Values with WinHex

Objectives

WinHex has many of the same features as FTK Imager, such as disk imaging, reading the file structure in images of storage devices and virtual hard disks, and calculating MD5 and SHA-1 hash values, which makes it useful as a forensics validation tool. Unlike FTK Imager, WinHex can be used to edit hex values in file headers that have been deliberately altered, deleted, or placed in hidden disk partitions. In this lab, you examine the exported files from Lab 9.1 and use WinHex to validate the hash values in the Excel file.

After completing this lab, you will be able to:

- Use WinHex to calculate MD5 and SHA-1 hash values
- Use WinHex to validate hash values

Materials Required:

This lab requires the following:

- Windows 8 or 8.1 Professional
- WinHex (installed in Step 1)
- The C9Proj1 Exported Files.csv file from Lab 9.2

> Estimated completion time: **20 minutes**

Activity

In this lab, you use WinHex to validate the exported file hashes calculated in Lab 9.2:

1. Install WinHex (using the **winhex.zip** file on the DVD), and start it.

2. Click **File, Open** from the menu, click the **Look in** list arrow, navigate to the **C:\Work\ Labs\Cases\C9Proj1\Export** folder, click the **CREDITS.txt** file, and click **Open**.

3. Repeat Step 2 and open the **HISTORY.txt** file in WinHex. You should see two tabs in the right pane, one for each file you have opened (see Figure 9-6). Notice the information in the right pane, including file size.

Figure 9-6 Viewing files in WinHex

Courtesy of X-Ways AG, www.x-ways.net

4. Click the **CREDITS.txt** tab, and click **Tools, Compute Hash** from the menu. Click **SHA-1 (160 bit)** in the drop-down list, and click **OK** to see the SHA-1 hash value (see Figure 9-7).

Figure 9-7   Viewing the SHA-1 hash value in WinHex

Courtesy of X-Ways AG, www.x-ways.net

5. To validate your results, compare the SHA-1 hash value in WinHex with the SHA-1 hash value in the C9Proj1 Exported Files.csv file to see whether they match. A match of hash values validates the exported files with another forensics tool. Click **Close** in the SHA-1 (160 bit) dialog box.

6. Repeat Step 4 with the **HISTORY.txt** file, and compare its SHA-1 hash value with the one in the C9Proj1 Exported Files.csv file to validate your results.

7. Click the **CREDITS.txt** tab, and click **Tools, Compute Hash** from the menu. Click **MD5 (128 bit)** in the drop-down list, and click **OK** to see the MD5 hash value. Compare this value with the one in the C9Proj1 Exported Files.csv file. Click **Close** in the MD5 (128 bit) dialog box.

8. Click the **HISTORY.txt** tab, and then click **Tools, Compute Hash** from the menu. Click **MD5 (128 bit)** in the drop-down list, and click **OK** to see the MD5 hash value. Again, compare the computed MD5 hash value with the value in the C9Proj1 Exported Files.csv file. Click **Close** in the MD5 (128 bit) dialog box.

9. Leave WinHex open as you answer the following review questions. When you're finished, close the Excel file and exit WinHex.

Review Questions

1. WinHex can calculate only SHA-1 and MD5 hash values. True or False?

2. WinHex can edit hex values in file headers. True or False?

3. What's the size in bytes of the HISTORY.txt file?

4. The hex values of the first 4 bytes are always the same for .txt files. True or False?

5. WinHex has which of the following features? (Choose all that apply.)

   a. Recovering data in deleted partitions

   b. File-decrypting tools

   c. Editing file hash values

   d. Creating images of storage devices

VIRTUAL MACHINE FORENSICS, LIVE ACQUISITIONS, AND NETWORK FORENSICS

Labs included in this chapter:

- Lab 10.1 Installing DEFT Linux in Oracle VirtualBox
- Lab 10.2 Using FTK Imager to Image and View Virtual Hard Drives
- Lab 10.3 Using Autopsy to Analyze a Virtual Hard Drive Image

Lab 10.1 Installing DEFT Linux in Oracle VirtualBox

Objectives

Oracle VirtualBox is a powerful type 2 hypervisor that runs on 32-bit or 64-bit versions of Windows, Linux, Mac OS X, Solaris, and OpenBSD. This free open-source product is available under the terms of the GNU General Public License (GPL). When it's installed on a 64-bit computer, it can run most 32-bit and 64-bit guest OSs, making it useful for digital forensics. In addition, it's used extensively, along with Microsoft Hyper-V and VMware, as an enterprise solution for hosting virtual desktop infrastructure (VDI) computers in large organization settings. In this lab, you install Oracle VirtualBox, install DEFT Linux as a guest OS, and copy the DEFT.vhd file to your Evidence folder for future analysis.

After completing this lab, you will be able to:

- Install VirtualBox and create a virtual hard disk
- Install a guest OS in VirtualBox

Materials Required:

This lab requires the following:

- Windows 8 or 8.1 Professional
- Oracle VirtualBox
- The DEFT boot DVD from Lab 4.3

Estimated completion time: **60–120 minutes,** depending on your computer's performance

Activity

In this lab, you install VirtualBox and create a DEFT virtual machine:

1. Start a Web browser, and go to **https://www.virtualbox.org/wiki/Downloads**. Download VirtualBox 4.3.28 for Windows hosts. In File Explorer, double-click the **VirtualBox-4.3.28-100309-Win.exe** file. If necessary, click **Run** in the Open File - Security Warning message box to begin the installation. In the Oracle VM VirtualBox 4.3.28 Setup window, click **Next**. Click **Next** twice, click **Yes** in the Warning: Network Interfaces message box, and click **Install** in the Ready to Install window. If necessary, click **Yes** in the UAC message box. In the "Would you like to add this device software?" window, click **Install**, and then click **Finish**. Oracle VirtualBox starts automatically.

2. If necessary, download and install the **VirtualBox 4.3.28 Oracle VM VirtualBox Extension Pack** to add support for USB devices. Click **Yes** in the UAC message box, and then click **OK** to finish the installation. Exit your Web browser.

3. In VirtualBox, click the **New** toolbar icon to start the Create Virtual Machine Wizard. In the Name and operating system window, type **Deft** in the Name text box. Click the **Type** list arrow and click **Linux** in the list, and then click the **Version** list arrow and click **Ubuntu (64 bit)** in the list, as shown in Figure 10-1. Click **Next**. In the Memory size window, type **1024** in the text box, and click **Next**.

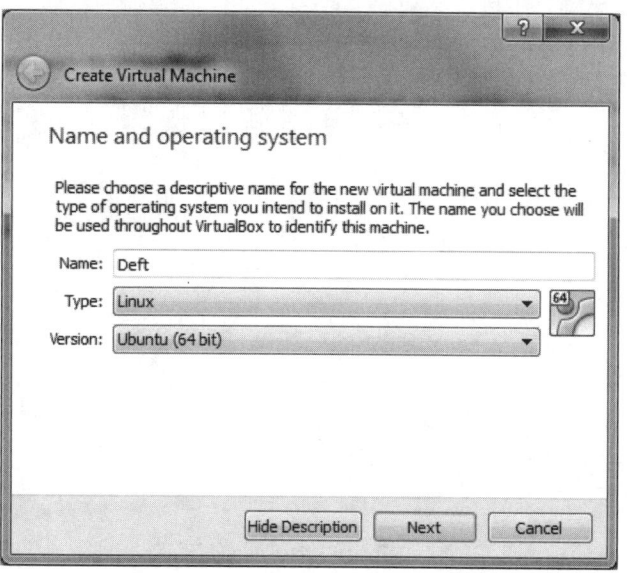

Figure 10-1   Entering a name and OS for the virtual machine

Source: Oracle VirtualBox, www.virtualbox.org

4. In the "Hard drive" window, click the **Create a virtual drive now** option button, and then click **Create**. In the "Hard drive file type" window, click the **VHD** (**Virtual Hard Disk**) option button, and then click **Next**. In the "Storage on physical hard drive" window, click the **Fixed size** option button, and then click **Next**. In the File location and size window, type **10 GB** in the text box, and click **Create** to configure the virtual hard drive, which might take a few minutes.

5. Place the DEFT DVD in your CD/DVD drive, and close the drive. Click the **DEFT** icon, if necessary, and click **Start**. In the Select start-up disk dialog box, click **Start** to start the virtual machine. Click the CD/DVD drive letter to boot from the DVD when prompted.

6. When the DEFT installation window opens, highlight **English** as the default language, and press **Enter**. Use the up and down arrow buttons to scroll to **Install DEFT Linux 8**, and press **Enter**.

7. In the Welcome window, click **Continue**, and in the "Preparing to install DEFT" window, click the **Install this third-party software** check box, and then click **Continue**. Click the **Guided - use entire disk** option button, if necessary, and click **Install Now**. In the "Where are you?" window, click **Continue**, and in the "Keyboard layout" window, click **Continue**.

8. In the "Who are you?" window, type **Student** in the "Your name" text box, type **password** in both "Choose a password" text boxes, click the **Log in automatically** option button (see Figure 10-2), and click **Continue**. The installation's progress is shown in the bar at the top. (Installation might take an hour or more). If the Auto capture keyboard and mouse pointer integration message boxes are displayed, you can close them.

9. In the Installation Complete window, click **Restart Now**. When prompted, remove the DEFT DVD and click **Enter**. The virtual machine restarts, and the DEFT desktop is displayed. (If you see an error message stating that a system program problem was detected, click **Cancel**.)

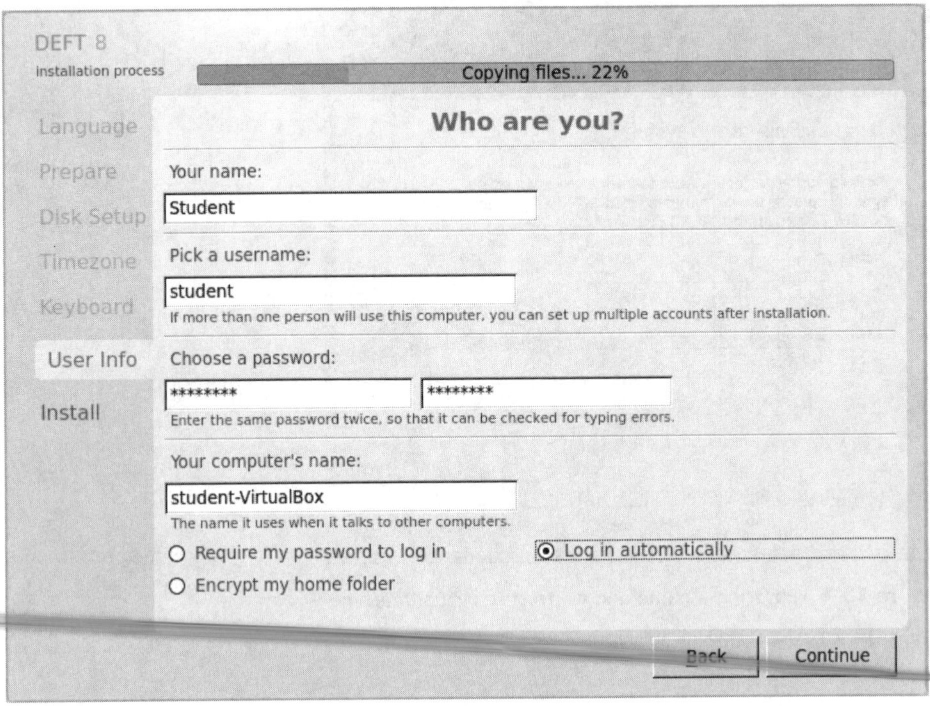

Figure 10-2   Entering user information

Source: Oracle VirtualBox, www.virtualbox.org

10. Click the **d** button at the lower left, click **System Tools**, click **Software Updater**, and click **Install Now** in the Software Updater dialog box. Type **password**, as shown in Figure 10-3, and click **Authenticate** to install new updates. (Your computer must be connected to the Internet to update DEFT.) Click **Restart** when prompted to finish the update installation.

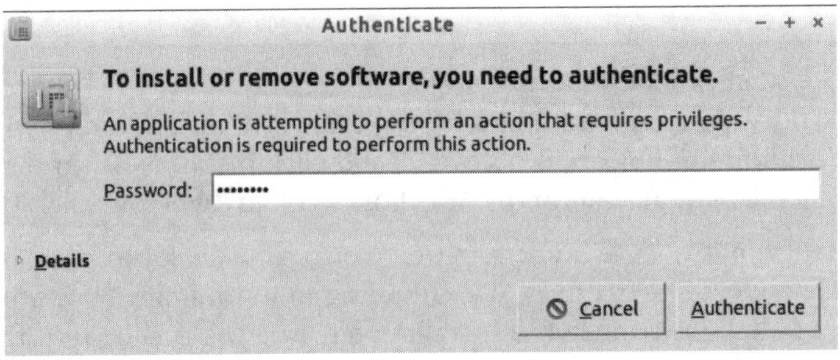

Figure 10-3   Authentication for software installation

Source: Oracle VirtualBox, www.virtualbox.org

 Some antivirus or firewall software tries to access the Internet through VirtualBox, so you might need to disable it during the update and then reenable it. Ask your instructor for details, if needed.

11. Double-click the **File Manager** icon on the DEFT desktop to view the Student user account and the system files and folders. Click **/** (the systemroot folder), and write down the system folder names to refer to in Lab 10.3. Click the **d** button, and browse through the menu to become familiar with the programs in DEFT.

12. Leave VirtualBox open as you answer the following review questions. When you're finished, click the **d** button in the lower-left corner of the virtual machine, click **Logout**, and click **Shutdown** to shut down the DEFT virtual machine.

13. In File Explorer, right-click the **Deft** virtual machine and click **Show**. Right-click the **DEFT.vhd** file and click **Copy**. In the Open Deft window, navigate to **C:\Work\Labs\ Evidence** and paste the **DEFT.vhd** file. This step copies the virtual hard drive image from the default VirtualBox location on your hard drive to the Evidence folder for forensic analysis later. When you're finished, exit VirtualBox.

Review Questions

1. How much free space is shown in File Manager?

2. In which folder is the Student user's home folder?

   a. /home

   b. Student

   c. Bin

   d. Documents

3. How many Web browsers does DEFT include?

   a. 1

   b. 2

   c. 3

   d. None

4. DEFT has no Office file viewer. True or False?

5. VirtualBox can run in both 32-bit and 64-bit OSs. True or False?

Lab 10.2 Using FTK Imager to Image and View Virtual Hard Drives

Objectives

AccessData FTK Imager can image virtual hard drives so that you can process them with forensics software that doesn't include this feature. In addition, you can use FTK Imager to mount a virtual hard drive and view the files and folders in an image. It can be useful for verifying files with hashes and extracting files and folders for detailed analysis. FTK Imager also shows MD5 and SHA-1 hash values, UNIX permissions, and file and folder timestamp information. In this lab, you create an .E01 image of the DEFT.vhd virtual hard drive and view its system folders.

After completing this lab, you will be able to:

- Create an .E01 image of a virtual hard drive
- Use FTK Imager to view a virtual hard drive image

Materials Required

This lab requires the following:

- Windows 8 or 8.1 Professional
- FTK Imager
- The DEFT.vhd file from Lab 10.1

Estimated completion time: 30–45 minutes

Activity

In this lab, you create an .E01 image of a virtual hard drive and view its system folders:

1. Start FTK Imager, clicking **Yes** in the UAC message box, if necessary.

2. Click **File**, **Create Disk Image** from the menu. In the Select Source dialog box, click the **Image File** option button, and then click **Next**. In the Evidence Source Selection dialog box, click **Browse**, navigate to the **C:\Work\Labs\Evidence** folder, click the **DEFT.vhd** file, and click **Open**. Click **Finish** to load the file.

3. In the Create Image dialog box, click **Add**, click the **E01** option button, and click **Next**. Type **C10Proj1** in the Case Number and Evidence Number text boxes, and click **Next**. In the Select Image Destination dialog box, click **Browse**, navigate to and click the **C:\Work\Labs\Evidence** folder, and then click **OK**. In the Image Filename (Excluding Extension) text box, type **C10Proj1** (see Figure 10-4), and then click **Finish**.

4. In the Create Image dialog box, click **C:\Work\Labs\Evidence\C10Proj1 [E01]** in the Image Destination(s) list box (see Figure 10-5), and then click **Start** to start the imaging process.

5. When the imaging is finished, write down the MD5 and SHA-1 hash values, click **Close** in the Drive/Image Verify Results dialog box, and click **Close** again to exit. These values are also stored in your Evidence folder in the C10Proj1.E01.txt file.

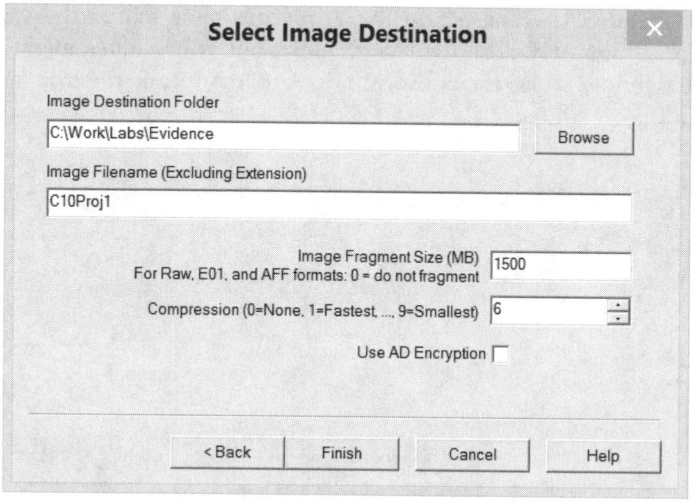

Select Image Destination   X

Image Destination Folder

C:\Work\Labs\Evidence   Browse

Image Filename (Excluding Extension)

C10Proj1

Image Fragment Size (MB)   1500
For Raw, E01, and AFF formats: 0 = do not fragment

Compression (0=None, 1=Fastest, ..., 9=Smallest)   6

Use AD Encryption ☐

< Back   Finish   Cancel   Help

Figure 10-4   The Select Image Destination dialog box

©2015 AccessData Group, Inc. All Rights Reserved.

Create Image   X

Image Source

C:\Work\Labs\Evidence\DEFT.vhd

Starting Evidence Number: 1

Image Destination(s)

C:\Work\Labs\Evidence\C10Proj1 [E01]

Add...   Edit...   Remove

☑ Verify images after they are created   ☐ Precalculate Progress Statistics
☐ Create directory listings of all files in the image after they are created

Start   Cancel

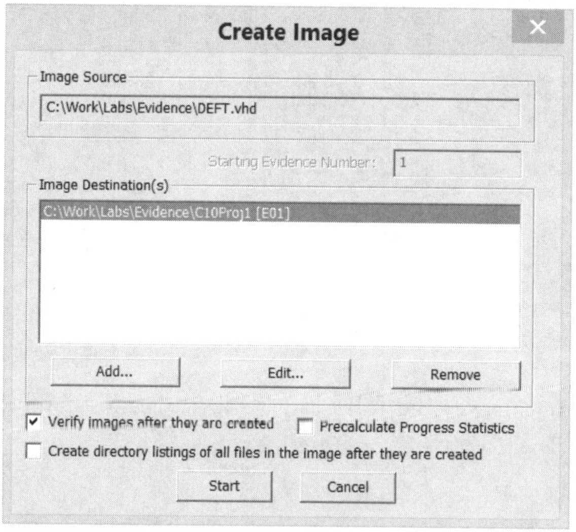

Figure 10-5   The Create Image dialog box

©2015 AccessData Group, Inc. All Rights Reserved.

6. Click **File, Add Evidence Item** from the menu. In the Select Source dialog box, click the **Image File** option button, and then click **Next**. In the Select File dialog box, click **Browse**, navigate to the **C:\Work\Labs\Evidence** folder, click the **C10Proj1.E01** file, and click **Open**. Click **Finish** to add the file to the Evidence folder.

7. In the left pane, expand **C10Proj1.E01, Partition 1[9215MB], NONAME [ext4]**, and **[root]** to view the DEFT virtual hard drive and its system files and folders.

8. Verify that the MD5 and SHA-1 hashes in the Properties pane match the values you wrote down in Step 5. Figure 10-6 shows an example, but your values might differ. If necessary, resize the window to see the entire values. A match means the evidence added to FTK Imager hasn't been altered.

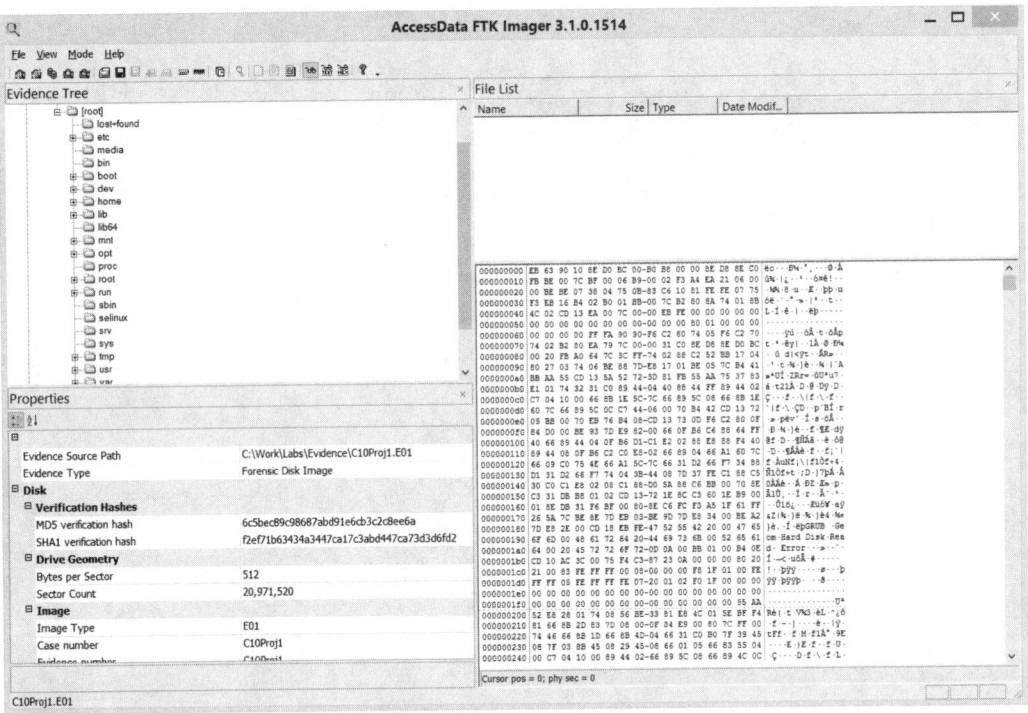

Figure 10-6   Viewing the calculated hash values

©2015 AccessData Group, Inc. All Rights Reserved.

9. Leave FTK Imager open as you answer the following review questions. When you're finished, exit FTK Imager.

Review Questions

1. How many hard drive partitions are in the `C10Proj1.E01` virtual hard drive image?

    a. 1

    b. 2

    c. 3

    d. 4

2. FTK Imager can create images of virtual hard drives only in the `.E01` format. True or False?

3. What file system is used in the `C10Proj1.E01` virtual hard drive image?

4. In what folder are the system folders?

 a. root

 b. NONAME

 c. bin

 d. boot

5. FTK Imager displays UNIX permissions. True or False?

Lab 10.3 Using Autopsy to Analyze a Virtual Hard Drive Image

Objectives

Autopsy supports the forensic analysis of virtual hard drives, using many common image formats, such as .img, .dd, raw, and .E01. This feature enables forensics investigators to examine virtual machines outside the hypervisor without the possibility of altering potential evidence. In addition, you can use the search tools in Autopsy to locate keywords, files, folders, Office documents, and other evidence. In this lab, you process the C10Proj1.E01 file containing the DEFT.vhd virtual hard drive and look for system folders and Office documents.

After completing this lab, you will be able to:

• Load a virtual hard drive image in Autopsy

• Find virtual machine system folders

10

Materials Required

This lab requires the following:

• Windows 8 or 8.1 Professional

• Autopsy for Windows

• The C10Proj1.E01 file from Lab 10.2

Estimated completion time: **360–420 minutes**

This lab might take more than 5 hours because of the image's large file size. Setting up the image file to process overnight is recommended.

Activity

In this lab, you load the C10Proj1.E01 file in Autopsy, and then look for evidence:

1. Start Autopsy. In the Welcome window, click **Create New Case**.

2. Type **C10Proj2** in the Case Name text box. Click **Browse**, navigate to and click the **C:\Work\Labs\Cases** folder, click **Select** to enter this path in the Base Directory text box, if necessary, and then click **Next**. Type **C10Proj2** in the Case Number text box and your initials in the Examiner text box, and then click **Finish**.

3. In the Add Data Source dialog box, click **Browse**, navigate to **C:\Work\Labs\Evidence**, click the **C10Proj1.E01** file, click **Open**, and then click **Next**. Click **Next** to accept the default ingest modules, and then click **Finish** to begin processing the image file, which could take 4 to 5 hours. Watch the progress bar in the lower-right corner to determine when the process is finished.

4. Click the **Keyword Search** button, type **student** in the text box, and click **Search** to look for any files related to the student user account name. Figure 10-7 shows the results.

Name	Location	Modified Time	Change Time
student	/img_C10Proj1.E01/:vol_vol2/home/student	2015-04-26 12:32:08 EDT	2015-04-26 12:32:08 EDT
.xsession-errors	/img_C10Proj1.E01/vol_vol2/home/student/.xsession-errors	2015-04-26 12:29:31 EDT	2015-04-26 12:29:31 EDT
gnome-exe-thumbnailer.files	/img_C10Proj1.E01/vol_vol2/home/student/.thumbnails/g...	2015-04-22 02:29:11 EDT	2015-04-22 02:29:11 EDT
.xsession-errors.old	/img_C10Proj1.E01/vol_vol2/home/student/.xsession-erro...	2015-04-26 12:14:54 EDT	2015-04-26 12:29:30 EDT
.testing.writeability	/img_C10Proj1.E01/vol_vol2/home/student/.gconf/.testing...	2015-04-26 12:30:00 EDT	2015-04-26 12:30:00 EDT
Local State	/img_C10Proj1.E01/vol_vol2/home/student/.config/google...	2015-04-23 09:21:01 EDT	2015-04-23 09:21:01 EDT
00000000	/img_C10Proj1.E01/vol_vol2/home/student/.config/google...	2015-04-22 02:20:39 EDT	2015-04-22 02:20:39 EDT
Preferences	/img_C10Proj1.E01/vol_vol2/home/student/.config/google...	2015-04-23 09:21:01 EDT	2015-04-23 09:21:01 EDT
.com.google.Chrome.tPgMvq	/img_C10Proj1.E01/vol_vol2/home/student/.config/google...	2015-04-23 09:21:01 EDT	2015-04-23 09:21:01 EDT
.com.google.Chrome.Jy0A82	/img_C10Proj1.E01/vol_vol2/home/student/.config/google...	2015-04-23 09:21:01 EDT	2015-04-23 09:21:01 EDT
run.log	/img_C10Proj1.E01/vol_vol2/home/student/.cache/lxsessi...	2015-04-26 12:32:08 EDT	2015-04-26 12:32:08 EDT
f_000026	/img_C10Proj1.E01/vol_vol2/home/student/.cache/google...	2015-04-23 09:20:49 EDT	2015-04-23 09:20:49 EDT
f_00002a	/img_C10Proj1.E01/vol_vol2/home/student/.cache/google...	2015-04-23 09:20:50 EDT	2015-04-23 09:20:50 EDT
9754602c51f5a427e6cdc019f6ae9ac3/	/img_C10Proj1.E01/vol_vol2/home/student/.cache/menus...	2015-04-26 12:14:16 EDT	2015-04-26 12:14:16 EDT
9754602c51f5a427e6cdc019f6ae9ac3	/img_C10Proj1.E01/vol_vol2/home/student/.cache/menus...	2015-04-26 12:14:16 EDT	2015-04-26 12:14:16 EDT
password.lst	/img_C10Proj1.E01/vol_vol2/usr/share/john/password.lst	2010-01-11 00:29:14 EST	2015-04-22 02:16:07 EDT
gnumeric-functions.mo	/img_C10Proj1.E01/vol_vol2/usr/share/locale/en_CA/LC_...	2012-06-23 04:56:18 EDT	2015-04-22 02:16:12 EDT
gnumeric-functions.mo	/img_C10Proj1.E01/vol_vol2/usr/share/locale/en_GB/LC_...	2012-06-23 04:56:19 EDT	2015-04-22 02:16:12 EDT

Figure 10-7   Viewing search results

Source: www.sleuthkit.org

5. In the left pane, expand **C10Proj1.E01** and **vol2 (Linux (0x83): 2048-9662629887)** to view the systemroot folders, shown in Figure 10-8, and compare them with the list of folders you wrote down in Lab 10.1.

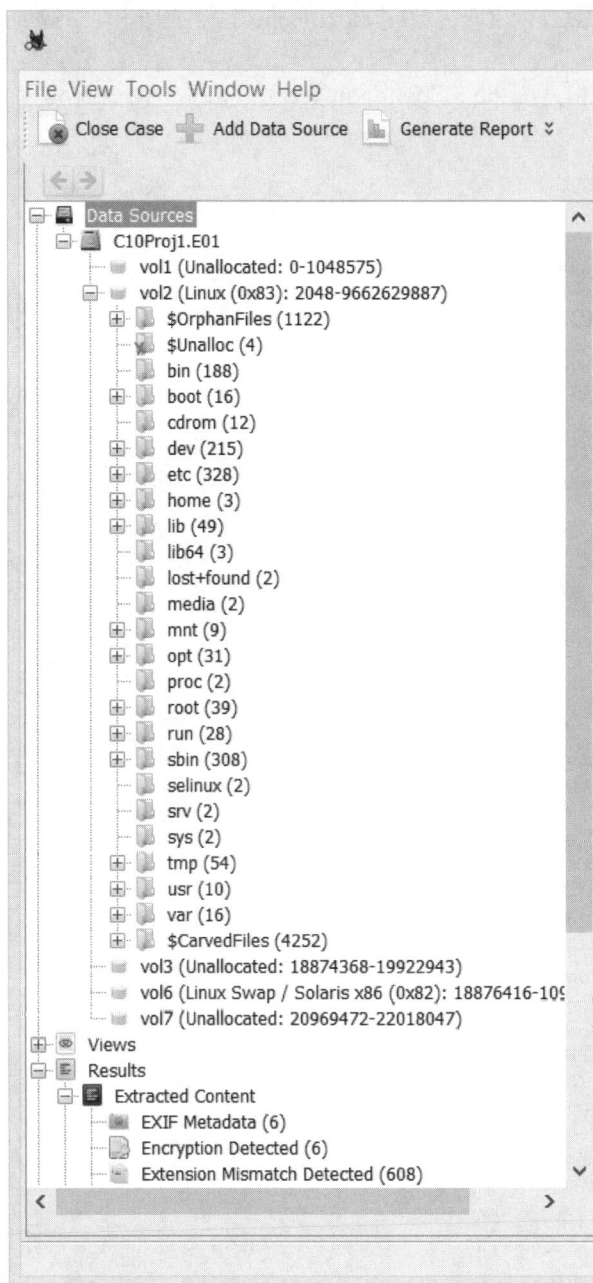

Figure 10-8   Viewing the systemroot folders

Source: www.sleuthkit.org

10

6. In the left pane, expand **Views, File Types,** and **Documents** and click the **Office** folder to see the files in it.

7. Leave Autopsy open as you answer the following review questions. When you're finished, exit Autopsy.

Review Questions

1. How many Excel files are in the Office folder?

2. How many Word documents (including those in unallocated space) are in the Office folder?

3. Autopsy can process virtual hard drives only in the .E01 format. True or False?

4. How many results did the search for the keyword "student" produce?

5. The C10Proj1.E01 virtual hard drive has only one partition. True or False?

E-MAIL AND SOCIAL MEDIA INVESTIGATIONS

Labs included in this chapter:

- Lab 11.1 Using OSForensics to Search for E-mail Messages and Mailboxes
- Lab 11.2 Using Autopsy to Search for E-mail Messages and Mailboxes
- Lab 11.3 Finding Google Searches and Multiple E-mail Accounts

Lab 11.1 Using OSForensics to Search for E-mail Messages and Mailboxes

Objectives

OSForensics can't process Outlook PST files, so investigators must search an entire image to find e-mail evidence. Ron Torvald is a possible suspect in a case involving cybercrime and theft of computer files. In this lab, you examine an image file to look for e-mail evidence of his criminal activity.

After completing this lab, you will be able to:

- Load an image containing e-mails in OSForensics
- Search e-mail messages in OSForensics

Materials Required

This lab requires the following:

- Windows 8 or 8.1 Professional
- OSForensics
- The MS E-mail Files.E01 file on the DVD

Estimated completion time: **30–60 minutes**

Activity

In this lab, you use OSForensics to search for e-mail evidence involving Ron Torvald:

1. Start OSForensics, and click **Yes** in the UAC message box. If necessary, click **Continue Using Free Version**. Click **Start** in the left pane, and click **Create Case** in the right pane.

2. In the New Case dialog box, type **C11Proj1** in the Case Name text box, enter your initials in the Investigator text box, and click the **Investigate Disk(s) from Another Machine** option button.

3. Click the **Custom Location** option button. Click **Browse**, navigate to and click the **C:\Work\Labs\Cases** folder, click the **Make New Folder** button, type **C11Proj1**, and click **OK** twice.

4. Copy the **MS E-mail Files.E01** file from the book's DVD to the C:\Work\Labs\Evidence folder. Click the **Add Device** button, click the **Image File** option button, click the **...** button, navigate to and click **C:\Work\Labs\Evidence**, click **MS E-mail Files.E01**, and click **Open**. Click **OK**.

5. In the left pane, click **Create Index**. In the Step 1 of 5 window, click the **Use Pre-defined File Types** option button, click to select all the file types, and click **Next**. In the Step 2 of 5 window, click the **Add** button. In the Add Start Location dialog box, verify that the **Whole Drive** option button is selected, and then click **OK**. Click **Next**, and in the Step 3 of 5 window, click **Start Indexing**. When OSForensics finishes indexing, click **OK** in the message box about the file limit (if necessary), and then click **OK** again.

6. Click the **Search Index** button in the left pane, type **Ron** in the Enter Search Words text box, and click **Search** in the right pane. The e-mail messages on Ron Torvald's computer are listed in the Emails tab with their file headers containing timestamp confirmation data (see Figure 11-1).

Figure 11-1   E-mail messages displayed with file headers

Source: PassMark Software, www.osforensics.com

7. Right-click the first e-mail message and click **Open** to view it in the OSForensics E-mail Viewer (see Figure 11-2).

11

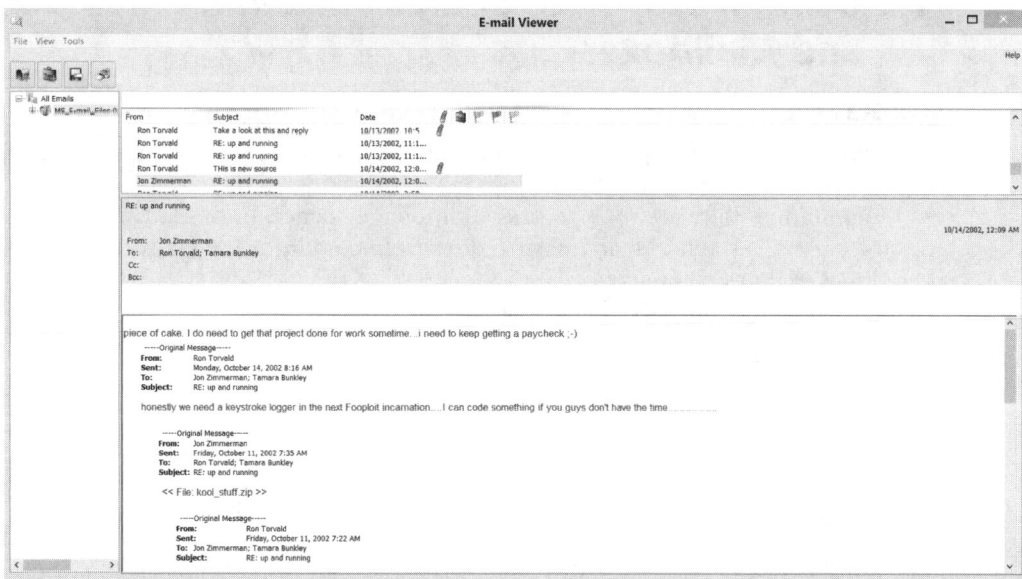

Figure 11-2   Opening an e-mail in the built-in viewer

Source: PassMark Software, www.osforensics.com

8. Use the scrollbar to view details, such as date, time, and subject. You can also select an e-mail in the upper-right pane to view any attached files. In the upper-right pane, find the e-mail from Jon Zimmerman dated 10/9/2002 at 5:28 a.m. Double-click the attached file **main_image.jpg** to open it with the internal viewer. In the left pane, expand **MS_E-mail_Files-0:\Outlook\MAILBOX.PST** and **Top of Personal Folders** to see the Deleted Items, Inbox, and Sent Items folders. Click the **Deleted Items** folder to see deleted e-mail messages.

 Files attached to e-mails have a paperclip symbol next to the timestamp.

9. Leave OSForensics open as you answer the following review questions. When you're finished, close all open windows, and exit OSForensics.

Review Questions

1. How many e-mails were deleted from Ron Torvald's Outlook mailbox?

2. How many e-mails with attached files did Ron receive?

3. Deleted e-mails with attachments can't be viewed. True or False?

4. How many e-mails did you recover by using "Ron" as a search keyword?

5. How many zipped files are attached to e-mails?

Lab 11.2 Using Autopsy to Search for E-mail Messages and Mailboxes

Objectives

Like OSForensics, Autopsy can't process Outlook PST files, so you must search an entire image to find e-mail evidence. In previous labs, you validated the results of forensic searches by using multiple software tools to find additional evidence. In this lab, you use Autopsy to search for e-mail evidence in an image and try to find additional e-mails that might not have been discovered in OSForensics.

After completing this lab, you will be able to:

• Load an image containing e-mails in Autopsy

• Use Autopsy to look for evidence in e-mails

Materials Required

This lab requires the following:

• Windows 8 or 8.1 Professional

• Autopsy for Windows

• The MS E-mail Files.E01 file on the DVD

Estimated completion time: **30–60 minutes**

Activity

In this lab, you search the MS E-mail Files.E01 file in Autopsy to find e-mail evidence:

1. Start Autopsy. In the Welcome window, click **Create New Case**.

2. Type **C11Proj2** in the Case Name text box. Click **Browse**, navigate to and click the **C:\Work\Labs\Cases** folder, click **OK** to enter this path in the Base Directory text box, and then click **Next**. Type **C11Proj2** in the Case Number text box and your initials in the Examiner text box, and then click **Finish**.

3. In the Add Data Source dialog box, click **Browse**, navigate to the **C:\Work\Labs\Evidence** folder, click the **MS E-mail Files.E01** file, and click **Open**. Click **Next** twice, and then click **Finish** to start analyzing the evidence.

4. Click the **Keyword Lists** button at the upper right, click the **Phone Numbers, IP Addresses, Email Addresses,** and **URLs** check boxes, and then click the **Search** button to begin searching for mailboxes and files that match the phone number, IP address, e-mail address, or URL patterns. Figure 11-3 shows the results.

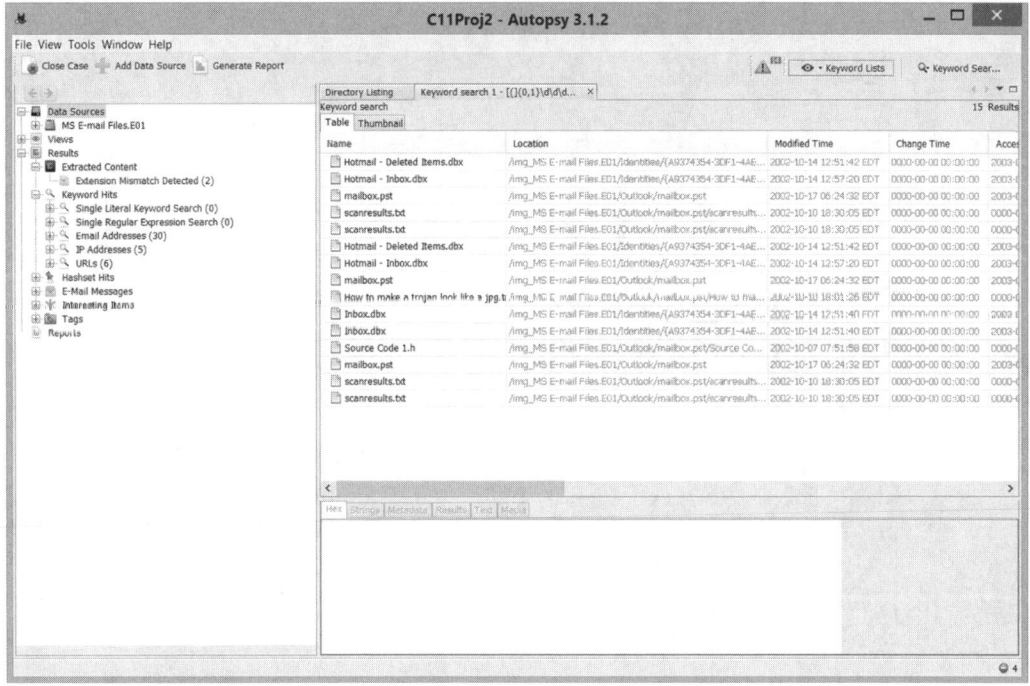

Figure 11-3 Viewing mailboxes found in an image

Source: www.sleuthkit.org

5. Click the **Keyword Search** button at the upper right, type **Ron Torvald**, and click **Search**.

6. Click the **Sent Items.dbx** folder to see the e-mails Ron Torvald sent; his name is highlighted in yellow in these e-mails. Use the scrollbar to view messages in the lower-right pane.

7. Click the **mailbox.pst** folder to see the e-mails Ron Torvald received; again, his name is highlighted in yellow. Use the scrollbar to view messages in the lower-right pane.

8. In the left pane, expand **E-Mail Messages** and **Default ([Default])**, and click the **Default** folder to see e-mails sorted in E-Mail To and E-Mail From columns, as shown in Figure 11-4.

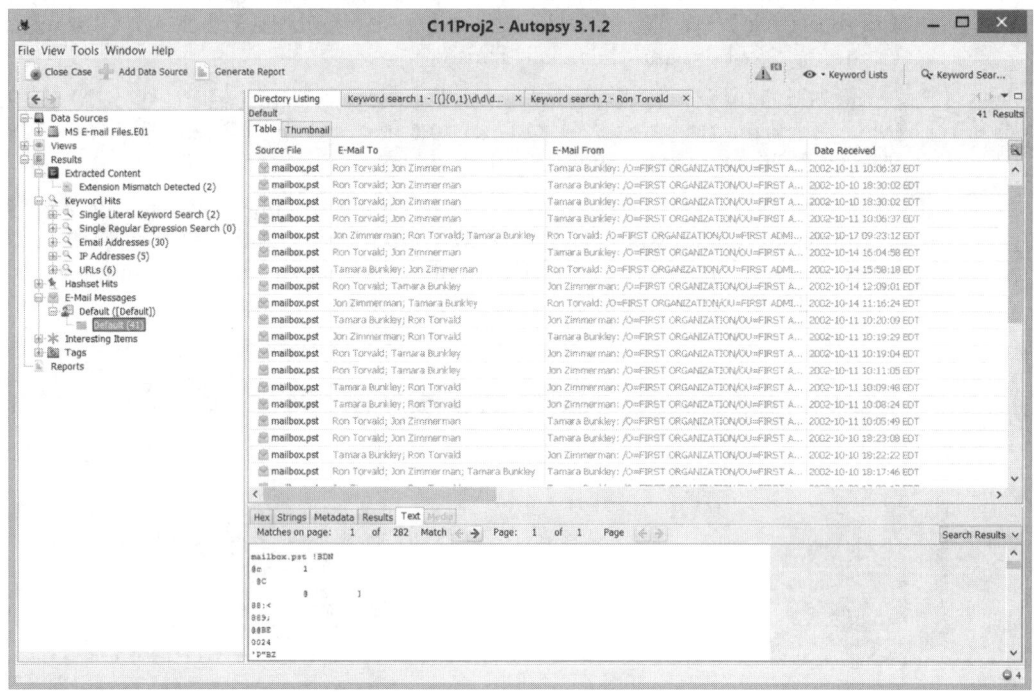

Figure 11-4   Viewing sorted e-mails

Source: www.sleuthkit.org

9. In the left pane, expand **Views**, **File Types**, and **Documents** to see e-mails with attached files. Click the **Images** folder, and click the **Thumbnail** tab in the right pane to see the pictures attached to e-mails. Click the **Table** tab, and scroll to the right to see the MD5 hash value for each graphics file.

10. Leave Autopsy open as you answer the following review questions. When you're finished, close all open windows, and exit Autopsy.

Review Questions

1. How many graphics files did you recover?

2. How many Hotmail e-mail addresses did you find?

3. No video files are attached to e-mails in the MS E-mail Files.E01 image. True or False?

4. What's the name of the Word document you recovered?

   a. new interfaces

   b. scanresults

   c. ACK CMD

   d. new100back

5. What IP address is associated with the Hotmail account?

Lab 11.3 Finding Google Searches and Multiple E-mail Accounts

Objectives

Frodo Baggins, a suspect in a digital crime, used his forensics skills to discover account passwords by using information he found in the Windows Registry. In this lab, you use Autopsy to find e-mail and Google search evidence showing that Frodo Baggins hacked a Windows computer's Registry to discover user account passwords.

After completing this lab, you will be able to:

- Find Google searches and associated text
- Find mailboxes associated with multiple e-mail accounts

Materials Required

This lab requires the following:

- Windows 8 or 8.1 Professional
- Autopsy for Windows
- The precious.001 file on the DVD

Estimated completion time: **60 minutes**

Activity

In this lab, you use Autopsy to find evidence of Google searches and multiple e-mail accounts on a Windows computer:

1. Copy the **precious.001** file from the book's DVD to the **C:\Work\Labs\Evidence** folder.

2. Start Autopsy. In the Welcome window, click **Create New Case**. Type **C11Proj3** in the Case Name text box. Click **Browse**, navigate to and click the **C:\Work\Labs\Cases** folder, click **OK** to enter this path in the Base Directory text box, and then click **Next**. Type **C11Proj3** in the Case Number text box and your initials in the Examiner text box, and then click **Finish**.

3. In the Add Data Source dialog box, click **Browse**, navigate to and click **C:\Work\Labs\ Evidence**, click the `precious.001` file, and click **Open**. Click **Next** twice, and then click **Finish** to start analyzing the evidence.

4. Click the **Keyword Lists** button at the upper right, click the **Phone Numbers, IP Addresses, Email Addresses,** and **URLs** check boxes, and then click **Search** to view all the mailboxes on this computer. Notice that the name Frodo Baggins is at the top of the Keyword search 1 list (see Figure 11-5).

Name	Location	Modified Time	Change Time	Ac
Frodo Baggins.wab	/img_precious.001/vol_vol2/Documents and Settings/Frod...	2004-12-29 18:33:54 EST	2005-01-04 16:53:14 EST	200
NTUSER.DAT	/img_precious.001/vol_vol2/Documents and Settings/Frod...	2006-01-03 18:11:06 EST	2004-12-31 16:14:03 EST	200
Addressbook.ldif	/img_precious.001/vol_vol2/Documents and Settings/Frod...	2005-01-02 14:58:36 EST	2005-01-04 16:53:12 EST	200
abook.mab	/img_precious.001/vol_vol2/Documents and Settings/Frod...	2005-01-02 15:10:40 EST	2005-01-04 16:53:14 EST	200
8BF5F7F0d01	/img_precious.001/vol_vol2/Documents and Settings/Frod...	2004-12-21 13:21:55 EST	2005-01-04 16:53:15 EST	200
Unalloc_4293_12027392_128318976	/img_precious.001/vol_vol2//$Unalloc/Unalloc_4293_1202...	0000-00-00 00:00:00	0000-00-00 00:00:00	000
Inbox.dbx	/img_precious.001/vol_vol2/Documents and Settings/Frod...	2004-12-30 11:51:45 EST	2004-12-30 11:51:45 EST	200
In.mbx	/img_precious.001/vol_vol2/Documents and Settings/Frod...	2004-12-30 05:51:45 EST	2004-12-30 07:07:26 EST	200
f0029229.dbx	/img_precious.001/vol_vol2/$CarvedFiles/f0029229.dbx	0000-00-00 00:00:00	0000-00-00 00:00:00	000
Digital Evidence Standards (Public).pp	/img_precious.001/vol_vol2/Documents and Settings/Sam...	2002-05-20 14:16:28 EDT	2005-04-11 11:56:16 EDT	200
Sent	/img_precious.001/vol_vol2/Documents and Settings/Frod...	2004-12-30 04:46:19 EST	2005-01-04 16:53:15 EST	200
9CC092FCd01	/img_precious.001/vol_vol2/Documents and Settings/Frod...	2004-12-21 13:28:56 EST	2005-01-04 16:53:15 EST	200
accesdatajessica.log	/img_precious.001/vol_vol2/Program Files/Trillian/users/d...	2004-12-17 18:52:05 EST	2005-01-04 17:08:27 EST	200
Saved Mail	/img_precious.001/vol_vol2/Documents and Settings/Frod...	2004-12-30 06:12:51 EST	2004-12-30 06:12:51 EST	200
PHONE TEST.txt	/img_precious.001/vol_vol2/WINDOWS/system/PHONE TE...	2003-10-01 23:30:10 EDT	2005-04-11 11:34:52 EDT	200
INSTALL.LOG	/img_precious.001/vol_vol2/Program Files/Yahoo!/Messen...	2004-12-10 12:35:46 EST	2005-01-04 17:14:22 EST	200
cookies.txt	/img_precious.001/vol_vol2/Documents and Settings/Frod...	2005-01-02 14:59:59 EST	2005-01-04 16:53:15 EST	200
Dd3.htm	/img_precious.001/vol_vol2/RECYCLER/S-1-5-21-1801674...	2004-12-29 18:36:50 EST	2005-01-01 14:05:31 EST	200
Personality Survey.htm	/img_precious.001/vol_vol2/Documents and Settings/Frod...	2004-12-29 18:36:50 EST	2005-01-04 16:53:13 EST	200

Directory Listing — Keyword search 1 - [(){0,1}\d\d\d... Keyword search — 362 Results — Table | Thumbnail

Hex | Strings | Metadata | Results | Text | Media

Figure 11-5   Viewing the search results

Source: www.sleuthkit.org

5. Click **Keyword Search** at the upper right, type **Frodo Baggins,** and click **Search**. Scroll through the results; you should find several mailboxes.

6. In the left pane, expand **E-Mail Messages** and **Default ([Default])**. Click the **Default** folder, and then click the first **Out.mbx.001** mailbox in the right pane to see the message in the lower-right pane, as shown in Figure 11-6.

Some results are duplicated because of the combined keyword searches 1 and 2.

NOTE

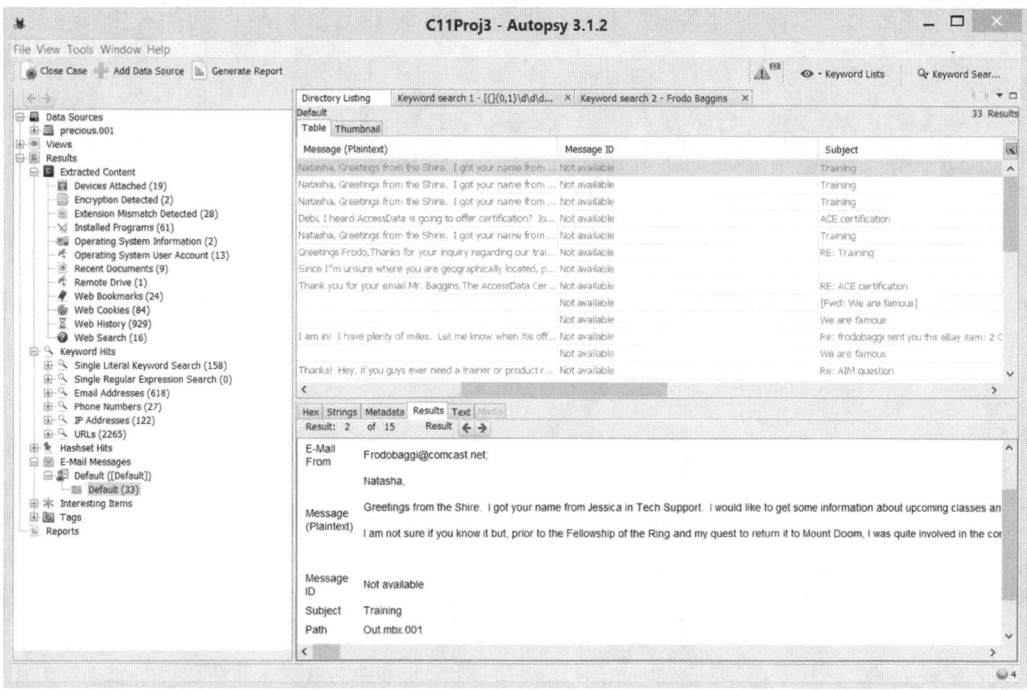

Figure 11-6   Viewing the text of an e-mail

Source: www.sleuthkit.org

7. Click the **Text** tab at the bottom to see the e-mail header information, including the Message ID, which uniquely identifies the message in the e-mail server database.

8. In the left pane, click **Web Search** under Extracted Content to see Google searches with the text Frodo typed and the Web pages returned in the search results.

9. Leave Autopsy open as you answer the following review questions. When you're finished, exit Autopsy.

Review Questions

1. How many e-mail messages, including duplicates, did you find?

2. How many different Frodo Baggins e-mail addresses did you recover?

3. Frodo Baggins didn't have an AOL e-mail account. True or False?

4. How many Google searches for the term "computer forensics" were made?

5. MD5 hash values are displayed automatically in the default mailbox view. True or False?

MOBILE DEVICE FORENSICS

Labs included in this chapter:

- Lab 12.1 Examining Cell Phone Storage Devices
- Lab 12.2 Using FTK Imager to View Text Messages, Phone Numbers, and Photos
- Lab 12.3 Using Autopsy to Search Cloud Backups of Mobile Devices

Lab 12.1 Examining Cell Phone Storage Devices

Objectives

Most cell phones support removable memory storage devices, such as MicroSD and MiniSD flash devices, that can store up to 128 GB of data. These devices can contain personal information, photos, and other data that can be useful in a forensics investigation. Creating an image of these devices separately from imaging cell phones is recommended. Recovering cell phone data can be challenging because no single standard exists for how and where phones store messages, and file systems vary from manufacturer to manufacturer. In this lab, you use Autopsy to process a forensic image of a Motorola cell phone and its MicroSD storage device.

After completing this lab, you will be able to:

- Process an image of a cell phone and its storage device in Autopsy
- Examine forensic data on cell phones and their storage devices

Materials Required

This lab requires the following:

- Windows 8 or 8.1 Professional
- Autopsy for Windows
- The `Motorola.E01` file on the DVD

Estimated completion time: **120–180 minutes,** depending on your computer's performance

Activity

In this lab, you examine a Motorola cell phone image to look for forensic evidence:

1. Copy the **`Motorola.E01`** file from the DVD to the **C:\Work\Labs\Evidence** folder on your computer.

2. Start Autopsy. In the Welcome window, click **Create New Case**.

3. Type **C12Proj1** in the Case Name text box. Click **Browse,** navigate to and click the **C:\Work\Labs\Cases** folder, click **OK** to enter this path in the Base Directory text box, and then click **Next**. Type **C12Proj1** in the Case Number text box and your initials in the Examiner text box, and then click **Finish**.

4. In the Add Data Source dialog box, click **Browse,** navigate to the **C:\Work\Labs\ Evidence** folder, click the **`Motorola.E01`** file, and click **Open**. Click **Next** twice, and then click **Finish** to start analyzing the evidence.

5. In the left pane, click **Motorola.E01** to view the phone's OS folders and the MicroSD storage device. In the right pane, click the **motorola** folder, and then click the **Metadata** tab at the bottom to see the MicroSD storage device (see Figure 12-1). A red × next to files means they were deleted. The Unallocated entry in the Flags(Dir) column means these files are in unallocated space on the storage device. Click the first two deleted files to see the recovered JPG files on this storage device.

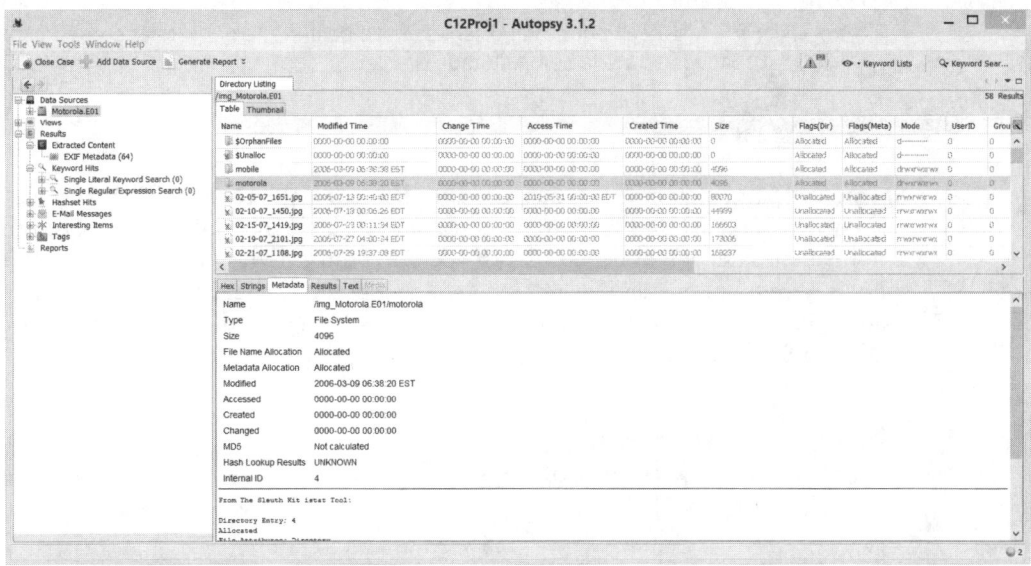

Figure 12-1 Viewing cell phone data in Autopsy

Source: www.sleuthkit.org

6. Scroll down the upper-right pane, and click the **$MBR** file. Its icon is grayed out, indicating it's a hidden system file. This file is the Master Boot Record and contains the file system information needed to mount the storage device. If necessary, click the **Text** tab at the bottom to see the file system for the storage device. The SANVOL name shown in Figure 12-2 means this device was manufactured by SanDisk, which can help forensics investigators identify the storage device.

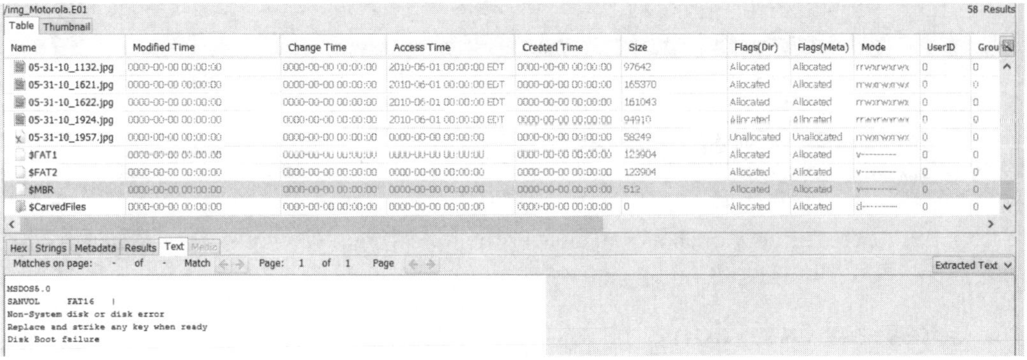

Figure 12-2 Viewing file system information

Source: www.sleuthkit.org

7. Click the **$CarvedFiles** folder to see data on graphics files that has been carved from unallocated space. Click the **Thumbnail** tab in the upper-right pane and scroll to see all the recovered and blank (unrecovered) images in the cell phone's memory storage.

Most cell phones and tablets have built-in memory storage in addition to what's available on storage devices.

8. In the left pane, expand **Extracted Content,** if necessary, and click **EXIF Metadata.** In the upper-right pane, click the first graphics file, and click the **Text** tab at the bottom to see Exif information, as shown in Figure 12-3. If you scroll through this information, you see that the photos were taken by the Motorola phone's built-in camera. Click the **Table** tab in the upper pane, if necessary. The camera information for these images is displayed in the Device Model and Data Source columns.

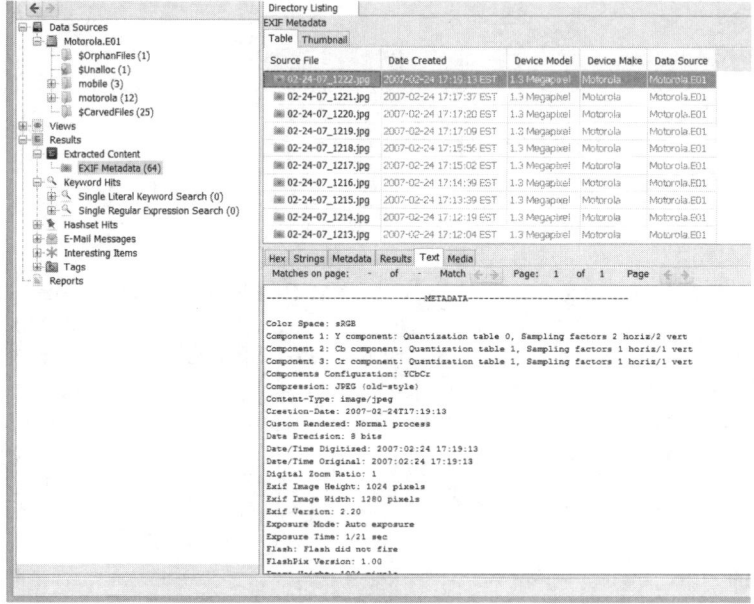

Figure 12-3   Viewing Exif information

Source: www.sleuthkit.org

9. Leave Autopsy open as you answer the following review questions. When you're finished, exit Autopsy.

Review Questions

1. How many photos in the cell phone's memory (not the MicroSD device's memory) could be viewed?

2. How many folders did you find on the MicroSD storage device?

   a. 12

   b. 10

   c. 64

   d. 25

3. Which file system is in use on the MicroSD storage device?

    a. NTFS

    b. FAT32

    c. FAT16

    d. HPF+

4. What's the resolution of the cell phone's camera?

    a. Can't be determined from the evidence

    b. 3.0 MP

    c. 4.0 MP

    d. 1.3 MP

5. Which column do you check to determine whether a file is in unallocated space?

Lab 12.2 Using FTK Imager to View Text Messages, Phone Numbers, and Photos

Objectives

Recovering forensic data from cell phones and other mobile devices can be challenging because of the wide variety of platforms used, such as Apple iOS, Google OS, Android, Windows Mobile, and other proprietary OSs. Some forensics tools capture data by using USB adapters or tablet devices that create an .E01 or a raw image that can be processed by most forensics tools. AccessData Mobile Phone Examiner (MPE) creates .ad1 images that can be processed by Forensic Toolkit or FTK Imager to recover evidence. FTK Imager is useful for screening devices before having to use expensive and often time-consuming forensics tools. In this lab, you process the MPE image of a LG 6000 cell phone to look for evidence.

After completing this lab, you will be able to:

- Process an MPE image in FTK Imager
- Use FTK Imager to look for cell phone evidence

Materials Required

This lab requires the following:

- Windows 8 or 8.1 Professional
- FTK Imager
- The LG_6000_4d76e052.ad1 file on the DVD

Estimated completion time: **30–45 minutes**

Activity

In this lab, you examine a cell phone image in FTK Imager:

1. Copy the **LG_6000_4d76e052.ad1** file from the DVD to the **C:\Work\Labs\Evidence** folder on your computer.

2. Start FTK Imager, clicking **Yes** in the UAC message box, if necessary.

3. Click **File**, **Add Evidence Item** from the menu. In the Select Source dialog box, click the **Image File** option button, and then click **Next**.

4. In the Select File dialog box, click **Browse**, navigate to the **C:\Work\Labs\Evidence** folder, click the **LG_6000_4d76e052.ad1** file, click **Open**, and then click **Finish**.

5. In the Evidence Tree pane, expand **LG_6000_4d76e052.ad1**, **External-File-System [AD1]**, and **LG VX6000**. Click the **LG VX6000** subfolder and then the **Phonebook** folder.

6. Click the **Last dialed numbers** folder. The most recent numbers stored in the phone's memory are shown in the File List pane on the right (see Figure 12-4). Use the scrollbar, if needed, to view all the numbers.

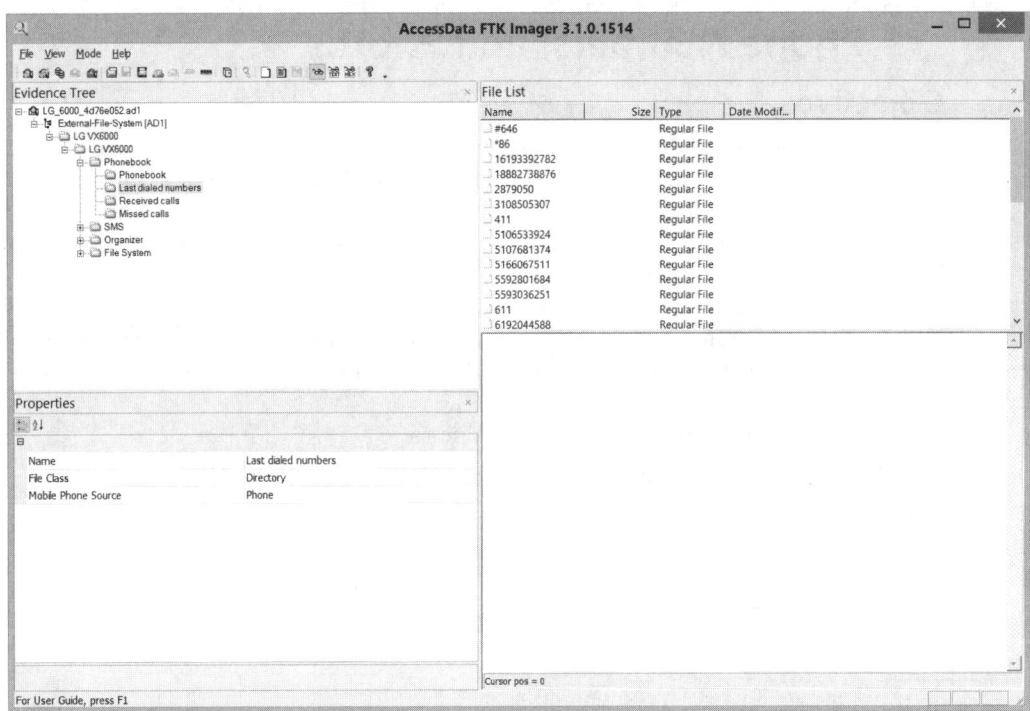

Figure 12-4   Viewing the most recent phone numbers dialed

7. Click the **Received calls** folder to see inbound calls. This image file doesn't show time and date of these calls, but you can get this information from the service provider or through MPE. Next, click the **Missed calls** folder to see inbound calls that weren't answered.

8. In the Evidence Tree pane, expand **File System**, and then click the **sms** folder to view text messages sent to the phone. In the File List pane, click the **mediacan000.dat** file, and read its contents in the lower-right pane (see Figure 12-5).

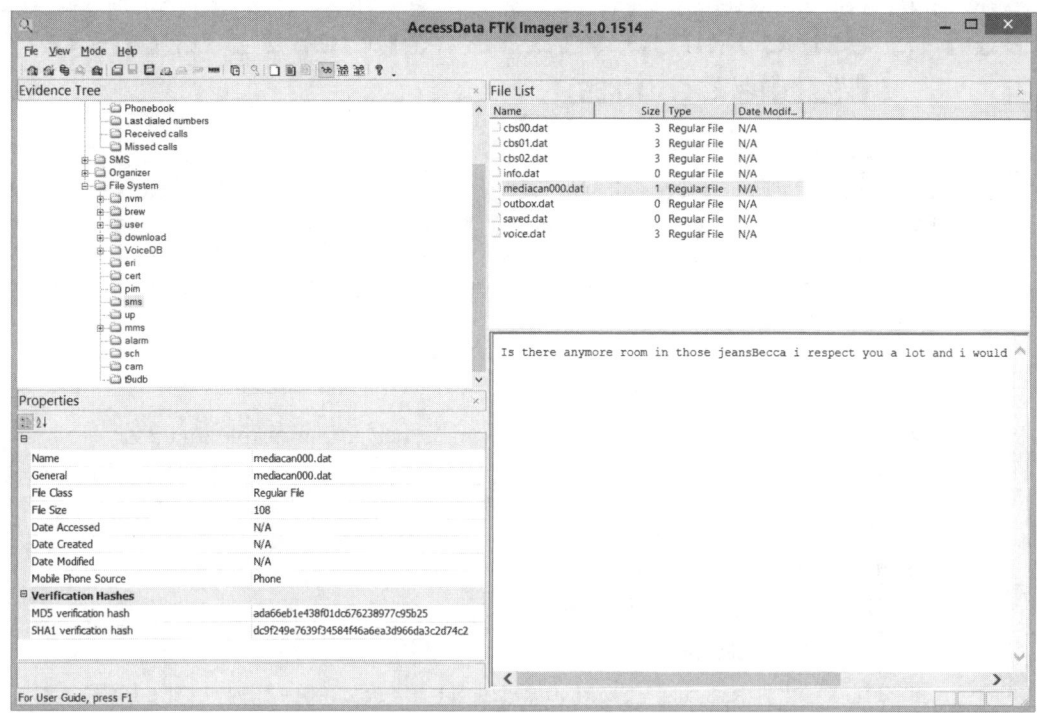

Figure 12-5 Viewing the contents of a text message

©2015 AccessData Group, Inc. All Rights Reserved.

9. Click the **eyeglass** toolbar icon, if necessary, and then click the **cam** folder in the Evidence Tree pane to look for photos taken by the phone's camera. Click each .jpg file in the File List pane to see it in the viewer.

10. Leave FTK Imager open as you answer the following review questions. When you're finished, exit FTK Imager.

Review Questions

1. How many phone numbers with a valid number of digits were dialed on this phone?

   a. 24

   b. 28

   c. This information can't be determined based on the data recovered.

   d. No numbers were dialed.

2. How many inbound calls couldn't be identified?

3. FTK Imager can be used to determine outgoing call dates and times on cell phones. True or False?

4. How many photos were taken by this phone's camera?

5. How many dialed calls were local numbers, not long distance?

Lab 12.3 Using Autopsy to Search Cloud Backups of Mobile Devices

Objectives

In Chapter 12 of the textbook, you processed a case involving the seizure of cloud backup images of Randall's and Sarah's mobile devices. You need to look for additional bank information or funding indicating that a money-laundering scheme was used to avoid taxes. In this lab, you examine the `InCh12Randall.001` and `InCh12Sarah.001` images to look for this information.

After completing this lab, you will be able to:

- Search cloud backups in Autopsy

- Use Autopsy to search for evidence linked between multiple images

Materials Required

This lab requires the following:

- Windows 8 or 8.1 Professional

- Autopsy for Windows

- The `InCh12Randall.exe` and `InCh12Sarah.exe` files on the DVD

Estimated completion time: **60 minutes**

Activity

In this lab, you use Autopsy to search mobile device images for evidence involving money transfers between bank accounts:

1. Copy the **InCh12Randall.exe** and **InCh12Sarah.exe** files from the DVD to your **C:\Work\Labs\Evidence** folder and extract them. (This process might take a few minutes.) Start Autopsy for Windows. In the Welcome window, click **Create New Case**. Type **C12Proj3** in the Case Name text box, verify that **C:\Work\Labs\Cases** is displayed in the Base Directory text box, and then click **Next**.

2. In the New Case Information dialog box, type **C12Proj3** in the Case Number text box and your initials in the Examiner text box, and then click **Finish**.

3. In the Add Data Source dialog box, click **Browse**, navigate to the **C:\Work\Labs\ Evidence** folder, click the **InCh12Randall.001** file, click **Open**, and then click **Next**.

4. Click **Next** to accept the default ingest modules, and then click **Finish** to start analyzing the evidence, which will take a few minutes. Watch the progress bar in the lower-right corner to determine when the process is finished.

5. Click the **Add Data Source** button. In the Add Data Source dialog box, click **Browse**, navigate to the **C:\Work\Labs\Evidence** folder, click the **InCh12Sarah.001** file, click **Open**, and then click **Next**.

6. Click **Next** to accept the default ingest modules, and then click **Finish** to start analyzing the evidence, which will take a few minutes. When it's finished, you should see the two image files in the Directory Listing pane on the right, as shown in Figure 12-6.

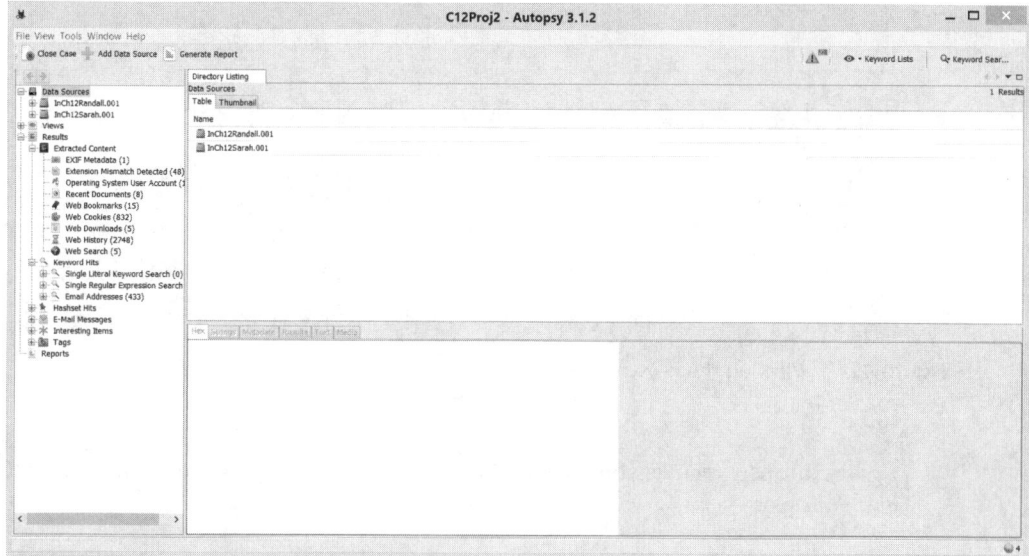

Figure 12-6   Image files loaded in Autopsy

Source: www.sleuthkit.org

12

7. Click the **Keyword Lists** button at the upper right. Click the **Phone Numbers, IP Addresses, Email Addresses**, and **URLs** check boxes, and then click the **Search** button. Wait until the search is finished before going on to the next step.

8. Click the **Keyword Search** button, type **Wells Fargo**, and click **Search**. Click **Keyword Search** again, type **Offshore Accounts**, and click **Search**. Click the **Keyword search 3 - Offshore Accounts** tab, if necessary, and click the first e-mail listed. The pane at the bottom shows the keyword highlighted in yellow (see Figure 12-7)

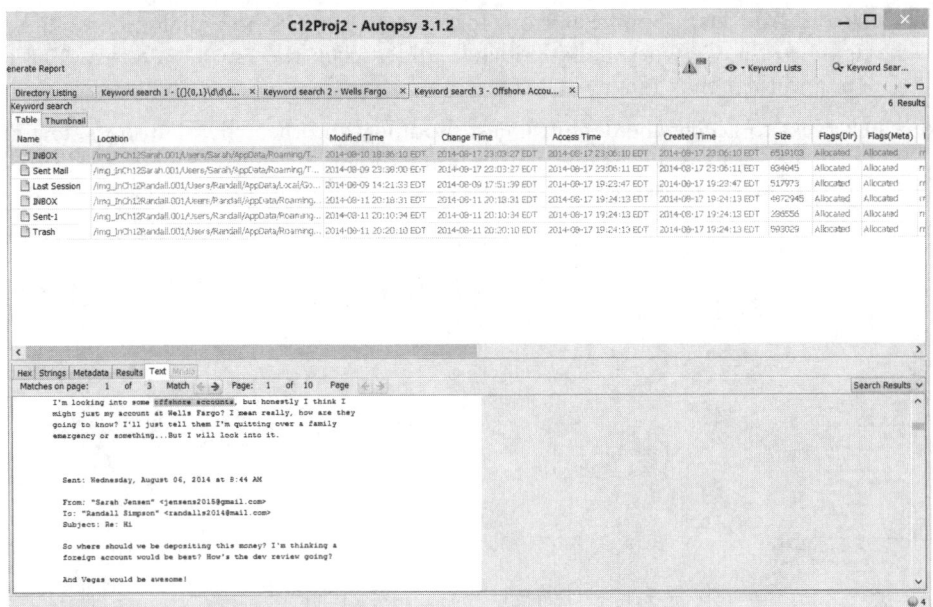

Figure 12-7 Viewing the keyword search results

Source: www.sleuthkit.org

9. Leave Autopsy open as you answer the following review questions. When you're finished, exit Autopsy.

Review Questions

1. How much money did Randall Simpson tell Sarah to ask her boss to fund?

2. What phone number was recovered in the evidence?

3. How many e-mails were recovered in the Default folder?

   a. 866

   b. 341

   c. 225

   d. 6782

4. No photos were recovered on either mobile device. True or False?

5. Evidence shows that both Randall and Sarah were involved in transferring money. True or False?

CHAPTER THIRTEEN

CLOUD FORENSICS

Labs included in this chapter:

- Lab 13.1 Examining Dropbox Cloud Storage
- Lab 13.2 Examining Google Drive Cloud Storage
- Lab 13.3 Examining OneDrive Cloud Storage

Lab 13.1 Examining Dropbox Cloud Storage

Objectives

Dropbox cloud storage uses several files on a client computer to store information. An important one is the `filecache.dbx` file, which stores information on shared directories associated with a Dropbox user account and file transfers between Dropbox and the client's system. Dropbox files on a system indicate a source of forensic evidence.

After completing this lab, you will be able to:

- Look for Dropbox account information
- Search for files transferred with Dropbox

Materials Required

This lab requires the following:

- Windows 8 or 8.1 Professional
- Autopsy for Windows
- The Dropbox account folder on the DVD

Estimated completion time: **20–40 minutes,** depending on your computer's performance

Activity

In this lab, you examine a Dropbox account to look for evidence:

1. Copy the **Dropbox** folder from your DVD to the **C:\Work\Labs\Evidence** folder, and start Autopsy. In the Welcome window, click **Create New Case.**

2. Type **C13Proj1** in the Case Name text box, and then click **Next.** Type **C13Proj1** in the Case Number text box and your initials in the Examiner text box, and then click **Finish.**

3. In the Add Data Source dialog box, click **Logical Files** in the "Select source type to add" list box, and then click **Add.** Navigate to and click **C:\Work\Labs\Evidence**, click the **Dropbox** folder, click **Select**, click **Next** twice, and then click **Finish.**

4. Click the **Keyword Search** button, type **users** in the text box, and click **Search** to look for the username associated with this Dropbox account. Figure 13-1 shows the results.

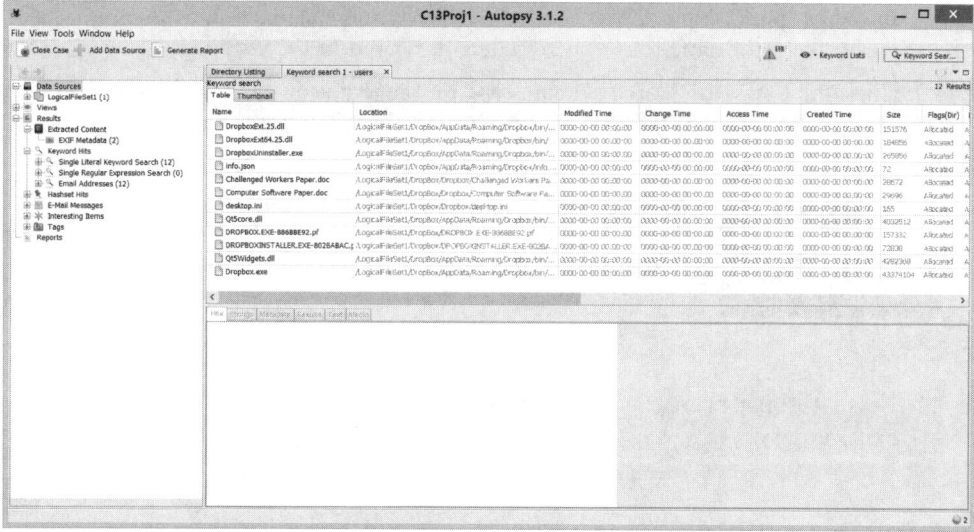

Figure 13-1   Viewing Dropbox search results

Source: www.sleuthkit.org

5. Click the **DROPBOXINSTALLER.EXE-802BABAC.pf** file, which is the Dropbox prefetch file. You can then see the username LAURIE in the lower pane.

6. Click the **Keyword Search** button, type **LAURIE** in the text box, and click **Search** to look for other information associated with this user account.

7. In the left pane, expand **LogicalFileSet1** and **DropBox**, and click the **Dropbox** folder under AppData to see the files that were synced with cloud storage.

8. Click the **Thumbnail** tab in the right pane to see the images transferred with Dropbox (see Figure 13-2). If necessary, scroll to see all the files.

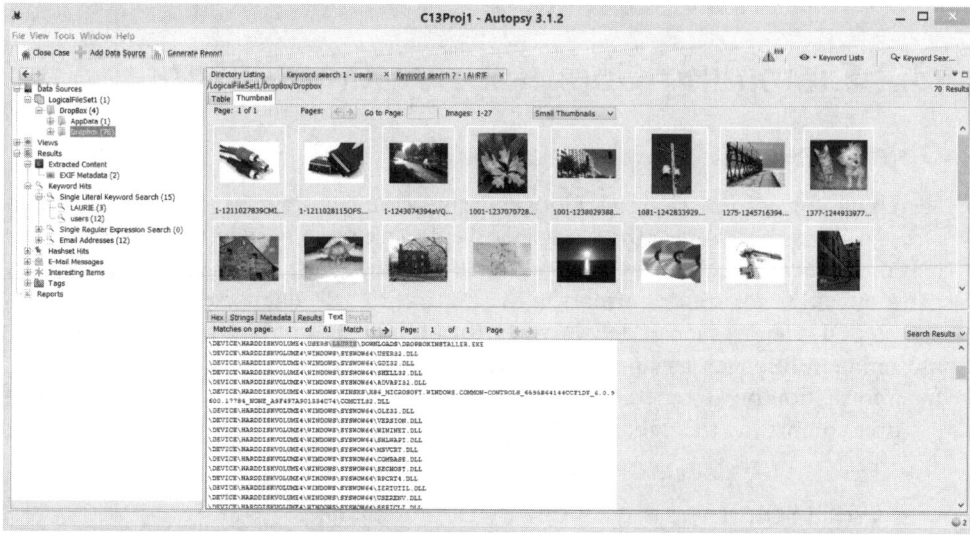

Figure 13-2   Images transferred with Dropbox

Source: www.sleuthkit.org

9. In the left pane, expand **Views** and **File Types,** and then click **Documents.** Click the **Table** tab in the right pane to see the documents stored in the cloud.

10. Click the **Keyword Search** button, type **filecache.dbx** in the text box, and click **Search** to look for this file containing information on shared directories and file transfers.

 The `filecache.dbx` file is in base-64 format, so you need specialized software to read it. One tool for this purpose is Dropbox Reader. For more information on this free tool, go to *www.net-security.org/secworld. php?id=11194.*

11. Leave Autopsy open as you answer the following review questions. When you're finished, exit Autopsy.

Review Questions

1. How many Office files were recovered from this Dropbox account?

2. How many prefetch files are in this Dropbox account?

    a. 1

    b. 4

    c. 2

    d. 3

3. Autopsy can read the contents of the `filecache.dbx` file. True or False?

4. What usernames are associated with this Dropbox account?

5. Name a tool that can be used to read files in base-64 format.

Lab 13.2 Examining Google Drive Cloud Storage

Objectives

Searching for information on Google Drive cloud storage is much easier than finding Dropbox information because Google Drive doesn't use a base-64 file format. It stores information on local cloud entries (such as filenames, MD5 hash values, and modified and created dates in UNIX timestamp format) in the `snapshot.db` database file. To view this file, you use an SQL viewer, such as DB Browser for SQLite. To convert UNIX timestamps, you can use online tools, such as EpochConverter (*www.epochconverter.com*). In this lab, you look for information on Google Drive transactions.

After completing this lab, you will be able to:

* Describe the Google Drive cloud storage structure
* Use an SQL viewer and convert UNIX timestamps

Materials Required

This lab requires the following:

- Windows 8 or 8.1 Professional
- Autopsy for Windows
- DB Browser for SQLite
- The Google Drive account folder on the DVD

Estimated completion time: **30–45 minutes**

Activity

In this lab, you examine a Google Drive account on a computer to look for evidence:

1. Copy the **Google Drive** folder from the DVD to the **C:\Work\Labs\Evidence** folder, and start Autopsy. In the Welcome window, click **Create New Case**.

2. Type **C13Proj2** in the Case Name text box, and then click **Next**. Type **C13Proj2** in the Case Number text box and your initials in the Examiner text box, and then click **Finish**.

3. In the Add Data Source dialog box, click **Logical Files** in the "Select source type to add" list box, and then click **Add**. Navigate to and click **C:\Work\Labs\Evidence**, click the **Google Drive** folder, click **Select**, click **Next** twice, and then click **Finish**.

4. Click the **Keyword Search** button, type **users** in the text box, and click **Search** to look for the username associated with this Google Drive account. Figure 13-3 shows the results. Notice the two Google Drive prefetch files in the right pane.

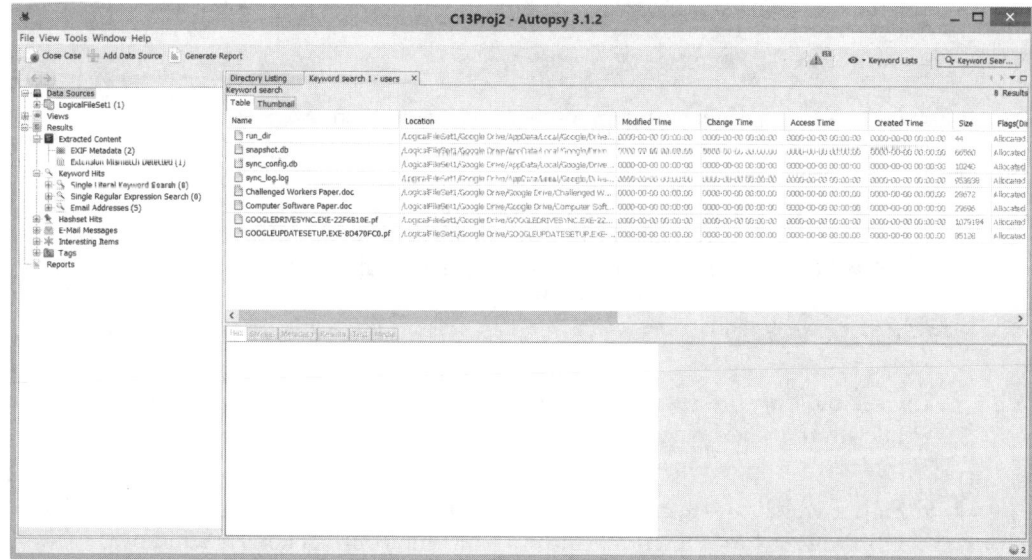

Figure 13-3   Viewing Google Drive search results

Source: www.sleuthkit.org

5. Click the **GOOGLEDRIVESYNC.EXE-22F6B10E.pf** file, a Google Drive prefetch file, to see the username for this account in the lower pane.

6. Click the **sync_log.log** file to see a detailed list of a user's cloud transactions. This log file isn't in a base-64 format, so you can view it with a text editor or the Autopsy built-in viewer.

7. Click the **Keyword Search** button, type **RawEvent** in the text box, and click **Search** to look for the create, modify, and deleted dates for this account's cloud transactions. Figure 13-4 shows the results.

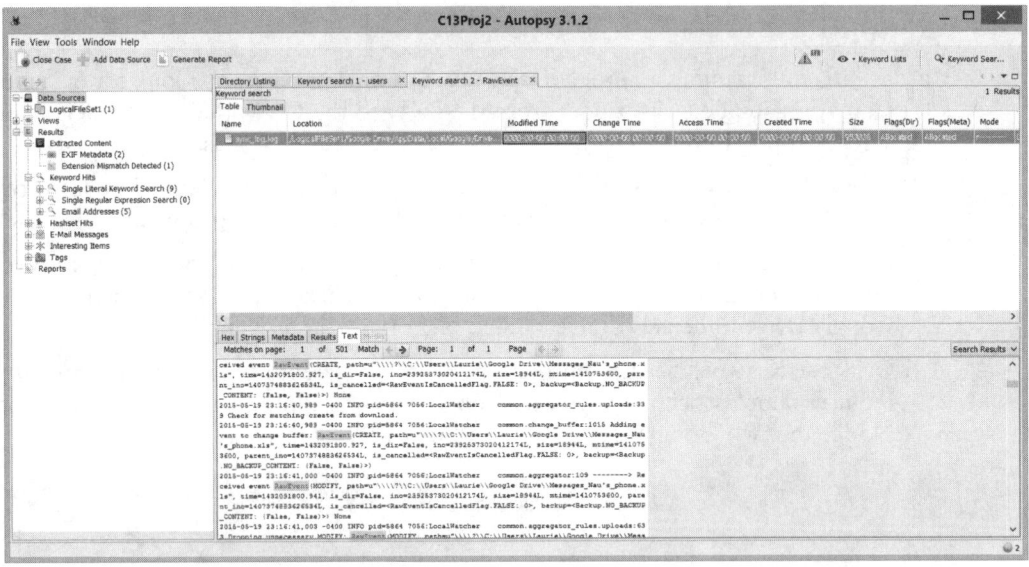

Figure 13-4   Viewing search results for the keyword RawEvent

Source: www.sleuthkit.org

The string values that indicate UNIX timestamps are RawEvent(CREATE, RawEvent(MODIFY, and RawEvent(DELETE.

TIP

8. Click the **Keyword search 1 - users** tab. Right-click the **snapshot.db** file, point to **Extract File(s)**, and click **Save** to extract this file to the C:\Work\Labs\Cases\C13Proj2\Export folder.

9. Start a Web browser, and go to **http://sqlitebrowser.org**. Download and install the correct DB Browser for SQLite (32-bit or 64-bit) for your version of Windows.

10. Start DB Browser for SQLite, and click **File, Open Database** from the menu. Navigate to **C:\Work\Labs\Cases\C13Proj2\Export**, click the **snapshot.db** file, and click **Open**.

11. Click the **Browse Data** tab to view Google Drive filenames with their modified and created UNIX timestamps, which show the last date and time data was synced with the cloud. To

convert the UNIX timestamps, start a Web browser, and go to **www.epochconverter.com**. Copy each timestamp from DB Browser for SQLite, and paste it in the text box at the top of the Epoch Converter page. Click the **Timestamp to Human date** button.

12. Leave all windows open as you answer the following review questions. When you're finished, exit Autopsy and DB Browser for SQLite, and close any open windows.

Review Questions

1. Which Google Drive file contains the list of deleted files?

   a. `snapshot.db`

   b. `sync_log.log`

   c. RawEvent

   d. Prefetch

2. In what folder are Google Drive user files kept?

3. There are no PDF files in this Google Drive account. True or False?

4. How many images were recovered from this account?

5. When was the `ademco.jpg` file modified?

Lab 13.3 Examining OneDrive Cloud Storage

Objectives

The OneDrive cloud service is included in Windows installations. The OneDrive user account used in this lab was recovered from the same computer as the one in Labs 13.1 and 13.2. However, because criminals might not use the same cloud service for all transactions, examining files to look for evidence of other cloud services can be useful. OneDrive stores information about file transactions in the `SyncDiagnostics.log` file. The SyncEngine files (with an `.etl` extension) manage synchronization between OneDrive and a user's computer. In addition, the `ONEDRIVESETUP.EXE-nnnnnnn.pf` prefetch file can be useful for finding client-linked folders storing documents and paths that tie the computer to a OneDrive cloud account. In this lab, you process a OneDrive account folder to look for evidence on usernames and file transactions.

You might find OneDrive folders and files listed as SkyDrive in older Windows versions. Searching for both names is best to make sure no information is overlooked.

TIP

After completing this lab, you will be able to:

- List the OneDrive files of interest to forensics investigators
- Search OneDrive for information on user accounts and file transactions

Materials Required

This lab requires the following:

- Windows 8 or 8.1 Professional
- Autopsy for Windows
- The OneDrive account folder on the DVD

Estimated completion time: **30–60 minutes**

Activity

In this lab, you examine a OneDrive account to look for evidence:

1. Copy the **OneDrive** folder from your DVD to the **C:\Work\Labs\Evidence** folder and start Autopsy. In the Welcome window, click **Create New Case**.

2. Type **C13Proj3** in the Case Name text box, and then click **Next**. Type **C13Proj3** in the Case Number text box and your initials in the Examiner text box, and then click **Finish**.

3. In the Add Data Source dialog box, click **Logical Files** in the "Select source type to add" list box, and then click **Add**. Navigate to and click **C:\Work\Labs\Evidence**, click the **OneDrive** folder, click **Select**, click **Next** twice, and then click **Finish**.

4. Click the **Keyword Search** button, type **users** in the text box, and then click **Search** to look for the username information associated with this OneDrive account (see Figure 13-5). Click the **42-f7a03bfb1c86c703.ini** file in the right pane to view the username for this OneDrive account. Click the **ONEDRIVESETUP.EXE-1224F619.pf** prefetch file to see the folders, system files, and paths linked with this OneDrive account.

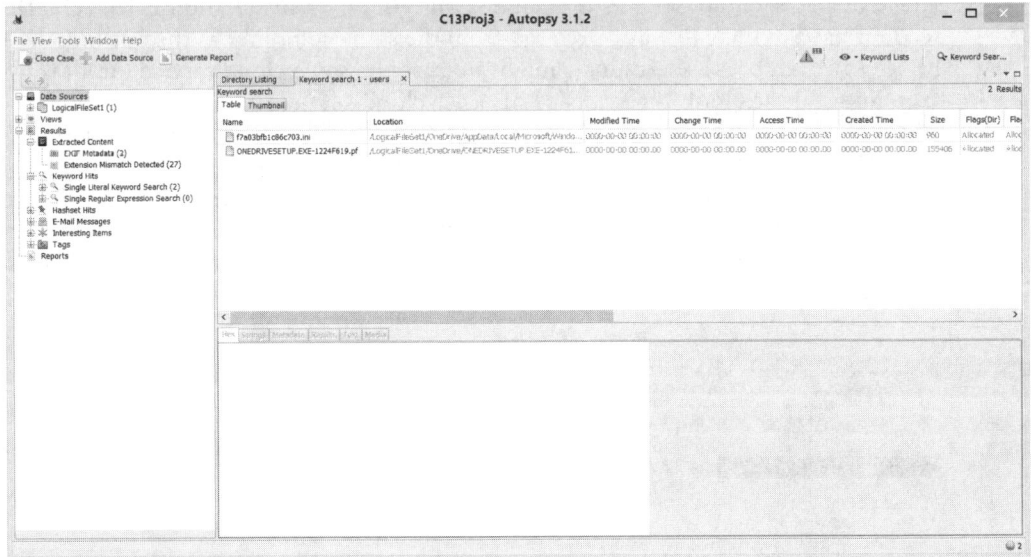

Figure 13-5   Viewing OneDrive search results

Source: www.sleuthkit.org

5. Click the **Keyword Search** button, type **SyncDiagnostics.log** in the text box, and then click **Search**. Click the **Table** tab, if necessary. Click the `SyncDiagnostics.log` file, and then click the **Strings** tab in the lower pane to see metadata about folder transactions associated with this OneDrive account (see Figure 13-6).

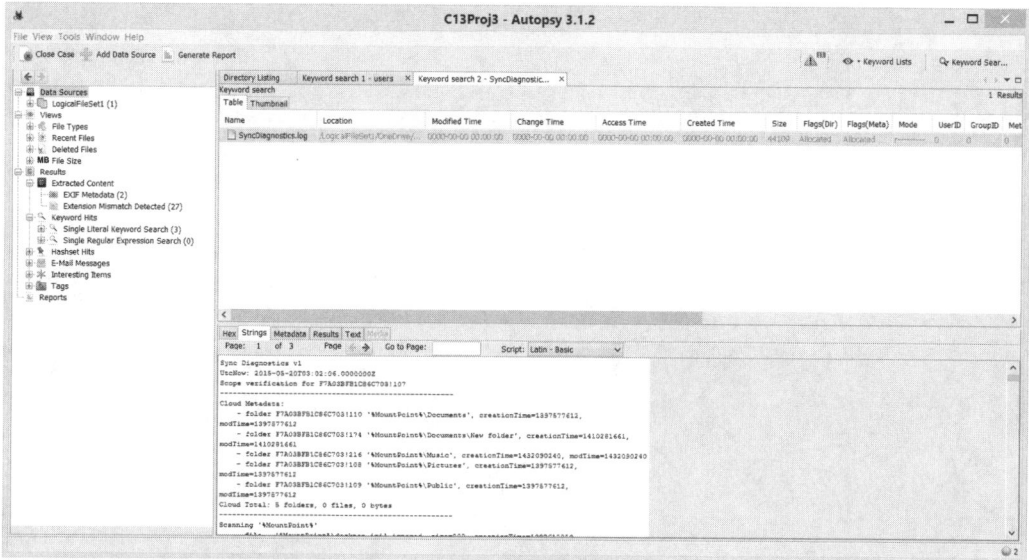

Figure 13-6 Information in the `SyncDiagnostics.log` file

Source: www.sleuthkit.org

6. Leave Autopsy open as you answer the following review questions. When you're finished, exit Autopsy.

Review Questions

1. How many Office documents were recovered from this OneDrive account?

2. How many JPEG files were recovered from this OneDrive account?

3. How many SyncEngine files are in this OneDrive account? (*Hint*: Use the Keyword Search tab.)

4. This OneDrive account has only one username associated with it. True or False?

5. Information about OneDrive file transactions is stored in the `SyncDiagnostics.log` file. True or False?

13

REPORT WRITING FOR HIGH-TECH INVESTIGATIONS

Labs included in this chapter:

- Lab 14.1 Investigating Corporate Espionage
- Lab 14.2 Adding Evidence to a Case
- Lab 14.3 Preparing a Report

Lab 14.1 Investigating Corporate Espionage

Objectives

Billions of dollars are lost each year to foreign competitors through economic espionage, usually involving employees attempting to make fast cash by selling trade secrets (*www.fbi. gov/about-us/investigate/counterintelligence/economic-espionage*). A patent search company called m57.biz specializes in researching patents before they're granted by the U.S. Patent Office. Charlie Brown, an employee of this company, is suspected of selling patent information to outside competitors, and private investigators have been asked to conduct a search of his desktop computer. The responding investigator created a forensic image of Charlie's computer and has given you this image for analysis.

After completing this lab, you will be able to:

- Search for evidence in preparation for a criminal case
- Use Autopsy search tools to find e-mail evidence

Materials Required

This lab requires the following:

- Windows 8 or 8.1 Professional
- Autopsy for Windows
- The `charlie-2009-12-11.E01` and `charlie-work-usb-2009-12-11.E01` files downloaded to your C:\Work\Labs\Evidence folder

This file might take several hours to process, depending on your computer's performance, so you might want to set it up to process overnight.

Estimated completion time: **180–240 minutes,** depending on your computer's performance

Activity

In this lab, you search the forensic image of Charlie Brown's computer for evidence of corporate espionage:

1. Start a Web browser, and go to **http://digitalcorpora.org/corp/nps/scenarios/2009-m57-patents/drives-redacted**. Download the `charlie-2009-12-11.E01` and the `charlie-work-usb-2009-12-11.E01` files to your C:\Work\Labs\Evidence folder.

2. Start Autopsy. In the Welcome window, click **Create New Case**. Type **C14Proj1** in the Case Name text box, and then click **Next**. Type **C14Proj1** in the Case Number text box and your initials in the Examiner text box, and then click **Finish**.

3. In the Add Data Source dialog box, click **Image File** in the "Select source type to add" list box. Click **Browse**, navigate to and click **C:\Work\Labs\Evidence**, click the `charlie-2009-12-11.E01` file, click **Open**, and then click **Next**. Click **Next** to accept the default ingest modules, and then click **Finish**. Autopsy begins processing the image, which might take several hours.

4. When the processing is finished, click the **Keyword Lists** button at the upper right. Click the **Phone Numbers, IP Addresses, Email Addresses,** and **URLs** check boxes, and then click **Search.** (The search might take a few minutes.) The information that's returned could be useful in finding persons of interest who have been in contact with the suspect or Web sites that were visited to conduct research related to a crime.

5. Click the **Keyword Search** button, click the **Exact Match** option button (if necessary), type **price,** and click **Search** to look for any text matching "price." Click the first result, and type **Sent** to look for any e-mails sent by Charlie that containing this keyword. You see the sentence "You know my price." Scroll up to see the entire e-mail, including the recipient, jaime@project2400.com (see Figure 14-1). This e-mail suggests that Charlie has information he wants to sell. Notice that the recipient is instructed to delete the e-mail.

 Jamie is using an alias e-mail address—jaime@project2400.com—in addition to the address jamie@project2400.com. Criminals often use aliases to confuse forensics investigators or law enforcement agents.

NOTE

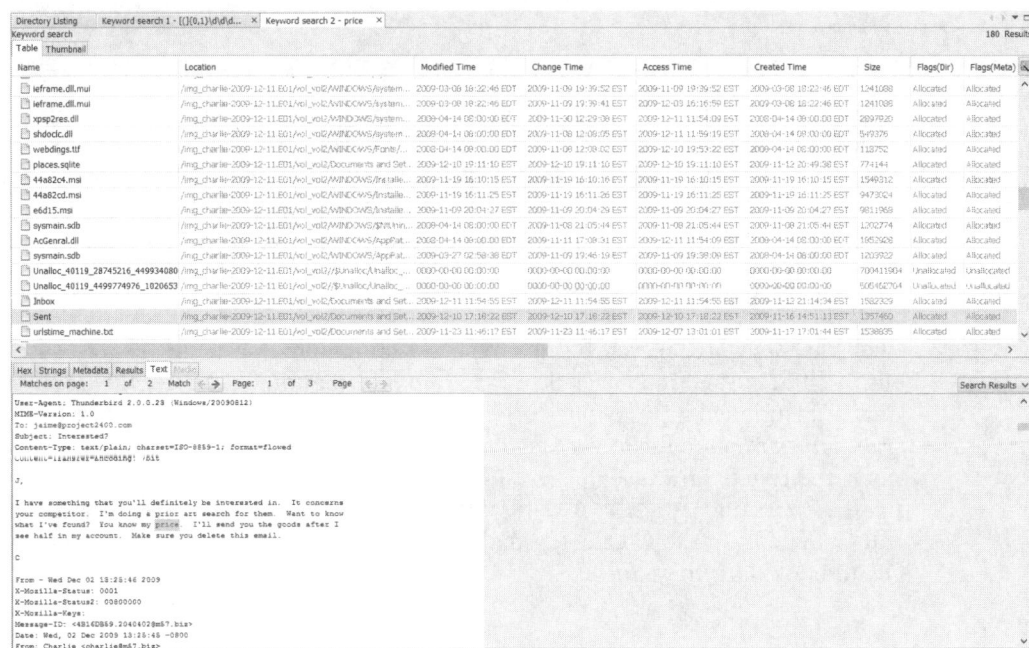

Figure 14-1   The keyword "price" in an e-mail sent by Charlie

Source: www.sleuthkit.org

6. Click the **Keyword Search** button, type **jamie@project2400.com,** and click **Search** to look for any other e-mails sent to Jamie. Scroll to make sure you see all the e-mails in the results.

7. Now that you have established that Charlie and Jamie are communicating with each other, expand **E-Mail Messages** and **Default ([Default])** in the left pane, and then click the **Default** folder to view all e-mail messages. Click the **E-Mail To** column header to sort e-mails by username and find the messages sent to jamie@project2400.com. Click the last e-mail message, which shows that Charlie received a deposit and provided a password for a steganography program containing the information he sold to Jamie (see Figure 14-2).

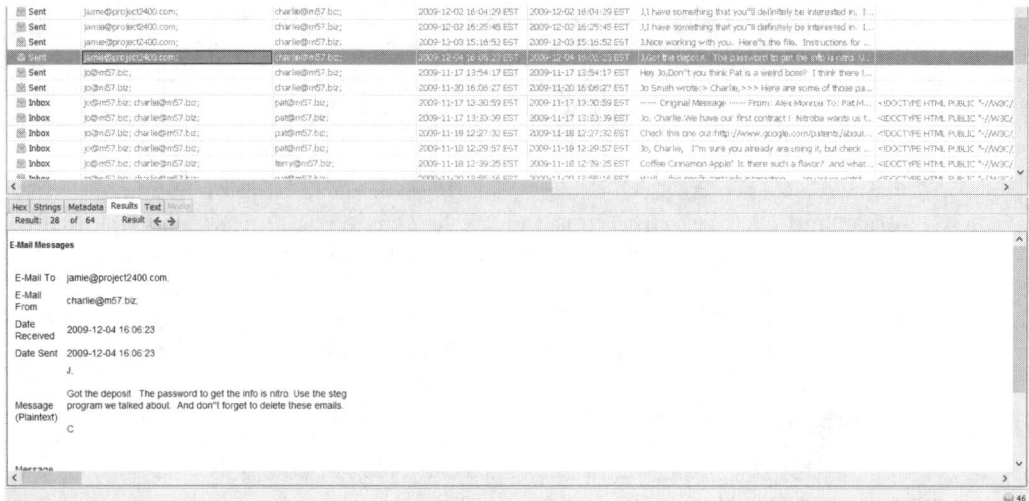

Figure 14-2 Confirmation of a money transfer to Charlie

Source: www.sleuthkit.org

8. Press **Shift,** and click the first e-mail sent to Jamie to select all the e-mails as a group. Right-click them, point to **Tag Files,** and click **Tag and Comment.** In the Create Tag dialog box, type **Information Sold to Project 2400,** and click **OK** to create bookmarks for these e-mails. In the right pane, click the **E-Mail From** column header, and Shift+click e-mails from Jamie to Charlie. Right-click this group, point to **Tag Files,** and click **Tag and Comment.** In the Create Tag dialog box, type **E-mails from Jamie to Charlie,** and click **OK** to bookmark them.

9. Click the **Keyword Search** button, type **steganography,** click the **Exact Match** option button (if necessary), and click **Search** to find information on the steganography program Charlie mentioned in his e-mail to Jamie. Click the `readme.txt` file, and view the program information in the lower pane (see Figure 14-3). Click the `_CACHE_003` file, which stores the results of a Google search for "steganography freeware tools." Shift+click the `readme.txt` and `_CACHE_003` files. Right-click them, point to **Tag Files,** and click **Tag and Comment.** In the Create Tag dialog box, type **Steg Program Information,** and click **OK** to bookmark these files.

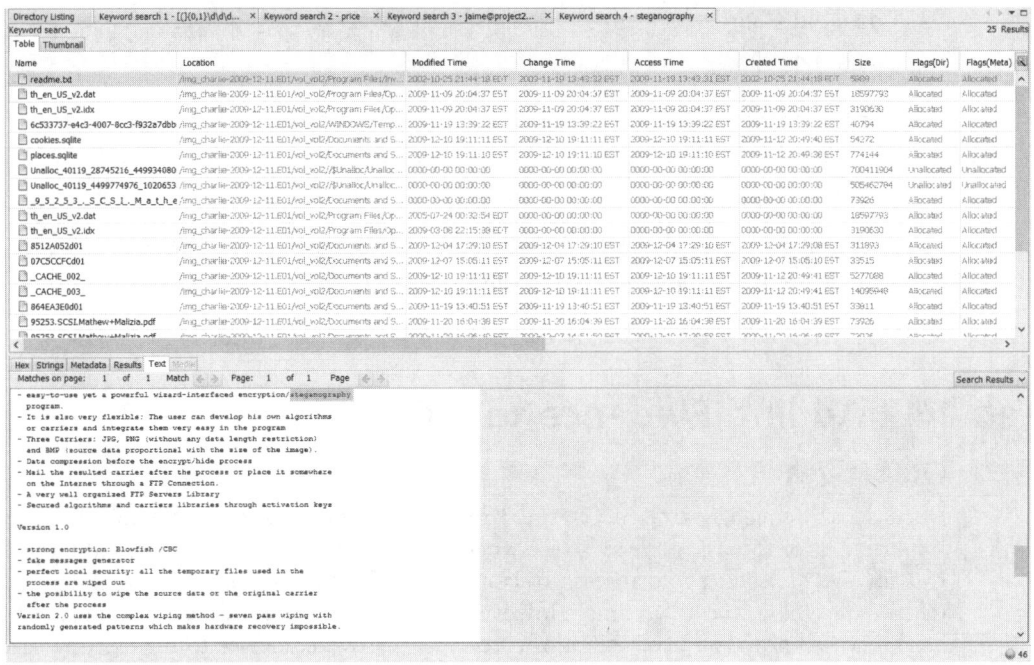

Figure 14-3 Viewing information on a steganography program

Source: www.sleuthkit.org

10. In the left pane, click **Web Search** to look for other Google searches for steganography programs. There are three results. Shift+click these results, and then right-click them, point to **Tag Files**, and click **Tag and Comment**. In the Create Tag dialog box, type **Google Searches for Steg Programs**, and click **OK** to bookmark these results. Scroll through the Web Search results, and notice that Charlie also searched for an open-source hex editor. Shift+click these results, and then right-click them, point to **Tag Files**, and click **Tag and Comment**. In the Create Tag dialog box, type **Hex Editor Searches**, and click **OK** to bookmark them.

11. In the left pane, click **Devices Attached** to look for any attached storage devices. You see that Charlie attached an Alcor Micro Corp flash drive, a SanDisk Cruzer Micro U3 device, and a Lacie Ltd Mobile hard drive to his computer. Shift+click all three devices, and then right-click them, point to **Tag Files**, and click **Tag and Comment**. In the Create Tag dialog box, type **External Storage Devices**, and click **OK** to bookmark them.

12. Leave Autopsy open as you answer the following review questions. When you're finished, leave Autopsy open for the next lab.

Review Questions

1. When did Charlie send a password to Jamie?

    a. 2009-11-19

    b. 2009-12-02

    c. 2009-12-03

    d. 2009-12-04

2. When did Charlie perform a Google search for steganography programs?

   a. 2009-11-19

   b. 2009-12-02

   c. 2009-12-03

   d. 2009-12-04

3. In Autopsy, you can bookmark files but not external devices. True or False?

4. How many e-mails did Charlie send to Jamie?

5. How much did Jamie agree to pay Charlie?

Lab 14.2 Adding Evidence to a Case

Objectives

During a subsequent search of Charlie Brown's desk, an investigator found a USB device and submitted it for forensic analysis to see whether it contains any evidence indicating that Charlie was involved in selling information to competitors. Normally, you process all digital evidence that's recovered at the same time. However, you had already processed the image of Charlie's hard drive, so now you need to add this recently discovered device to the existing case.

After completing this lab, you will be able to:

- Add new evidence to an existing case
- Search for evidence common to more than one device

Materials Required

This lab requires the following:

- Windows 8 or 8.1 Professional
- Autopsy for Windows
- The `charlie-work-usb-2009-12-11.E01` file downloaded in Lab 14.1

Estimated completion time: **60–90 minutes**

Activity

In this lab, you add an image of a USB device to the evidence recovered earlier from Charlie's desk:

1. If necessary, start Autopsy, and click **Open Recent Case**. Click the **C14Proj1** case name, and then click **OK** to load the case. Click the **Add Data Source** button, click **Browse**, click the `charlie-work-usb-2009-12-11.E01` file, click **Open**, and then click **Next**. Click **Next** to accept the default ingest modules, and then click **Finish** to add the image of the USB device. This process takes a few minutes.

2. When the image has finished processing, expand **charlie-work-usb-2009-12-11.E01** and **vol2 (NTFS/exFAT (0x07): 1-1059061248)** in the left pane, and then click the **Email** folder. This folder contains the backup of Charlie's e-mails from November 16, 2009, to

December 4, 2009, and all the e-mails were copied to the USB drive from December 3 to December 4, 2009. Scroll down and click the **Charlie_2009-12-01_1302_Sent. txt** file. The message shown in the lower pane was sent from Charlie to Alix and says that he'll be able to afford a nice vacation soon (see Figure 14-4).

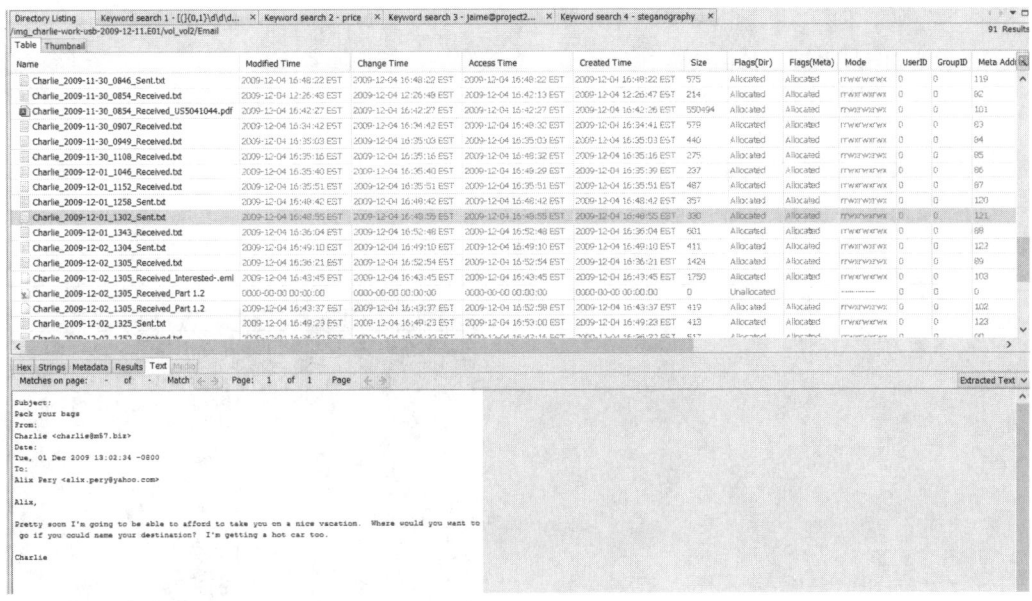

Figure 14-4   Viewing the e-mail to Alix

Source: www.sleuthkit.org

3. Click the **Charlie_2009-12-02_1304_Sent.txt** file to see the first e-mail to Jamie that offered information for money. Obviously, Charlie wants this e-mail deleted after Jamie reads it. Right-click the file, point to **Tag Files**, and click **Tag and Comment**. In the Create Tag dialog box, type **USB Backup of Charlie's E-mail**, and click **OK** to add it to the bookmarked files.

4. Scroll down and click the **Charlie_2009-12-03_0951_Received.txt** file, which is the e-mail from Jamie offering Charlie "50 large" if the file is good. Right-click the file, point to **Tag Files**, and click **Tag and Comment**. In the Create Tag dialog box, type **USB Backup of Charlie's E-mail**, and click **OK** to add it to the bookmarked files. Click the **Charlie_2009-12-03_1216_Sent.txt** file to see the message Charlie sent to Jamie with the file he sold attached. Right-click the file, point to **Tag Files**, and click **Tag and Comment**. In the Create Tag dialog box, type **USB Backup of Charlie's E-mail**, and click **OK** to add it to the bookmarked files. Click the next file, which contains the astronaut1.jpg file attached to the previous e-mail, as denoted by the same time-stamp (see Figure 14-5). Shift+click both e-mails and the attached JPG file, and then right-click them, point to **Tag Files**, and click **Tag and Comment**. In the Create Tag dialog box, type **File Transferred to Jamie**, and click **OK**.

14

Figure 14-5   Viewing the file transferred to Jamie

Source: www.sleuthkit.org

5. Click the remaining e-mails to find any other incriminating messages. Click the **Charlie_2009-12-04_0941_Sent.txt** file to see an e-mail to Andy that's black-mailing him for $100,000 on a pending patent. Figure 14-6 shows the results. It seems to be another unrelated act of economic espionage involving Charlie. The next file contains the zipped file Charlie sent Andy.

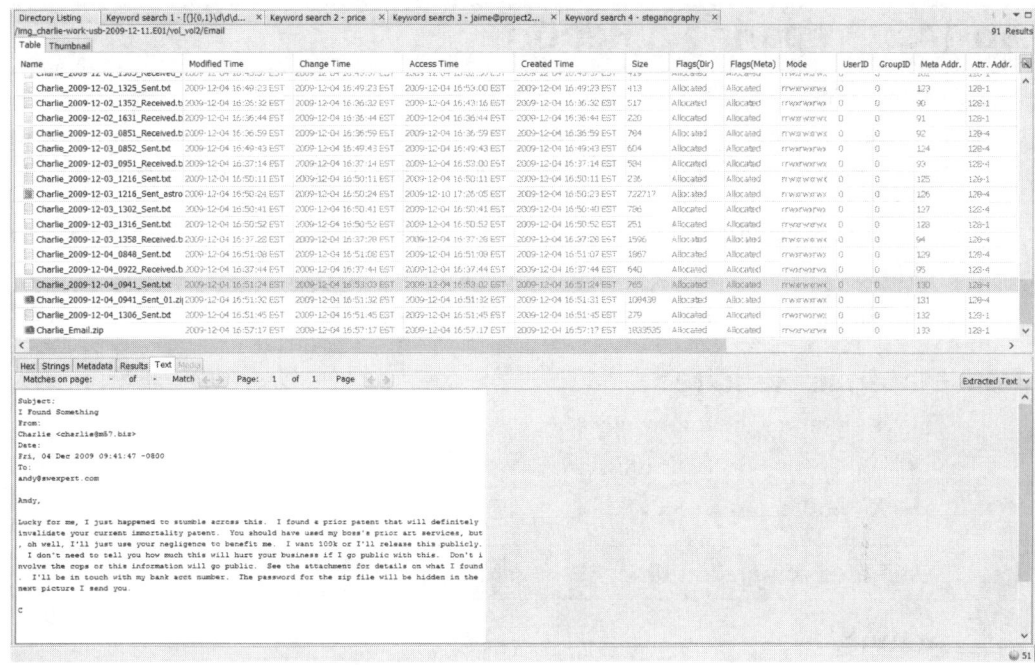

Figure 14-6   Viewing the blackmail message

Source: www.sleuthkit.org

6. Click the `Charlie_2009-12-04_1306_Sent.txt` file to see Charlie's response to Jamie; it acknowledges that he received the money and gives Jamie the password to unlock the file. Again, Charlie asks Jamie to delete the e-mail. Shift+click the `Charlie_2009-12-04_0941_Sent.txt`, `Charlie_2009-12-04_1306_Sent.txt`, and `Charlie_2009-12-04_0941_Sent_01.zip` files. Right-click these files, point to **Tag Files**, and click **Tag and Comment**. In the Create Tag dialog box, type **New Blackmail Evidence**, and click **OK**.

7. Leave Autopsy open as you answer the following review questions. When you're finished, leave Autopsy open for the next lab.

Review Questions

1. When did Charlie first approach Jamie to offer competitor information?

   a. 2009-11-19

   b. 2009-12-02

   c. 2009-12-03

   d. 2009-12-04

2. Only one graphics file was recovered from the USB device. True or False?

3. What's the domain name in Andy's e-mail address?

4. What's the name of the file Charlie sent Jamie?

5. Charlie sent Andy a password via e-mail. True or False?

14

Lab 14.3 Preparing a Report

Objectives

Now that you have processed Charlie's hard drive and USB device, you need to generate a report for the owner of m57.biz. This report helps you prepare for meeting with the owner and supports your investigation's findings.

After completing this lab, you will be able to:

- Generate a report on the results of a forensic analysis
- Find information in an HTML-formatted report

Materials Required

This lab requires the following:

- Windows 8 or 8.1 Professional
- Autopsy for Windows

Estimated completion time: **15–30 minutes**

Activity

In this lab, you generate a report with the bookmarked files you added in Labs 14.1 and 14.2 and review the results:

1. If necessary, start Autopsy, and click **Open Recent Case**. Click the **C14Proj1** case name, and then click **Open** to load the case. Click **Generate Report** at the upper left.

2. In the Select and Configure Report Modules dialog box, click the **Results-HTML** option button, and then click **Next**.

3. In the Configure Artifact Reports dialog box, click **All Results**, and then click **Finish**. A green checkmark is displayed in the progress bar when the report is finished.

4. Click the **Results-HTML** link to view the report. Figure 14-7 shows the results.

Figure 14-7   An Autopsy report

Source: www.sleuthkit.org

5. In the left pane under Report Navigation, click **Tagged Files** to see bookmarked files with their comments, timestamps, file sizes, and MD5 hash values.

6. In the left pane, click **E-Mail Messages** to see e-mail information, including to and from addresses, subjects, timestamps, and location on the storage device.

7. Leave the Autopsy report open as you answer the following review questions. When you're finished, exit Autopsy, and close all open windows.

Review Questions

1. The EXIF Metadata item in the Autopsy report shows the MD5 hash values for each graphics file that was recovered. True or False?

2. What OS was installed on Charlie's computer?

3. How many USB devices were attached to Charlie's computer?

4. Encrypted files were found on Charlie's USB device. True or False?

5. What hex editor did Charlie install on his computer?

14

CHAPTER FIFTEEN

EXPERT TESTIMONY IN DIGITAL INVESTIGATIONS

Labs included in this chapter:

- Lab 15.1 Conducting a Preliminary Investigation
- Lab 15.2 Investigating an Arsonist

Lab 15.1 Conducting a Preliminary Investigation

Objectives

Arsonists often return to the scenes of fires they started and take photos to remember the event or gloat about their handiwork. Several years ago, the fire marshal determined that multiple fires around the cities of Roslyn and Winthrop were the work of an arsonist. This arsonist challenged the police to capture him before his next fire in notes left at the crime scenes and signed "Trogdor the Burninator." The police believe the suspect is using a computer at a local company and have permission from the company's owner to examine the computer on site to determine whether there's any evidence on the hard drive. In this lab, you conduct a preliminary investigation of the hard drive image before getting a warrant to seize the computer.

After completing this lab, you will be able to:

- Use FTK Imager to conduct a preliminary investigation
- Export file hashes to validate recovered evidence

Materials Required

This lab requires the following:

- Windows 8 or 8.1 Professional
- Microsoft Excel 2013
- FTK Imager
- The `Firestarter.zip` file on the DVD

Estimated completion time: **30–60 minutes**

Activity

In this lab, you conduct a preliminary investigation of the `Firestarter.dd` image to look for potential evidence:

1. Copy the **`Firestarter.zip`** file from the DVD to your **C:\Work\Labs\Evidence** folder. Double-click the zipped file to extract it to the same folder.

2. Start FTK Imager, clicking **Yes** in the UAC message box, if necessary. Click **File, Add Evidence Item** from the menu.

3. In the Select Source dialog box, click the **Image File** option button, and then click **Next**.

4. In the Select File dialog box, click **Browse**, navigate to the **C:\Work\Labs\Evidence\ Firestarter** folder, click the **`Firestarter.dd`** file, click **Open**, and then click **Finish** to add the image to FTK Imager.

5. In the Evidence Tree pane, expand **Firestarter.dd, FIRESTARTER [FAT32]**, and **[root]** to view the Firestarter image (see Figure 15-1).

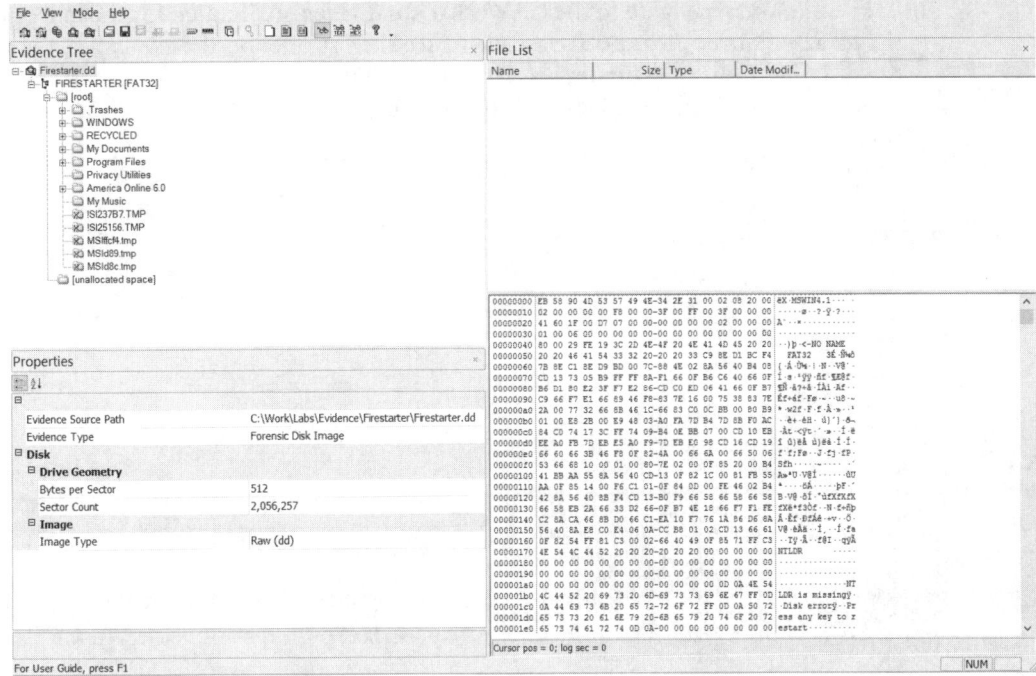

Figure 15-1   Viewing the Firestarter image

6. Open File Explorer, and create a **Chapter 15** subfolder in the C:\Work\Labs\Evidence folder. Right-click `Firestarter.dd` in the Evidence Tree pane of FTK Imager and click **Export Directory Listing**. Navigate to the **C:\Work\Labs\Evidence\Chapter 15** folder, type **Preliminary Search** in the File name text box, click **Save**, and click **Close** in the Creating Directory Listing [100%] dialog box to export the list of files.

7. Right-click **FIRESTARTER[FAT32]** in the Evidence Tree pane and click **Export File Hash List**. In the Save As dialog box, type **Firestarter File Hashes** in the File name text box, and click **Save**.

15

8. In File Explorer, navigate to the **C:\Work\Labs\Evidence\Chapter 15** folder. Double-click the **`Preliminary Search.csv`** file to see the list of exported filenames, the paths on the disk, and other file attributes. Drag the column borders to the right to increase the width and see all the details (see Figure 15-2).

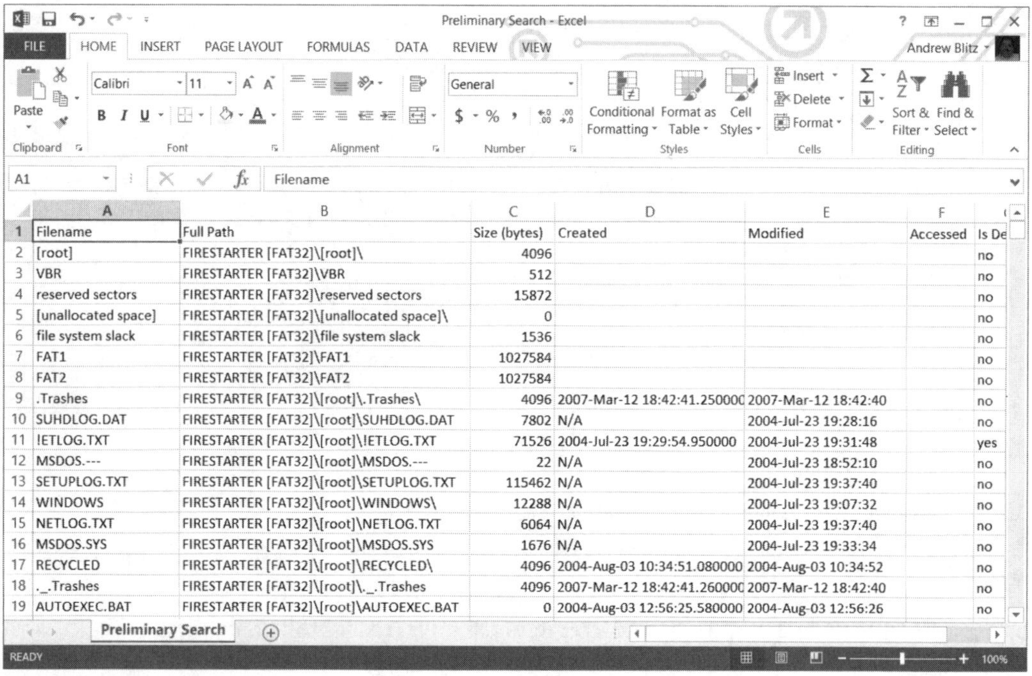

Filename	Full Path	Size (bytes)	Created	Modified	Accessed	Is De
[root]	FIRESTARTER [FAT32]\[root]\	4096				no
VBR	FIRESTARTER [FAT32]\VBR	512				no
reserved sectors	FIRESTARTER [FAT32]\reserved sectors	15872				no
[unallocated space]	FIRESTARTER [FAT32]\[unallocated space]\	0				no
file system slack	FIRESTARTER [FAT32]\file system slack	1536				no
FAT1	FIRESTARTER [FAT32]\FAT1	1027584				no
FAT2	FIRESTARTER [FAT32]\FAT2	1027584				no
.Trashes	FIRESTARTER [FAT32]\[root]\.Trashes\	4096	2007-Mar-12 18:42:41.250000	2007-Mar-12 18:42:40		no
SUHDLOG.DAT	FIRESTARTER [FAT32]\[root]\SUHDLOG.DAT	7802	N/A	2004-Jul-23 19:28:16		no
!ETLOG.TXT	FIRESTARTER [FAT32]\[root]\!ETLOG.TXT	71526	2004-Jul-23 19:29:54.950000	2004-Jul-23 19:31:48		yes
MSDOS.---	FIRESTARTER [FAT32]\[root]\MSDOS.---	22	N/A	2004-Jul-23 18:52:10		no
SETUPLOG.TXT	FIRESTARTER [FAT32]\[root]\SETUPLOG.TXT	115462	N/A	2004-Jul-23 19:37:40		no
WINDOWS	FIRESTARTER [FAT32]\[root]\WINDOWS\	12288	N/A	2004-Jul-23 19:07:32		no
NETLOG.TXT	FIRESTARTER [FAT32]\[root]\NETLOG.TXT	6064	N/A	2004-Jul-23 19:37:40		no
MSDOS.SYS	FIRESTARTER [FAT32]\[root]\MSDOS.SYS	1676	N/A	2004-Jul-23 19:33:34		no
RECYCLED	FIRESTARTER [FAT32]\[root]\RECYCLED\	4096	2004-Aug-03 10:34:51.080000	2004-Aug-03 10:34:52		no
._.Trashes	FIRESTARTER [FAT32]\[root]\._.Trashes	4096	2007-Mar-12 18:42:41.260000	2007-Mar-12 18:42:40		no
AUTOEXEC.BAT	FIRESTARTER [FAT32]\[root]\AUTOEXEC.BAT	0	2004-Aug-03 12:56:25.580000	2004-Aug-03 12:56:26		no

Figure 15-2 Viewing the directory listing

9. Minimize this window. In File Explorer, double-click the **`Firestarter File Hashes.csv`** file in the C:\Work\Labs\Evidence\Chapter 15 folder. In Excel, increase the width of the MD5 and SHA1 columns to view the entire hash signatures of the files in the image (see Figure 15-3).

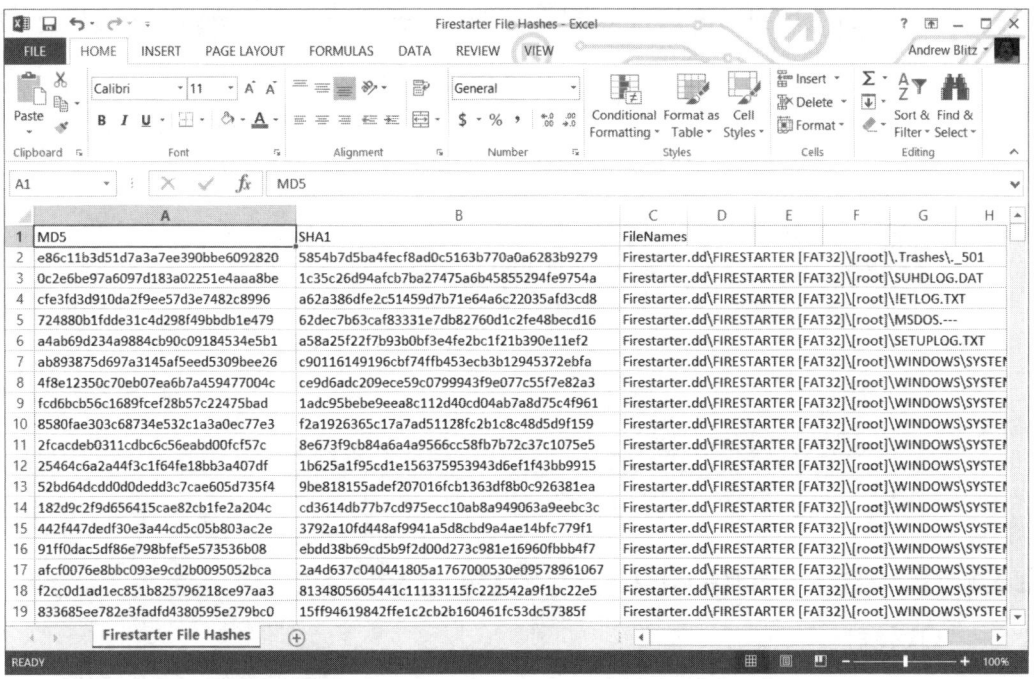

Figure 15-3   Viewing file hashes

10. Leave the Excel files and FTK Imager open as you answer the following review questions. When you're finished, exit FTK Imager, but leave the two Excel files open.

Review Questions

1. What's the volume serial number of the Firestarter.dd image?

   a. FIRESTARTER

   b. 2,056,257

   c. 2D3C-19FE

   d. Can't be determined from the evidence

2. What date was the Windows file system in the Firestarter.dd image last accessed?

   a. 3/22/2009

   b. 7/23/2004

   c. 7/24/2004

   d. 3/13/2007

15

3. What deleted Office file was found in the `Firestarter.dd` image? (*Hint*: Check the RECYCLED folder.)

   a. `!NFO2`

   b. `!C0.TXT`

   c. `Dc3.XLS`

   d. `DC3.doc`

4. What's the size in bytes of the FAT folders?

   a. 4096

   b. 1536

   c. 15,872

   d. 1,027,584

5. FTK Imager can recover all deleted files. True or False?

Lab 15.2 Investigating an Arsonist

Objectives

After conducting a preliminary investigation, you suspect you have found the arsonist and the computer used to document his crimes. During your analysis of the `Firestarter.dd` file, you recovered images of fires in a folder named Pleasure. You also found folders named walmart and Lumbermill, which could indicate scenes of previous fires. In this lab, you use Autopsy to analyze the `Firestarter.dd` image and gather evidence to build a case. Your findings will be presented in a report to the district attorney with a copy of the file hashes calculated in FTK Imager to validate the evidence.

After completing this lab, you will be able to:

- Search for evidence in preparation for a criminal case
- Use Autopsy search tools to find evidence and create a report

Materials Required

This lab requires the following:

- Windows 8 or 8.1 Professional
- Microsoft Excel 2013
- Autopsy 3.1.2 for Windows
- The `Firestarter.dd` file from Lab 15.1

This file could take a few hours to process, depending on your computer's performance, so you might want to set it up to process overnight.

Estimated completion time: **180–240 minutes,** depending on your computer's performance

Activity

In this lab, you process the Firestarter image to find and bookmark evidence of arson and use it to generate a report:

1. Start Autopsy. In the Welcome window, click **Create New Case**. Type **C15Proj2** in the Case Name text box, and then click **Next**. Type **C15Proj2** in the Case Number text box and your initials in the Examiner text box, and then click **Finish**.

2. In the Add Data Source dialog box, click **Image File** in the "Select source type to add" list box. Click **Browse**, navigate to and click **C:\Work\Labs\Evidence**, click the **Firestarter.dd** file, click **Open**, and then click **Next**. Click **Next** to accept the default ingest modules, and then click **Finish**. Autopsy begins processing the image, which could take a few hours.

3. When the processing is finished, click the **Keyword Lists** button at the upper right. Click the **Phone Numbers, IP Addresses, Email Addresses**, and **URLs** check boxes, and then click **Search**. (The search might take a few minutes.)

4. Click the **Keyword Search** button, click the **Regular Expression** option button, type **fire**, and click **Search**. Click the **Thumbnail** tab to see the images in the results, including one of a Walmart (see Figure 15-4). Shift+click to select all images, and then right-click them, point to **Tag Files**, and click **Tag and Comment**. In the Create Tag dialog box, type **Images of Recent Fires**, and click **OK** to bookmark them.

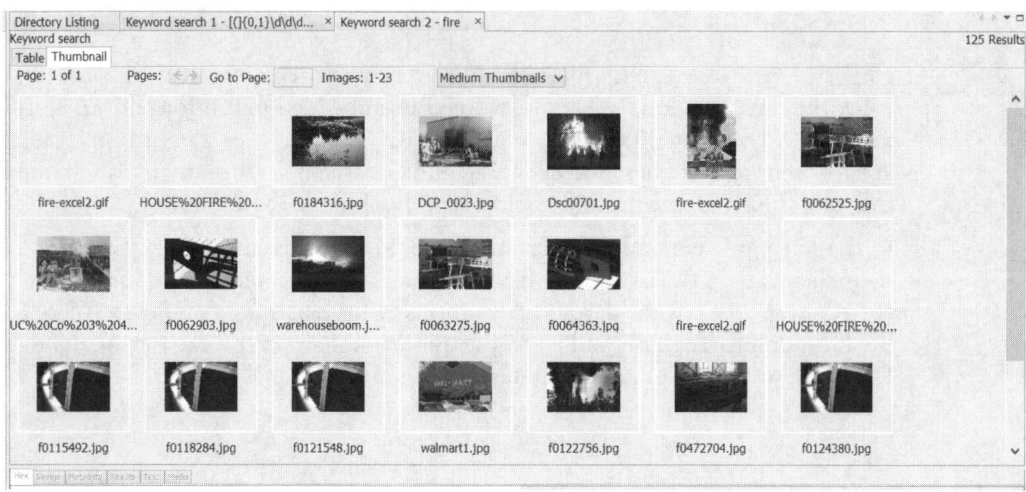

Figure 15-4   Images of fires

Source: www.sleuthkit.org

5. Click the **Keyword Search** button, click the **Exact Match** option button (if necessary), type **Burninator**, and click **Search**. Click the first result, and notice that a file has been recovered from the carved files. It's in the Location column and contains statements from Trogdor the Burninator that "Burninating the Walmarts is a GOOD idea" and "One should also burninate the countryside" (see Figure 15-5). Unfortunately, files recovered from carved space and orphan files can't be bookmarked.

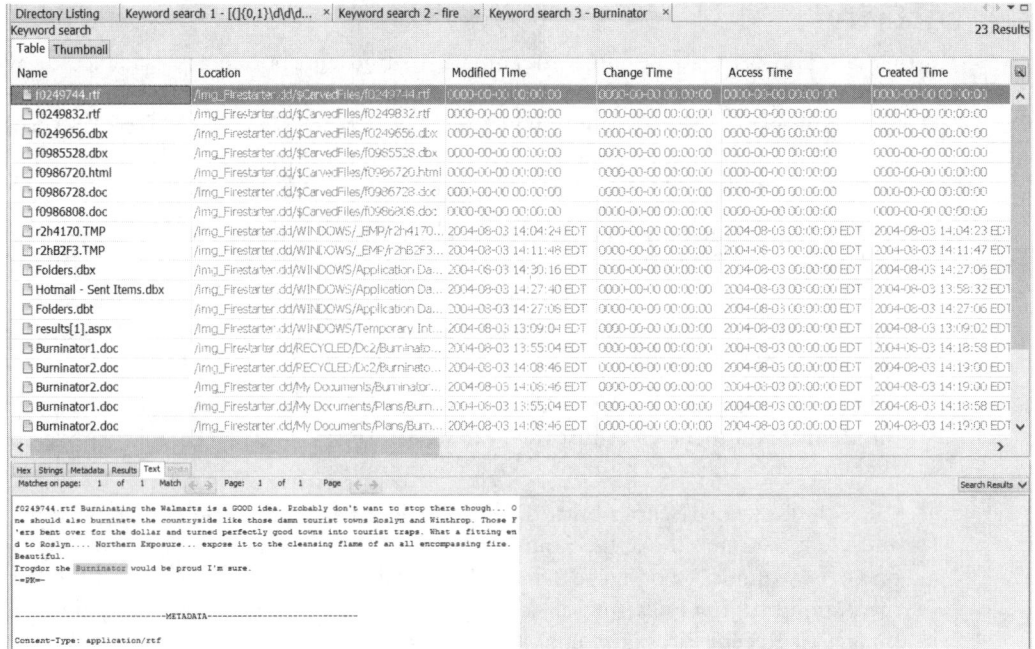

Figure 15-5 Incriminating text in a carved file

Source: www.sleuthkit.org

6. Click the **r2h4170.TMP** file, which contains the same text as the first carved file. Click the next files, one at a time, to see the embedded text information. Shift+click the **r2h4170.TMP** and **chat.log** files to select all these files as a group. Right-click the group, point to **Tag Files**, and click **Tag and Comment**. In the Create Tag dialog box, type **Incriminating Statements**, and click **OK** to bookmark these files.

7. In the left pane, expand **Firestarter.dd** and **My Documents**. Click the **Data** folder, and then click the **_ATE1.XLS** file. It was deleted, as indicated by the red ×. The recovered spreadsheet contains the dates and locations of fires, as shown in Figure 15-6. Right-click the file, point to **Tag File**, and click **Tag and Comment**. In the Create Tag dialog box, type **Deleted Excel File Containing Dates of Fires**, and click **OK**.

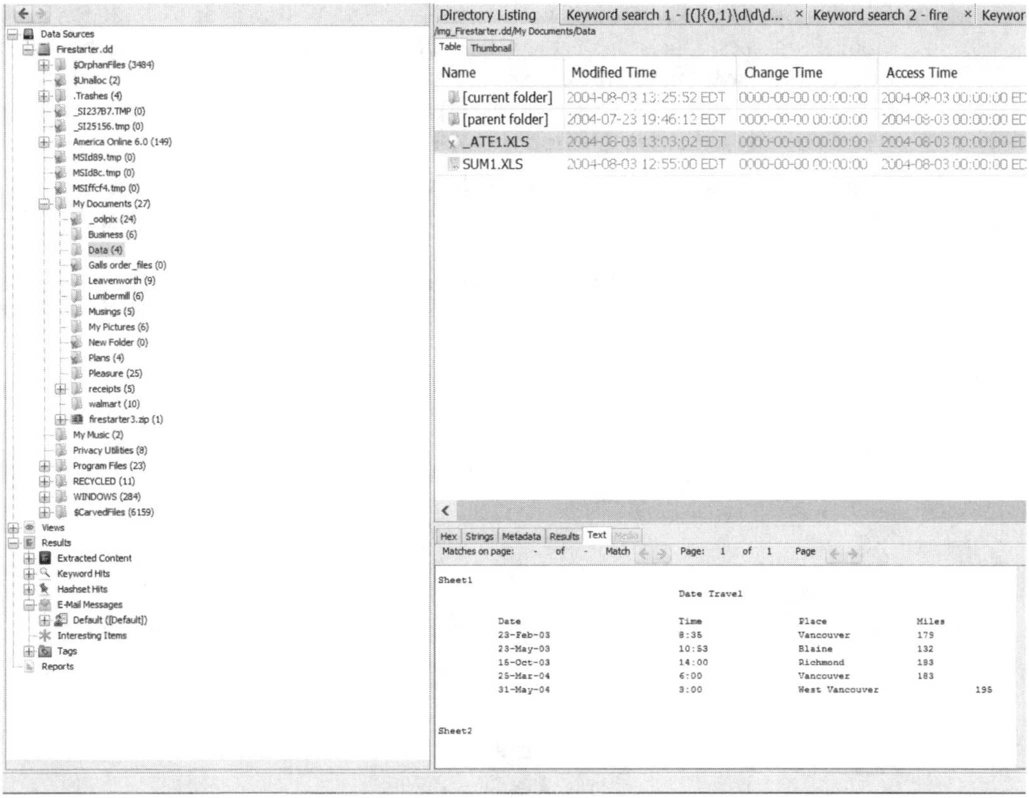

Figure 15-6 Dates and locations of fires

Source: www.sleuthkit.org

8. Click the **Pleasure** folder. It contains JPEG files, and some are named "fire." Click the **Thumbnail** tab to see all the images (see Figure 15-7). Shift+click to select all the files, and then right-click them, point to **Tag Files,** and click **Tag and Comment.** In the Create Tag dialog box, type **Images of Recent Fires,** and click **OK.**

15

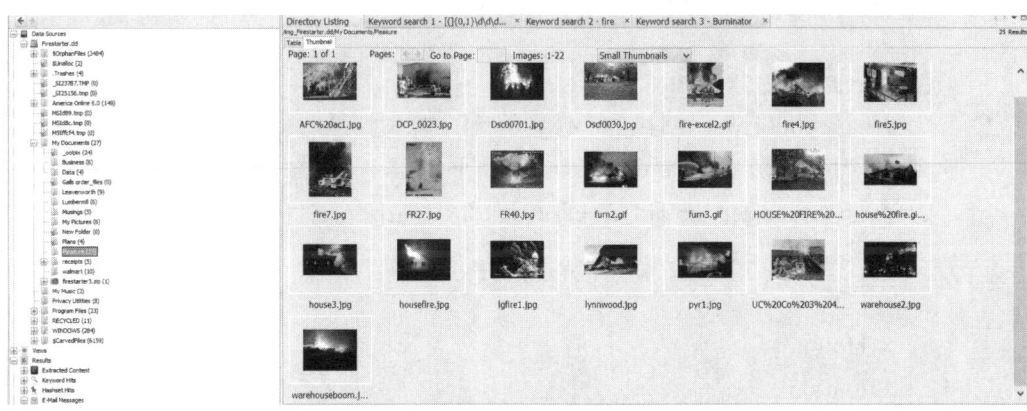

Figure 15-7 Viewing more images of fires

Source: www.sleuthkit.org

9. Expand **Extracted Content**, if necessary, and click **Web Search** to look for incriminating Google searches. Click the **Table** tab, if necessary, to see the searches. Notice that most involve the words "fire," "firestarter," and "burn." Select all the relevant files, and then right-click them, point to **Tag Files**, and click **Tag and Comment**. In the Create Tag dialog box, type **Google Searches for Fire**, and click **OK**.

10. At this point, you have collected enough evidence. Click **Generate Report** at the upper left. In the Select and Configure Report Modules dialog box, click the **Results-HTML** option button, and then click **Next**. In the Configure Artifact Reports dialog box, click **All Results**, if necessary, and then click **Finish**. A green checkmark is displayed in the progress bar when the report is finished. Click the **Results-HTML** link to see the report (see Figure 15-8).

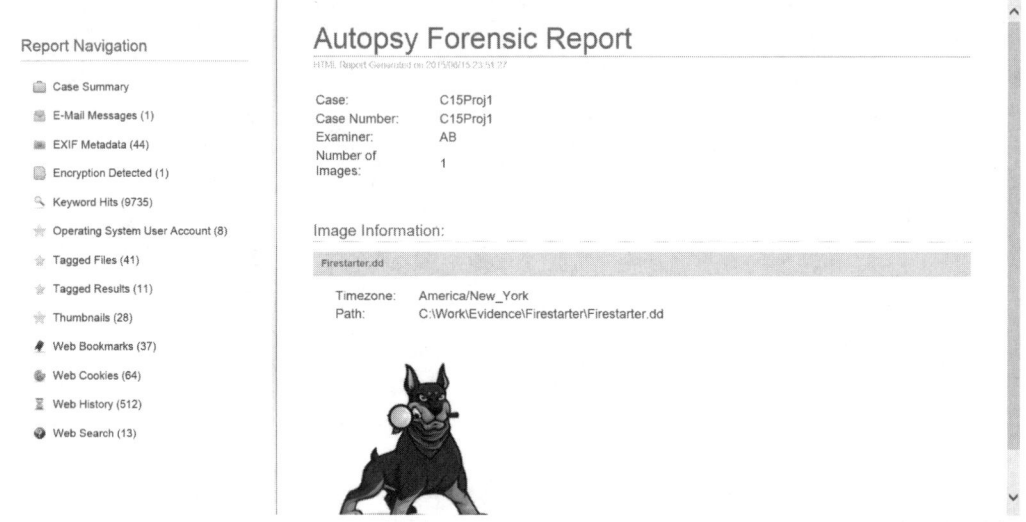

Figure 15-8　Viewing the Autopsy report

Source: www.sleuthkit.org

11. Leave the Autopsy report open as you answer the following review questions. (You might also need to look at keyword search results.) When you're finished, exit Autopsy and close all open windows.

Review Questions

1. Which photo was taken before a fire?

2. Which file was found to be encrypted?

3. What e-mail service did Trogdor the Burninator use?

   a. Yahoo

   b. Gmail

   c. Hotmail

   d. Outlook.com

4. How many search results were returned for the keyword "Burninator"?

5. No Exif metadata was recovered from the `Firestarter.dd` image. True or False?